Integrating Educator Well-Being, Growth, and Evaluation

Educator growth, well-being, and evaluation are often disconnected. How can we weave them together to better champion adult learning needs so educators can thrive and remain in their roles?

In this important resource, bestselling authors Lori Cohen (*The PD Book*) and Elizabeth Denevi (*Learning and Teaching While White*) present a framework for creating a healthy ecosystem of school transformation: equity, well-being, growth, and evaluation. The authors discuss each foundation in depth and provide research-informed practices, tools, and case studies for easy implementation. Resources include reflections to co-create a vision for equity, a sample coaching/mentoring conversation arc, steps for implementing a growth structure, the Teacher–Student Relationship Quality (TSRQ) Matrix, the Integrated Classroom Practices for Equity rubric, and more.

Whether you're a school leader, mentor, or teacher evaluator, this accessible guide will help you create a transformative school environment to sustain and grow effective, empowered educators.

Lori Cohen has over 25 years of experience in education as a teacher, instructional coach, school leader, and professional development facilitator. As a consultant and coach, she has partnered with educators, schools, and organizations worldwide to transform teaching, learning, and school leadership. Lori is the co-author (with Elena Aguilar) of *The PD Book: 7 Habits That Transform Professional Development*.

Elizabeth Denevi works with schools, colleges, and universities to increase equity, promote diversity pedagogy, and implement strategic processes for growth and development. She has served as a classroom teacher as well as an equity director, leadership coach, and director of professional development. She is also an assistant clinical professor at Lewis & Clark College in the Graduate School of Education and Counseling. She is co-author (with Jenna Chandler Ward) of *Learning and Teaching While White: Antiracist Strategies for School Communities*.

Equity and Social Justice in Education Series

Paul C. Gorski, Series Editor

Routledge's Equity and Social Justice in Education series is a publishing home for books that apply critical and transformative equity and social justice theories to the work of on-the-ground educators. Books in the series describe meaningful solutions to the racism, white supremacy, economic injustice, sexism, heterosexism, transphobia, ableism, neoliberalism, and other oppressive conditions that pervade schools and school districts.

Embracing the Exceptions: Meeting the Needs of Neurodivergent Students of Color
JPB Gerald

Identity-Conscious Practice in Action: Shaping Equitable Schools and Classrooms
Liza Talusan

Social Studies for a Better World, Second Edition: A Guide for Elementary Educators
Noreen Naseem Rodríguez and Katy Swalwell

Teaching Storytelling in Classrooms and Communities: Amplifying Student Voices and Inspiring Social Change
Maru Gonzalez, Michael Kokozos, and Christy Byrd

Igniting Real Change for Multilingual Learners: Equity and Advocacy in Action
Carly Spina

Anti-Oppressive Universal Design for Teachers: Building Equitable Classrooms
Diana Ma

Integrating Educator Well-Being, Growth, and Evaluation: Four Foundations for Leaders
Lori Cohen and Elizabeth Denevi

Integrating Educator Well-Being, Growth, and Evaluation

Four Foundations for Leaders

Lori Cohen and Elizabeth Denevi

Routledge
Taylor & Francis Group
NEW YORK AND LONDON

Designed cover image: © Lori Cohen

First published 2026
by Routledge
605 Third Avenue, New York, NY 10158

and by Routledge
4 Park Square, Milton Park, Abingdon, Oxon, OX14 4RN

Routledge is an imprint of the Taylor & Francis Group, an informa business

© 2026 Lori Cohen and Elizabeth Denevi

The right of Lori Cohen and Elizabeth Denevi to be identified as authors of this work has been asserted in accordance with sections 77 and 78 of the Copyright, Designs and Patents Act 1988.

All rights reserved. No part of this book may be reprinted or reproduced or utilized in any form or by any electronic, mechanical, or other means, now known or hereafter invented, including photocopying and recording, or in any information storage or retrieval system, without permission in writing from the publishers.

Trademark notice: Product or corporate names may be trademarks or registered trademarks, and are used only for identification and explanation without intent to infringe.

Library of Congress Cataloging-in-Publication Data
Names: Cohen, Lori (Teacher) author | Denevi, Elizabeth author
Title: Integrating educator well-being, growth, and evaluation : four foundations for leaders / Lori Cohen and Elizabeth Denevi.
Description: New York, NY : Routledge, 2026. | Series: Equity and social justice in education series | Includes bibliographical references.
Identifiers: LCCN 2025005329 (print) | LCCN 2025005330 (ebook) | ISBN 9781032871813 paperback | ISBN 9781003531296 ebook
Subjects: LCSH: Educators--Mental health | Well-being | Teacher-student relationships | Education--Evaluation | Mentoring in education
Classification: LCC LB2840 .C57 2026 (print) | LCC LB2840 (ebook) | DDC 371.1001/9--dc23/eng/20250512
LC record available at https://lccn.loc.gov/2025005329
LC ebook record available at https://lccn.loc.gov/2025005330

ISBN: 978-1-032-87181-3 (pbk)
ISBN: 978-1-003-53129-6 (ebk)

DOI: 10.4324/9781003531296

Typeset in Palatino
by KnowledgeWorks Global Ltd.

Contents

Acknowledgments vii

Introduction: Reimagining the Ecosystem
of Educator Support 1

1 Four Foundations of a Healthy School Ecosystem. 15

2 Equity: Lay the Foundation 29

3 Practices to Lay the Foundation 45

4 Well-Being: Nurture the Soil 64

5 Practices to Nurture the Soil 96

6 Growth: Cultivate Continuous Learning. 131

7 Practices to Cultivate Continuous Learning 163

8 Evaluation: Tend the Ecosystem 199

9 Practices to Tend to the Ecosystem. 224

10 Conclusion 247

Appendix A: Example Portrait of an Effective Educator 255
Appendix B: Professional Learning Choice Cohort Sample 259
Appendix C: Book Questions, Concepts, and Tools 261

Acknowledgments

From both of us
Thank you, Paul Gorski, for being a warm demander for us. Your high expectations and enduring belief in our work were critical to both the quality and completion of this project. To Lauren Davis, thank you for your encouragement and support. Thank you to all of our focus group participants, pre-readers, and those who gave us early feedback on our framework: Megan Barrett, Bawaajigekwe Boulley, Tanisha Brandon-Felder, Nita Creekmore, Carley Dryden, Drew Dillhunt, Maria Dyslin, Bianca Espinosa, Carter Graham, Miryam Harvey, Sarah Housley, Natalie Holz, Torian Hodges-Finch, Jasmine Locke, Annie Lamberto, Janet Lee, Malia Lee, Melissa Kantor, Laura Ross, Rob Robinson, Margaret Ramsey, KD Parman, Phelana Pang, and Krystal Wu. Our manuscript took better shape with each piece of insight and feedback. Finally, we express our gratitude to Dr. Dwayne Chism for his collegiality and scholarship.

From Elizabeth
Thank you to Lori, my amazing co-author, for your commitment to our process first and foremost. While we knew writing this book would be challenging, it was such an affirming journey because of your collaboration, expertise, and great sense of humor. I look forward to our continued partnership.

To all my students, my gratitude for your willingness to share your experiences and to help me think more comprehensively about how to fix a very broken system. You are my inspiration and my hope, and you provided so much of the energy to complete this project.

Finally, thank you to my family, who stood by my side as we wrote the manuscript. You always asked about how things were going and never complained about all of my time away to write.

And the experiences my children have had in educational institutions always provide a "rubber meets the road" reality for the work I do. I appreciate their insights into their own learning and accounts of how their teachers impacted them.

From Lori

I want to acknowledge Elizabeth for being willing to go on this ride with me. From welcoming me when I first moved to Portland, to modeling what this journey could look like, to geeking out on evaluation (which planted the seeds for this book), I am deeply grateful. Throughout this process, I've loved how our thinking has evolved—from teacher evaluation to reimagining the entire ecosystem. Thank you for an incredible and inspiring collaboration.

Rebecca Blackmer, you've been a partner in every creative process—pushing my thinking in profound ways and refining the smallest details. Your friendship and partnership have been invaluable to my growth. Tamisha Williams, you embody well-being and what it means to live well. Your work supporting others inspires how I think about community care. Thank you for being a thought partner throughout this writing journey, before and beyond. Rebecca Ritter, your partnership in reimagining the educator ecosystem has been invaluable; I'm inspired by all you've done and continue to do.

There are so many educators who challenge the notion of "this is the way we've always done it" and envision doing school differently. I'm grateful to be in your orbit. You make the vision we propose come to life in daily ways. To the Academic Committee from years ago at The Bay School—those who dared to reimagine what's possible with teacher support and evaluation—thank you for your boldness and collaboration in a process that laid the foundation for so much to follow.

Finally, Amy, you turned our yard into a flourishing marvel—tiny maps drawn to scale, countless hours of weeding and pruning, a garden that feeds our family, and a sunny oasis for the dog. Your slow, steady work is a counternarrative to these troubling times, a fractal of steady little efforts that grow into something much larger and more beautiful.

Introduction: Reimagining the Ecosystem of Educator Support

How We Got Here

While working together to develop our Assessing for Equity workshop series, we were lamenting our frustration with evaluation cycles for teachers. We both had been at schools that had made multiple efforts to improve professional growth, but those efforts were often piecemeal. For example, one year we might add a peer observation process, but we never connect it to the actual professional cycle for all faculty. Or we might have an engaging professional development session on student feedback, but then we just went on with business as usual. Lori had successfully led her site through an evaluation redesign process, but the full program implementation happened after she left. So, while we both experienced effective practices, they were never integrated into a more comprehensive professional growth system. And these various evaluation processes were not designed with equity in mind.

In fact, most large-scale evaluation systems are not. They don't start by acknowledging the historical and social context that impacts teachers and their work with students. They don't name the effects of bias and discrimination that affect instruction. Most evaluations typically offer a series of criteria that are disconnected from the lived experiences of students, families, and teachers. And those criteria echo a color-evasive approach (Annamma et al., 2017), sometimes referred to as "colorblind," that has been pervasive throughout the educational system in the United States. Early in our leadership careers, we remember taking existing tools and trying to infuse important considerations of diversity and equity. Elizabeth focused on the topic of "student engagement" with teachers to raise issues of how race might be impacting patterns of participation. Classroom observations revealed noticeable racialized data, but it was like pulling teeth to get teachers to attend to those patterns. And while working with white teachers, any mention of how their race might be impacting student achievement brought on waves of defensiveness. Lori asked teachers to create their professional goals with an equity lens, but for many, equity felt like an add-on rather than a foundation for growth. The school claimed a commitment to diversity, equity, and inclusion, but in practice, these efforts were scattershot.

More often than not, institutions have processes "on the books" that aren't followed. We hear this over and over from new leaders who really try to create meaningful accountability practices, but who are met with resistance from faculty who say, "This is the first time anyone has ever evaluated me!" and "No one has ever said that about my teaching!" Or evaluation is used selectively—such as when a teacher is really struggling or having a conflict with the school's mission or leadership. Often termed "gotcha" evaluations, teachers frame evaluation as a deficit process, set up to catch them doing something wrong, as opposed to a process to help them grow and develop.

Our focus here will be to offer an ecosystem for the assessment of teaching and learning that will incorporate all of the necessary ingredients needed to build and sustain a healthy system of feedback and accountability. We will begin with equity as the foundation of this ecosystem rather than something grafted on as a piecemeal set of efforts. We will discuss how educator well-being is essential to any change efforts a school is undertaking; students won't be well if the adults who lead them are not. We will share the manifold ways growth can take hold when educator well-being is centered and well-defined, and we will share the ways evaluation is the outcropping of these prior focal areas, not a top-down, disconnected set of practices.

As it stands now in schools, here is what we have noticed pertaining to equity, well-being, growth, and evaluation:

- Institutions get "top-heavy" in one or more of these areas (equity, well-being, growth, evaluation) and/or have gaps in one or more of these areas. For example, there may be a strong coaching program, but it is absolutely disconnected from the professional growth cycle. Or there is a faculty meeting that offers suggestions for supporting teacher mental health for 45 minutes—but then the meeting ends, and it's back to the grind.
- Institutions/leaders follow trends without thinking of the long-term implications. We also call this "chasing shiny objects"—jumping on the latest fad without ensuring that it's grounded in effective practice backed by sound data.
- Institutions/leaders are reactive rather than proactive and responsive. Practices are adopted to put out the latest fire as a defensive measure as opposed to observing larger patterns and responding more holistically. While the reaction may address a short-term issue, it will not solve the bigger problem and will not anticipate what might be coming next, creating the hamster-wheel effect so many teachers describe: "We just keep spinning our wheels."
- Leadership takes on too much at one time (usually in September–October) versus adopting a deliberate, prioritized approach. This creates a cycle of overwhelm, and it both drains leadership and diminishes faculty morale. It also sets up a pattern of a back-to-school/fall term with all kinds of new initiatives that are dead or ignored by the spring. Then, the next fall brings on a new set of initiatives with no accounting for past work. Rinse, repeat.
- Leadership makes excuses: "Just never enough time." This is a constant refrain, and we want to really dive into

what this means. How can it be that we spend hours and hours on campus, often 12-hour days, but there's not enough time to ensure our instructional practices are equitable and serve all children? *What's really going on when we say there isn't enough time?* We know that leaders mean this—they are overwhelmed, and the problems we are trying to address are big. But they aren't new. We have a serious rut in the proverbial road here that needs addressing.

We will note that over our decades in education, we have seen more mention of equity in various tools. But just as the aforementioned examples show, so often it's just a blanket statement of "be equitable" without any of the specifics needed to actually address inequity. Without concrete, observable steps to address inequity, well-being, and growth, these general statements will not be able to effectively support change because they don't explicitly name how bias shows up in the interactions between teachers, students, and families.

This failure to locate issues of inequity in the academic system creates the cycle of "racism without racists" so acutely researched by Dr. Bonilla-Silva (Bonilla-Silva, 2022; Pollock, 2008): "Contrary to the popular belief that educators across the world have typically been agents for progressive racial change, the weight of the evidence suggests that most educational systems and most educators operate to maintain racial hierarchy rather than to challenge it" (p. 334). Educators will acknowledge the existence of systemic inequities, but they will generally do one of two things with that acknowledgment: Blame others or succumb to the inevitability/overwhelming nature of oppression. This sounds like, "If only this student would…" locating the problem with the student and expecting them to either fix themselves or the problem. Or it might be, "That family/community is just not committed to education." This kind of deficit thinking is pervasive in our school systems (Gorski & Swalwell, 2023). Then there is the expression of equity overwhelm, which can sound like, "What do you expect me to do? I'm just a teacher," or "We're just one school. There's only so much we can do!" Either response fails to take accountability for the impact of inequity, leaving these patterns of discrimination undisturbed.

Juxtaposed to these deficit ideologies and diffuse calls to "be more equitable," there are excellent tools for assessing equitable classroom practices. Yet these rubrics and checklists, many of which we will offer in the pages ahead, are not *embedded* in evaluation processes. A leader here or there might use a culturally responsive classroom observation tool, but that's only if they heard about it in a workshop or maybe it was part of an instructional leadership class they had. A teacher may be working hard to address issues of stereotypes in their classroom, but their leader doesn't have the skills needed to actually engage, support, and extend the teacher's work. These inconsistencies produce a similar effect as the general calls for equity: The system—as designed—remains firmly in place.

We pay lip service to a number of elements in our schools: We say we want to increase "diversity," and once we have hired a few teachers of color, we think the deeper work is done. We hold teacher appreciation events, provide a few baskets of snacks at the staff meeting, and call our teachers "well." We boast about our schools having instructional coaches, but we don't create the time for teachers to meet with them or to create the trust needed for coaches to do their work effectively and with support. We provide an evaluation packaged in a lengthy checklist and call it "done" for a couple of years. All of these efforts toward educator support are transactional. The more intentional, transformative work interweaves these elements with the acknowledgment that the work can be small, slow, messy, and complex, but also more thoughtful and better poised to make lasting change in schools.

Our Pivot: From Transactional to Transformative

We have been inspired by the work of Dr. Shawn Ginwright, author of *The Four Pivots: Reimagining Justice, Reimagining Ourselves* (2022). Ginwright offers a vision for making our educational institutions places where diversity and belonging drive our collaborative work and create meaningful and just learning environments. He is clear about the impact of inequality: "Inequality, in all its forms, doesn't only block opportunities, it also breeds individualism, distrust, skepticism, and fear ... Inequality erodes our ability to imagine any other way, and it conditions us to only focus on surface solutions to deep problems" (p. 7). He makes the critical point that just getting rid of harm is not the same as healing from the impact of inequality and offers Dr. M. L. King's notion of "beloved community" as a force for healing via connection and empathy, "leaning into new possibilities, different ways of relating ... more loving when we are hated, more generous in times of scarcity, more inclusive when we want to close ranks" (pp. 15–16). To create this kind of community, we must pivot—make a "small change in direction from a single point where we are ... not a complete abandonment of what we know, but it braids together what we know with how we feel and who we wish to be" (p. 16). Of the four core pivots he describes, we have been most influenced by his notion of a pivot in our connection—*from transactional to transformative relationships:*

> Most of us have been trained to lead and work with others in highly technical ways. Transactional relationships are efficient for work and productivity but insufficient for healing. Transformative relationships in our professional and personal lives cultivate deeper human connection through vulnerability, empathy, and listening. *(p. 18)*

In this text, we pivot to a more transformative vision for evaluation because our current transactional approaches are hurting our students and burning out our teachers and leaders. We operate from a place of reactivity over proactivity, such as:

- managing student behavior (transactional) versus considering how to cultivate classroom culture (transformational)
- making boilerplate statements after a crisis (transactional) rather than considering practices for healing and repair when ruptures happen (transformational)

- leading schoolwide initiatives because they are part of the latest trend in education (transactional) rather than assessing what students specifically need to learn at their best (transformational)

When we take a transformational approach to reimagining our school's ecosystem, we ask ourselves, "How do we design for what we want to see? What small, incremental changes might have an impact on the larger ecosystem?" and "How do we shake ourselves out of what has been done before to imagine a new reality for educator well-being, growth, and evaluation?" We hope this text can weave together new kinds of connections, new possibilities where we can create a more integrated ecosystem devoted to healthy, supported, and engaged educators who will be able to ensure that all of our students can grow and thrive.

Many practitioners, scholars, and researchers write about adult wellness, coaching and growth models, educator well-being, equity, and evaluation. But we have not seen a book that interweaves how these pieces fit together in a systematic way. We can't answer the biggest challenges in education unless we put the pieces of the puzzle together coherently and cohesively. We allow the pendulum in education to shift from extreme to extreme, engaging in "either/or" debates that don't permit a more integrated, both/and approach. During the pandemic, we had an opportunity to remake education. We did, and then we didn't. We can't just solve educational equity challenges through focusing on well-being or through growth or through evaluation—we need all these elements to inform one another, to support a healthier ecosystem within our schools.

A Fractal Approach to Systems Transformation

When we considered metaphors for our book's framework, we thought of various examples from the natural world, such as a garden or a forest. We wanted a metaphor that represented something dynamic, evolving, and iterative, requiring ongoing tending and care. We settled on the idea of an ecosystem.

We started kicking around the idea of a terrarium, a mini ecosystem, as our metaphor. While terrariums can be a bit precious, highly curated, and even at times artificial (e.g., some of the DIY terrariums we researched come with tiny plastic dinosaurs, including the one we built together), they also give us a window into how ecosystems function: how a balance of human activity and external factors plays a role in a shaping an ecosystem's development. While this metaphor may not work in every instance (and we'll ask for your grace about this), we like this metaphor because a terrarium is a type of fractal, a microcosm of the larger world. The lessons we derive from fractals can help us think about what we create, and replicate, in schools.

Fractals are complex patterns of similarity across different scales, meaning the same basic shape or pattern is repeated at every level of magnification. Examples include broccoli, pine cones, snowflakes, coastlines, the branching of trees, and blood vessels. In her book, *Emergent Strategy: Shaping Change, Changing Worlds* (2017), author, facilitator, and pleasure activist adrienne maree brown writes about fractals as microcosms for social change; she emphasizes the importance of small, intentional actions in creating broader systemic transformation.

As brown articulates, the patterns of behavior, values, and practices we establish on a small scale are mirrored on a larger scale within organizations, communities, and societies. Just as fractals are interconnected and dependent on their repetitive patterns, social transformation relies on the interconnected actions of individuals and groups working toward a common vision. For instance, a leader with a clear vision of equity, who is self- and relationally aware, and who fosters trust and psychological safety can influence their team to become a more cohesive unit that collectively leads toward a shared vision. This leadership team can work collaboratively to consider how to scale their efforts to influence change schoolwide. They can discuss and plan ways to bring the school's vision for equity to life. They can practice and model the dispositions and skillsets they hope teachers will emulate. The leadership team can partner with teachers to co-create conditions that center on human dignity, trust, and psychological safety. Leaders can continue to model a growth orientation, like asking for and applying feedback; teachers can do the same in classrooms with students. Through developing self-efficacy schoolwide, educators can co-create collective efficacy, having a more powerful impact on how students see themselves as learners and change agents. Leaders can reflect on areas of strength and areas in need of growth and tend to the site's ecosystem accordingly.

Patterns replicated in small-scale systems, like terrariums, are akin to the kinds of systems we strive to remake in schools. Schools are ecosystems where everything informs everything else. In terrariums, the type of foundation one chooses impacts the soil composition, and the soil composition influences which life will grow and thrive. Growth depends on how the diversity of life, weather patterns, light, moisture, and human activity contribute to the health or demise of the system. In schools, we can apply a similar line of thinking: What's at the foundation informs the culture of the community, and the culture informs what learning will look like, and so on. By understanding and applying these fractal principles, we can create small-scale changes that ripple outward, leading to systemic transformation in our schools.

This book will be your guide to developing and nurturing the ecosystem at your site, finding the entry point that works for you and your school/organization, balancing human activity with the external factors that impact how we operate in schools, and tending to the community in ways that allow educators and students to be affirmed and flourish in their full dignity.

Fractals in Practice

The examples and anecdotes in this book are a composite of our experiences, the experiences of those we have coached, led, and supervised, and schools we have worked for and with. We have changed the names and identities of these people and places. Any similarities to your experiences and school sites may confirm or affirm the realities where you work, but we are careful not to call out specific places or people. The examples we share are emblematic of many schools and education-facing organizations worldwide. While we refer to ourselves (Elizabeth and Lori) as "we" throughout the book, we'll default to the third person any time we're sharing an example from our own experiences.

One school we worked with, for example, Abundance Academy, committed to this fractal approach to making change. Abundance Academy, a pre-K-8 alternative school, has a mission to "Empower and bring out the brilliance of every child." The school was created to help students with learning differences become empowered self-advocates as they transitioned back into mainstream schooling. As the school grew and simultaneously weathered the most challenging conditions of the early 2020s, its culture and climate was fracturing; teachers were burning out. Roles were not clearly defined, so leaders were often doing more than what was expected. Not all students were receiving inclusive instructional practices. The formal evaluation process was too cumbersome for teachers and evaluators, and it was disconnected from other parts of the school's professional growth system.

Using the limited resources available, leaders at Abundance Academy worked incrementally to make changes rather than fix everything all at once. In a three-year timeframe, the school's leaders

- conducted staff empathy interviews about school climate and created a faculty forum to address educators' concerns
- invited outside agencies to provide training on coaching and empowered all mentors and leaders to implement coaching in their work
- worked in committees to create effective teaching tools and agreed upon inclusive practices that were expected in all classrooms
- spent two years building, piloting, and iterating on an evaluation process that was more integrated in teaching and learning at the school

The process was clunky, had many setbacks and iterations, and involved a lot of piloting and feedback sessions, but leaders remained committed to their school's mission and values.

When we met with a focus group consisting of Abundance Academy evaluators and evaluees at the end of this process, each person shared similar sentiments. Focus group participants shared that evaluation still needs work, but also how much of the evaluation model's success was because of the intentional steps the school took to get there, and involving teachers along the way, to cultivate a culture of trust, growth, and feedback. One teacher's anecdote stood out the most from these focus groups: Ginny, a second-year teacher, described what her year was like undergoing Abundance's pilot evaluation process:

> I was terrified to have a committee of evaluators observe my class ... During the committee's last observation, I thought my class was a disaster. But when I debriefed with the committee, we were able to reflect on what went well, what still needed addressing, and how I have the skills to do it. I wasn't afraid to be vulnerable. Leaders didn't let me off the hook for where I could still be growing. We took the time to build trust so that getting feedback wasn't scary. The committee valued me, had my back, and held me to high expectations. I never thought that could happen in a school.

Ginny's story is an outlier compared to what we typically hear from new and experienced teachers. Classroom teachers bring a lot of fear to the evaluation process for a host of reasons. For newer teachers in particular, it can feel like their job is on the line any time they have a bad lesson, bad day, or bad week. Throw a top-down, pre-packaged evaluation system into the mix and that just elevates the anxiety teachers bring to an overly demanding profession. In the case of Ginny's school, leaders took a collaborative approach to her evaluation, providing her with an array of perspectives on her teaching. This collaborative approach minimized Ginny's fear. At the same time, evaluators were able to hold Ginny accountable for her growth, balancing trust and responsibility in the process. By prioritizing intentionality and shared accountability, leaders at Abundance Academy created conditions where feedback became an opportunity for learning and development—demonstrating that small, intentional shifts can lead to transformative change.

Who We Are

Lori is a white, Jewish, queer, cisgender female whose career began in the late 1990s, the time when multiculturalism was celebrated and colorblindness was the norm. She has been a longtime classroom teacher, instructional coach, site-based leader, teacher trainer, and eventually consultant working with schools worldwide. In her time as an educator, she has seen the impact that structural and systemic oppression has played in shaping how schools function and has dedicated her career to doing her work through an equity lens, moving from colorblindness to critical perspectives on racism and structural inequities. Early in her career, she developed a passion for teaching teachers and began working with pre-service and early-career educators on teaching through the lenses of equity and inclusion. When Lori became a site administrator, she guided her school through a series of processes that impacted the ecosystem at her site: co-developing a mentoring program, a coaching program, the portrait of an effective educator and teacher effectiveness criteria, and a comprehensive overhaul of teacher evaluation. Throughout the years of building these systems, and interweaving growth and evaluation with a foundation of equity, Lori and her colleagues were able to shift culture and hold teachers to high expectations. Since that time, she has worked with schools and organizations across the globe to reimagine equity, well-being, growth, and evaluation.

Elizabeth started her career as a classroom teacher, and it was not until she began teaching an ethnic studies class in California that she understood the impact of her race (white) and ethnicity (Italian-American) on her work in schools. After completing her doctorate on her positionality as a white teacher and the role of racial literacy in classrooms, she served as an equity director in Washington, DC. There she began to explore the role of anti-bias education in developing curriculum, professional development, and peer feedback. She had the opportunity to extend her understanding of how additional aspects of her identity connected to her leadership, especially as a neurotypical, cisgender female. In her next role, she focused on teacher evaluation, equity pedagogy, and student feedback. All of her previous positions helped to frame the work she does now as a professor in a leadership studies department committed to the development of future school leaders.

While we are both passionate about equity and reimagining evaluation, we also recognize the limitations of our perspectives, particularly as white women, the dominant demographic in education in the United States (Chandler-Ward & Denevi, 2023). While we bring a broad range of experiences and perspectives to this work, we also hold ourselves accountable by increasing our lenses on the topics we write about, collaborating with colleagues of color, and prioritizing the work and research of historically marginalized experts throughout these pages.

Who This Book Is For

First and foremost, this book is for educators at any level who want to radically reimagine the educator ecosystem, who have a bold vision for equity and justice, and who are committed to supporting and retaining teachers through intentional efforts. We have designed this text for people who are charged with equity, well-being, growth, and/or evaluation and need tools and structures to systematize their efforts, including:

- site leaders
- department leaders who evaluate
- anyone who evaluates teachers or designs professional learning and growth
- anyone who has gone through a terrible or non-existent evaluation
- induction mentors and instructional leaders
- anyone who supports teacher success within a school building or from an outside agency

In the chapters that follow, you can expect an equity-based, accessible, comprehensive guide for sustaining and growing effective, culturally responsive, and empowered educators.

The flow of the book is organized by each element of the ecosystem. In one chapter, you'll receive theoretical approaches, key considerations, and examples; in the subsequent chapter, you'll receive practical tools and processes to support you in making incremental changes in your communities.

We'll culminate this book by providing a process for you to integrate all these elements into your context. We also hope you do this work in collaboration with your teams and communities, which will strengthen the potential for transformation. If you're the only one at your site reading this book, we hope you'll find community and resonance within this book's pages, providing a path for what you might leverage. Ultimately, we hope you will recognize that there are multiple entry points to transforming educational institutions and that change is possible when we start small and take a fractal approach to reimagining the educator ecosystem.

References

Annamma, S., Jackson, D. D., & Morrison, D. (2017). Conceptualizing color-evasiveness: Using dis/ability critical race theory to expand a colorblind racial ideology in education and society. *Race Ethnicity and Education*, *20*(2), 147–162. https://doi.org/10.1080/13613324.2016.1248837

Bonilla-Silva, E. (2022). *Racism without racists: colorblind racism and the persistence of racial inequity in America* (6th ed.). Rowman & Littlefield.

brown, a. m. (2017). *Emergent strategy: Shaping change, changing worlds*. AK Press.

Chandler-Ward, J., & Denevi, E. (2023). *Learning and teaching while White: Antiracist strategies for school communities*. Routledge.

Ginwright, S. (2022). *The four pivots: Reimagining justice, reimagining ourselves*. North Atlantic Books.

Gorski, P., & Swalwell, K. (2023). *Fix injustice, not kids*. ASCD.

Pollock, M. (Ed.) (2008). *Everyday antiracism: Getting real about race in school*. The New Press.

1

Four Foundations of a Healthy School Ecosystem

The framework for this book emphasizes four foundations in the ecosystem of school transformation:

1. Equity: lay the foundation
2. Well-being: nurture the soil
3. Growth: cultivate continuous learning
4. Evaluation: tend the ecosystem

By laying a solid foundation with equity, nurturing the soil with well-being, cultivating continuous learning through growth, and tending the ecosystem via a thoughtful evaluation process, the guidance and examples in this book will exemplify how small, intentional actions at the micro level can lead to transformative changes at the macro level (Figure 1.1).

Reimagining the ecosystem of schools requires us to address the following questions:

Equity: lay the foundation

- How do we define equity?
- What does equity look and sound like in practice?

Evaluation:
Tend the Ecosystem
- How do we define evaluation?
- What is the model of evaluation that is aligned with equity, well-being, and growth?
- How will educators be evaluated?
- What will be the measures of effectiveness?
- How will evaluators be prepared for the process?
- How will leaders tend to the ecosystem of their sites, including their own evaluation?

Growth:
Cultivate Continuous Learning
- How do we define growth?
- How will educators grow?
- How might leaders support educator growth in ways that are equitable, differentiated, and personalized in support of well-being?
- What structures will promote growth?
- How do leaders model their own growth and promote a culture of learning?

Equity:
Lay the Foundation
- How do we define equity?
- What does equity look and sound like in practice?
- What conditions need to be in place to support educators thriving in an equity-centered environment?
- What do leaders need to know and practice to foster equity?

Well-Being:
Nurture the Soil
- How do we define well-being?
- What is the portrait of an educator at our site?
- What does an educator need to be fully affirmed in their dignity, experience, and professional practice?
- How does this portrait align with the vision for equity?
- What conditions need to be in place to support educators' well-being?
- What do leaders need to know and practice to foster well-being?

FIGURE 1.1 Ecosystem framework

- What conditions need to be in place to support educators thriving in an equity-centered environment?
- What do leaders need to know and practice to foster equity?

Well-Being: nurture the soil

- How do we define well-being?
- What is the portrait of an educator at our site?
- What does an educator need to be fully affirmed in their dignity, experience, and professional practice?
- How does this portrait align with the vision for equity?
- What conditions need to be in place to support educators' well-being?
- What do leaders need to know and practice to foster well-being?

Growth: cultivate continuous learning

- How do we define growth?
- How will educators grow?
- How might leaders support educator growth in ways that are equitable, differentiated, and personalized in support of well-being?
- What structures will promote growth?
- How do leaders model their own growth and promote a culture of learning?

Evaluation: tend the ecosystem

- How do we define evaluation?
- What is the model of evaluation that is aligned with equity, well-being, and growth?
- How will educators be evaluated?
- What will be the measures of effectiveness?
- How will evaluators be prepared for the process?
- How will leaders tend to the ecosystem of their sites, including their own evaluation?

Equity: Lay the Foundation

When we were learning how to make a terrarium, we found that the container serves as the foundation for the world you are hoping to build—the place where your vision will take root. When selecting this container, the size, location, materials, and lighting matter. Once the container has been selected, one is then prompted to add a small layer of rocks or pebbles for drainage; it is advisable to add a layer of activated charcoal to filter water and prevent odors. Then, this layer is covered with moss to keep the soil separate from the base layers. Finally, one adds nutrient-rich soil to create a fertile environment that supports growth. This foundation is the firmament for growth.

In our ecosystem framework, equity is the base layer on which everything else resides. In this layer, we first ask, "How do we define equity and belonging?" Gorski and Swalwell remind their readers that the "tricky thing about defining *equity* is that the people who commit their careers to enacting it don't always agree on what it means" (2023, p. 17). Toggling between addressing people's individual needs and the needs of the collective, a strong definition of equity transcends individual needs (though it is important to meet those needs) to a more systems-focused approach. Equity is also rooted in a bold vision, one that dares to remake the systems that historically have been inequitable. We also need a clear vision that is inspiring, specific, and has been agreed upon by the collective. While leaders themselves can identify the key components of equity and communicate those components within their school communities, a shared definition, particularly one that has input from those most historically marginalized, will make for a stronger foundation.

For a school to enact a bold vision, though, it is important that leaders are comfortable and willing to enact this vision. They may need to unlearn some typical habits of leadership that center on perfectionism. In the Equity chapters, we'll guide you through what it means to lay the foundation for equity, be a leader for equity, and develop a coherent vision to guide your site.

Well-Being: Nurture the Soil

Well-being is the soil, and the healthier the soil—the clarity of roles, the robustness of policy, the trust and psychological safety, and the specific efforts to support educators—the healthier the culture of the school. For the soil of well-being to be healthy, schools and organizations need structures and practices that center on human dignity—valuing the unique dimensions of people's identities—where all those in the community can fulfill their work with trust, psychological safety, and ongoing support. We need to acknowledge that some groups of people have historically benefitted and currently benefit from various systems that exploit, harm, oppress, and marginalize others. A healthy culture with a focus on well-being will cultivate educators who are more willing to grow, accept growth-oriented feedback, and be motivated to stay in the profession.

The well-being portion of our framework may also be the most dynamic. People from a range of backgrounds and historical advantages—from those who have seen the pendulum swings of education trends many times to those who cut their teaching teeth online in the pandemic—may require different types of support. As we continue to increase our understanding of identity and belonging, we will need to continue updating our thinking about how to best center the dignity of those we work with and continue to counter the myriad challenges educators face through supporting their well-being. Much like an ecosystem needs ongoing tending, so do educators need the types of tangible supports that allow them to grow.

Many schools discuss increasing well-being efforts, but they don't specify which dimensions of well-being they are going to address in any kind of systematic fashion; instead, leaders might focus on broad definitions of well-being or half-hearted efforts at the most stressful times of the school year rather than specific measures to manage workloads, cultivate self- and collective efficacy, or foster strong, supportive relationships. To address well-being, leaders need to ask: What are the components of an educator that are essential to employee well-being and effectiveness? How might factors like diversity, sustainability, and ongoing support ensure that educators exist in a trusting, psychologically safe ecosystem? What role might feedback play in this process?

Just as school and district leaders need to be brave and courageous practitioners for equity, they also need to be well. This doesn't just mean that leaders engage in daily exercise or put on a good front in times of crisis, but that they also have high levels of self and social awareness; that they are engaged in ongoing personal and professional development; that they are human, recognizing their limitations and strengths; that they set good boundaries; they seek feedback; and they center relationships. In the Well-Being chapters, we'll share the components of well-being that leaders have the most influence over, and what to do to support individual and collective efficacy through the lens of well-being.

Growth: Cultivate Continuous Learning

In ecosystems, a healthy soil that is consistently nurtured provides the firmament for growth. In schools, the research is clear that growth is not a one-time event, and one-and-done professional learning opportunities rarely lead to greater growth (Darling-Hammond et al., 2017). Growth is the result of sustained efforts, which might include self-directed learning, small learning communities, and 1:1 structures like coaching, or any other method that differentiates and embeds support into educators' day-to-day practices. This type of "nutrient cycling"—the type of support that sustains the school's ecosystem—allows teachers to be supported by skillful leaders, students to learn well with skillful teachers, and schools to be high-functioning places where learning is at the center. Growth opportunities that are embedded in one's job and sustained over time will allow an educator to learn, reflect, practice, receive feedback, and implement their learning through multiple iterations of the process. Growth is evident when it is connected to something tangible, such as a site's mission, vision for equity, portrait of an educator, or a set of expectations adopted by a site-, district-, or state-level entity.

Growth is a natural outcropping of well-being. If teachers are supported and cared for, if they receive the resources they need to be effective in the classroom, and if they are validated and cared for in their full dignity, then they will bring a reserve of energy, passion, creativity, and joy to classroom spaces. Similarly, if teachers are challenged to grow and are supported in achieving high expectations of effective, culturally responsive teaching for all their students, they will take pride in their work and be more motivated to learn and grow.

Leaders who model learning themselves are more likely to cultivate a culture where growth is possible. Leaders need to be supportive in allocating the time and resources to supporting educators' growth while also modeling what their own growth trajectories are, whether through how they design staff meetings, how they acknowledge and learn from mistakes, and/or how they share their goals and learning process with the community. A growth orientation sends a powerful message to students about the process of learning. If adults are modeling their own learning and growth through ongoing practice, then students will receive meaningful modeling of what the learning process might look like for them. Just as an ecosystem contains a diversity of life, in the Growth chapters, we'll provide you with a diverse array of approaches for how to cultivate the conditions and develop the structures that will best support growth.

Evaluation: Tend the Ecosystem

While ecosystems are naturally occurring, human activity has shaped the trajectory of the planet, and that trajectory is driving us to destruction. Similarly, as schools funnel students and families into very narrow definitions of success rather than tapping into the brilliance and capacities of all community members, we're on the path to destruction in the education system. As the blowback against equity efforts continues nationwide, fear increases and exhaustion kicks in. Those who were excited to spearhead more equity-focused efforts lose steam or become targets themselves, which means that either schools default to the status quo that was never designed to serve all students in the first place, or those most passionate about equity are driven out. But if humans created inequitable systems and have the capacity to reverse some of the most damaging impacts of climate change, why don't humans reimagine and tend to the ecosystems of schools?

It is essential to tend to the diversity of life in an ecosystem to support it to flourish and grow. This process requires intentionality. Whether pruning plant life, replacing the soil, assessing the light sources, or adjusting the temperature, ongoing maintenance is what supports a thriving ecosystem. Similarly, schools should require an evaluation framework that is as dynamic as the vibrant ecosystems we aim to cultivate within our schools.

The consensus on what defines a viable ecosystem or a sound evaluation system remains elusive among scientists and educators, respectively. Our framework promotes building the teacher support ecosystem from the ground up, with an evaluation system that emerges from the soil of its communities, decenters those with more historical advantages, and focuses on a process and set of practices that are inclusive of educators' backgrounds, experiences, and ways of knowing. We hope schools will take a critical approach to adopting their evaluation framework and consider how that framework advances equity, supports culturally responsive pedagogy, and affirms the dignity of all those involved in the process—students, educators, families, and leaders. And if the framework doesn't support efforts toward greater equity, we hope leaders will have the courage to create something that does.

A Call to Leaders

One of the challenges we find any time we work with schools is that the teachers and department leaders are excited and galvanized to make the necessary changes for more equitable practices. But we often find them saying, "My principal or Head of School should attend this workshop." The same might go for the framework model we're proposing. Or perhaps you are a leader reading this book and thinking, "Yes, I want to do all this, but I don't think I have time or capacity—or support—to implement something like this." We get concerned with these kinds of "not me" statements because they move teachers and leaders away from their spheres of influence. We cede the control we do have and miss the opportunities that are right in front of us. As the author Alice Walker said, "We are the ones we have been waiting for" (Walker, 2006).

When we first embarked upon this project, we shared an early draft of the book's framework with a range of colleagues worldwide: school and district leaders, education consultants, classroom teachers, coaches, and state-level officials. When we asked colleagues to self-assess how their school, district, or organization was faring in relation to the four foundations of our framework, the results were all over the place but coalesced around several themes. For any of this work to take hold, leaders need the following:

- to be equipped with the knowledge, skills, and capacities to lead for equity
- to have the levels of self-awareness and social awareness to understand who they are and the communities they are leading
- to understand culturally responsive education models, pedagogy, and practice
- to be skillful facilitators and community builders
- to be warm demanders who hold their colleagues to high, attainable standards of equity
- to be collaborative, courageous, vulnerable, human-centered, and changemakers.

These leadership dispositions thrive on a clear vision and purpose, aiming to bring together community members through a collective call to transform education. This kind of leadership emphasizes understanding community members both as individuals and educators, upholds integrity through modeling the practices they hope to foster, and, above all, nurtures a culture of creativity, innovation, and risk-taking. We hope leaders who read this book will be as dynamic as the systems they are hoping to cultivate.

Throughout these pages, we'll get deeper into the framework we present, provide you with a range of resources and entry points to tending your own ecosystems, and support what a dynamic process for school transformation might look and sound like. However, we have a caveat: What we offer here is not a one-size-fits-all. There is no one way to create an ecosystem, just as schools don't have a cookie-cutter template for what they must include. We expect leaders to address the parts of their school's ecosystems that need the greatest attention. If a site's equity efforts have been strong so far, then well-being might be addressed. Or perhaps a school has gone through great efforts to develop a professional model that supports all teachers, but the culture of feedback is lacking or evaluation is nonexistent. Perhaps the blowback toward equity initiatives has created an exodus of teachers of color, and leaders need to clarify what they mean about equity. Wherever you're beginning, we hope you find an entry point that meets your needs, allowing the fractal approach we offer to shape the patterns that will transform education.

Landscape Assessment

Before you continue onto each layer of our ecosystem metaphor, it may be helpful to assess the landscape of your school, district, or organization to consider what areas you might need to develop and consider. Table 1.1 provides you with a brief self-assessment to determine what your baseline needs are before reading the chapters ahead. This leadership self-assessment will help you reflect on your effectiveness in leading practices related to equity, well-being, growth, and evaluation, providing insights into areas for your professional development and growth.

TABLE 1.1 Landscape Assessment: Self-Assessment for Equity, Well-Being, Growth, and Evaluation

Areas for Assessment	Statement	1—strongly agree			4—strongly disagree
Equity	Our site* has a clear definition of equity	1	2	3	4
	Our site clearly communicates its vision for equity	1	2	3	4
	Our site's environment supports educators thriving in an equity-centered atmosphere	1	2	3	4
	Our site's leadership actively works to unlearn typical habits that center on the dominant culture to hold a bold vision for equity	1	2	3	4
	The needs and voices of historically marginalized groups are centered in our school's equity initiatives	1	2	3	4

(Continued)

TABLE 1.1 Landscape Assessment: Self-Assessment for Equity, Well-Being, Growth, and Evaluation (*Continued*)

Areas for Assessment	Statement	1—strongly agree		4—strongly disagree	
Well-Being	Our site's values, goals, and mission align with the well-being of educators	1	2	3	4
	Educators at our site are clear about their roles, responsibilities, and expectations	1	2	3	4
	Our site addresses and fine-tunes conditions to support the well-being of educators	1	2	3	4
	Leaders cultivate trust and psychological safety as an ongoing practice	1	2	3	4
	Leaders are skilled at building, sustaining, and repairing relationships	1	2	3	4
	Leaders model the approaches to well-being they hope to foster at our site	1	2	3	4
Growth	Our site provides sustained and job-embedded professional learning opportunities	1	2	3	4
	Growth opportunities are aligned with our site's vision for equity and/or portrait of an educator	1	2	3	4
	Our site's leadership supports educators' growth by allocating time and resources for learning, practicing, and implementing knowledge, skills, and competencies	1	2	3	4
	Our site provides job-embedded growth opportunities like coaching, mentoring, professional learning communities, and/or self-directed forms of professional learning	1	2	3	4
	Our site fosters a culture of collaboration and shared responsibility among educators for student learning outcomes	1	2	3	4
	Our site leaders model a growth-orientation themselves	1	2	3	4

(*Continued*)

TABLE 1.1 Landscape Assessment: Self-Assessment for Equity, Well-Being, Growth, and Evaluation (*Continued*)

Areas for Assessment	Statement	1—strongly agree		4—strongly disagree	
Evaluation	The evaluation process in our school is comprehensive and fair	1	2	3	4
	Our evaluation process involves multiple measures to assess effectiveness	1	2	3	4
	Our evaluation process is collaborative, including student feedback	1	2	3	4
	The evaluation system at our site considers the context and specific needs of a diverse array of educators and students	1	2	3	4
	Our site's evaluation process respects and reflects the identities and cultural backgrounds of all engaged parties	1	2	3	4
	Our site connects evaluation outcomes to specific opportunities for professional growth	1	2	3	4
	Our site's evaluation process is dynamic and adaptive in promoting continuous improvement	1	2	3	4

* For the purposes of this survey, the word "site" encompasses schools, districts, and education-focused entities/organizations.

Now that you have had a chance to consider where your school, district, or organization falls in relation to this framework, grab your metaphorical gardening gloves and let's dig in.

Summary

This chapter provides an overview of the ecosystem framework for school transformation built upon four interdependent foundations: equity, well-being, growth, and evaluation. Each foundation represents a vital component of a thriving school ecosystem: Equity lays the foundation for belonging and justice; well-being nurtures the soil to sustain trust, psychological safety, and human dignity; growth fosters a culture of continuous learning and professional development; and evaluation tends the ecosystem by ensuring accountability and alignment with community values. The chapter underscores that transformation starts with small, intentional actions—fractals—guided by a collective vision and leadership that models courage, vulnerability, and compassion. Through this framework, the book emphasizes the importance of addressing systemic inequities and fostering environments where educators and students alike can thrive. A self-assessment tool at the end of the chapter invites leaders to reflect on their readiness to engage with these foundational elements.

For Further Reflection

1. Equity: How does your school or organization involve historically marginalized voices in defining and implementing its equity vision?
2. Well-being: What structures are in place to support educators' well-being and sense of belonging, and how might they be improved?
3. Growth: How does your organization ensure that professional learning opportunities are job-embedded and aligned with its mission and equity goals?
4. Evaluation: In what ways can your evaluation system incorporate multiple measures and approaches to reflect the identities and cultural contexts of all stakeholders while promoting continuous improvement?

References

Darling-Hammond, L., Hyler, M. E., & Gardner, M. (2017). Effective Teacher Professional Development. Learning Policy Institute. Retrieved from https://edpolicy.stanford.edu/sites/default/files/publications/professional-learning-learning-profession-status-report-teacher-development-us-and-abroad_0.pdf

Gorski, P., & Swalwell, K. (2023). *Fix injustice, not kids*. ASCD.

Walker, A. (2006). *We are the ones we have been waiting for: Inner light in a time of darkness*. New Press.

Equity:
Lay the Foundation

Equity is about fairness in both processes and outcomes, acknowledging historical, social, and institutional forces that create an unequal playing field. It requires addressing the structural roots of disparities, redistributing resources and opportunities, and transforming both spoken and unspoken norms to ensure every community member can thrive. Equity demands moving beyond surface-level initiatives and enacting deeply practices, policies, and leadership that challenge deficit thinking and disrupt systemic inequities.

2

Equity: Lay the Foundation

A few members of the leadership team at Beechwood School recently attended a math conference that focused on assessment and strengths-based pedagogical approaches to challenge the deficit thinking they had been hearing about from some teachers. In an effort to deepen conversations about school and department policies, the school was working to extend its diversity practices beyond heritage month celebrations and food festivals; while these events built a community across the school, they did little to shift inequitable practices in school and department policy. Upon their return from the math conference, leaders were eager to discuss ability groupings and the possibility of de-tracking the current math sequence. In particular, they wanted to focus on the advanced algebra course. Traditionally, in their placement conversations, the math department reviewed grades, teacher recommendations, and standardized test scores to determine who was eligible for the advanced class—and the department was very proud of their "objective" criteria. But after the conference, the leadership team wondered if this process might actually be creating a biased, inequitable selection process.

Leaders brought data to the math department to indicate that, for the past five years, the student population was not reflected in the higher-level math classes, especially with regard to race, gender, and students with IEPs and 504s. Leadership hoped to take a collaborative problem-solving approach to create more equitable conditions. They expressed their concerns and wondered if the current selection criteria might be contributing to the underrepresentation of their most marginalized students, especially when it came to Black and Latine students. While reviewing the data at a recent math team meeting, John, the advanced algebra section teacher, grew visibly uncomfortable. Out of frustration, he retorted, "So now are you asking us to lower our standards for those kids. That sounds pretty racist to me."

The principal replied, "No, I'm actually asking us to consider that our assessment process for the advanced math class may not be serving all our students or identifying who's actually ready for more advanced coursework."

John continued to defend the current system, and his colleague Suzie responded, "I'm good with all the diversity work we're doing, but don't mess with my autonomy and my grading. That doesn't feel fair." A few other department members nodded in agreement.

Sensing entrenched resistance, the principal offered to table the issue for now. Everyone left the meeting frustrated.

Sound familiar? As the adults defend their intentions and point fingers at each other, another year will go by in which students are unable to access the education they need and deserve. Department members are unable to see that equity has not been embedded in the academic program despite all of their efforts in the social festivals and community assemblies. The leadership team cannot assert their vision in the face of resistance and challenge. And they are stuck in an either/or cycle where either the teachers are racist or not, with no accounting of how their so-called objective assessment practices may not be what they think they are.

In order to create equitable schools that ensure all students can grow and thrive, we have to be committed to shifting the current status quo. Most of our major systems in school—discipline, state testing, assessment, and, of course, professional evaluation—were *not* designed with social justice in mind. In fact, we spend so much time and effort now trying to remake and re-envision these systems because they were actually built to reinforce inequality and preserve unfair social hierarchies. Yet our work to address these inequities often feels like we are just tinkering around the margins without making substantive change. That's because the central beliefs and tenets they were designed around are exclusionary and rooted in dominant cultures. And just to add insult to injury, these systems were often described through the lens of a false meritocracy where anyone can succeed if they just study/work hard enough (the ol' "pull yourself up by your bootstraps" argument), ignoring any systems of oppression that were firmly in place.

As opposed to starting from a "level" playing field, we begin by acknowledging how *unlevel* our educational playing field is and that teachers, students, and families are not coming to our schools with the same resources and opportunities (Pendharkar & Sparks, 2023). So, what must we account for to ensure that educational professionals can thrive so the students they serve can be successful? In our ecosystem metaphor, the base layer for shifting practice begins with equity. In a terrarium, the base layers include rocks, gravel, and activated charcoal; this foundation is also known as a "drainage layer," which helps maintain the overall balance of the ecosystem, ensuring that the life within can co-exist in a healthy, self-sustaining environment. Like the proper layers in a terrarium foundation, sustained change in education requires embedding equity into the foundations rather than the surface-level fixes or add-on initiatives that most schools employ as a checkbox measure. In order to be a threat to inequity, math departments like the one at Beechwood don't just need to address the issues inherent in math placement but also what lies at the foundation—the beliefs that educators hold and the policies that have been created—that prioritize the status quo over ensuring every student has the opportunity to learn. Without a solid foundation of equity, clearly defined, articulated, and carried forward with equity-centered leadership, a school's ecosystem will fail to thrive. This chapter will explore this foundation by identifying what leaders and educators need to do when setting a foundation of equity.

Defining Equity

We have found this definition of equity by Drs. Galloway and Ishimaru to be helpful because it attends not only to intentions but also to the actual impact of policies and procedures:

> Equity refers not merely to equal opportunity, but to fairness in processes and outcomes within the context of historical, economic, social, and institutional forces that have resulted in an unequal playing field for minoritized communities. An equity agenda requires addressing the structural roots of disparities, including the organizational processes and learning conditions that further accumulate the "education debt" owed to students marginalized by educational systems. Within this framework, achieving equity necessitates a redistribution of resources and opportunities coupled with transformations in spoken and unspoken norms that guide how people relate to one another.
>
> (Galloway & Ishimaru, 2019)

Like Beechwood, without a foundation of equitable teaching practices, the school is left with flimsy, surface "equity" initiatives that really only serve as window dressing as opposed to deeply embedded practices, routines, and policies. Their diversity and equity efforts are positioned as add-ons, such as a celebration, one-off presentation event, or as an extracurricular activity. Schools often don't realize that children can't learn when they lack identity safety or when they have experienced stereotype threat: the threat of being viewed through the lens of a negative stereotype, or the fear of doing something that would inadvertently confirm that stereotype (Cohn-Vargas & D. Steele, 2013; C. Steele, 2011). For example, Black students who are aware of the stereotype that they are not as "smart" or academically inclined as white students will often not ask for help due to the fear of confirming a teacher's low expectation for their performance. Similarly, Asian students get frustrated when teachers just assume that they are good at math and often report not getting the attention or help they need because everyone assumes they are fine.

One outcome of more intentional equity efforts is to increase students' sense of belonging. We have found alignment with how Cobb and Krownapple (2019) discuss belonging and dignity: the extent to which students/staff/families feel appreciated, validated, accepted, and treated fairly in a school environment. Belonging is also an important antidote to stereotype threat because students and teachers don't have to worry about being labeled or treated as less than their full representative selves. We have found several measures of perceptions of belonging and psychological engagement in school to be helpful. Both the Psychological Sense of School Membership Scale (Cobb & Krownapple, 2019) and the work of Cohn-Vargas et al. (2022) offer surveys that students can take to provide feedback to teachers and school leaders. Dr. Howard Stevenson (2014) distinguishes between a sense of belonging in schools where one gets to tell their story and embrace their difference instead of having to fit in or "shape shift" so others are not uncomfortable with one's difference or threatened by one's identity. Whatever definition or measure your institution decides to use for equity and belonging, it's imperative that school leaders have a clear vision that can be communicated widely.

Both teachers and students need to bring their full selves to the learning environment, and if they have to check an aspect of their authentic self at the door, then they can't bring their full potential to their work. If they have to try to protect themselves from harmful stereotypes and ongoing bias, their success will be impeded. That's why any professional growth cycle has to be based on a commitment to ensuring equity, supporting and sustaining educator well-being and dignity, and providing mechanisms to address inequity when it arises.

Starting with Leadership

In order to build a foundation of equity, school leaders need a way to assess their *own* skill level relative to inequitable school practices. Muhammad Khalifa (2016) developed a Culturally Responsive School Leadership (CRSL) framework in response to a growing recognition of the crucial role that leaders play in fostering cultures of school responsiveness to the evolving needs of its community. In practice, the CRSL framework might look like the following:

- Recognizing how policies or practices may be perpetuating oppression, and taking steps to root out and redress these policies/practices for equitable outcomes.
- Making substantive and reciprocal connections to the community beyond the school building.
- Making accommodations for students with learning needs or families whose backgrounds or work schedules might require translation services or other ways of getting information from the school.
- Working with a clear definition and examples of culturally responsive and sustaining practices; modeling these practices in meetings; and ensuring teachers are using these practices in their classrooms.
- Examining curricula alongside teachers and identifying/redressing the gaps in equitable representation.

These standards and practices are gaining traction in higher education institutions, principal leadership programs, and school districts across the United States, even in the midst of efforts to dismantle any kind of equity programming. As we bring educational leaders, district partners, and state agencies together, we see how communities are working collaboratively to address long-standing systemic issues. By centering CRSL in principal development programs and principal supervision, this framework advocates that leaders set the standard for equitable practices that center the dignity of every community member, putting well-being before policy and people before projects. Too often, we meet leaders who have no clear sense of their role in developing more equitable practices. They are quick to say they support equity, but when probed about what that actually means, they don't have examples.

Here is a case in point. Elizabeth was working with an instructional leadership team that was eager to build their antiracist curriculum. When she asked the team where they saw racism operating in current practices, they grew visibly uncomfortable. There were quick looks between the team members, some halting comments, and then the principal said, "Well, we aren't saying our curriculum is *racist*. We just know we can be doing a better job." This is yet another example of "surface" equity: a vague recognition that instructional practices may not be fair, but an inability to pinpoint where racial bias is operating. And without a clear articulation of the problem, it can be nearly impossible to develop effective strategies. So how can leaders ensure they can demonstrate these equity skills to their teachers and instructors?

In another instance, Jordie recently graduated from an administrative leadership program where the CRSL framework was interwoven throughout. He was excited to apply what he learned at the new middle school where he became the assistant principal. By the end of his first week, however, two major fights had broken out between students, and Jordie spent most of his time completing paperwork, communicating with the translators working with families of these students, and attending restorative circles with those involved in each campus conflict. On top of that, Jordie was working 12–14 hours a day, and even then, he couldn't manage to make time to send an email or connect with the other assistant principal next door, much less be the instructional leader he hoped he would be for teachers.

In reflective conversations with his coach, Jordie said, "I thought it would be different. In my leadership program, we have time to delve into the root causes of oppression. We have time to envision our instructional leadership. It was powerful. But in practice, that's out the window. Theory means little when you feel like you are drinking from firehose and two students are at each other's throats. You're not thinking of much else beyond getting them to stop."

Jordie's experience is like many leaders: The theory is great, perhaps empowering. But when it comes to the day-to-day demands of leadership, how might leaders do more deeply rooted equity work when they want to ensure the school is operating safely? We have been there ourselves. Culturally responsive and sustaining leadership is more than a set of beliefs; it is a way of being. When Jordie reflected further with his coach about one of the fights in the first week, he noticed that he wanted to understand the context rather than going straight to disciplinary action. He asked the Student Support Team about the barriers present for the students involved, and they explored what else might be at the root of this conflict and how to partner with the families and caregivers involved. He shared power through partnering with the school counselors, translators, and his peer colleagues about appropriate consequences rather than quick, punitive measures. While Jordie was certainly feeling the intensity and stress of moving from his practicum to a full-time job, he had applied more of the CRSL principles than he thought. The counselor shared how impressed she was by Jordie's patience and thoughtfulness throughout the process. "There are a lot of ways these situations can go," she said. "But you took the time to care about every person involved."

Whether through navigating student conflict or supporting new teachers, CRSL will look different for each context. And it should. Laying a foundation of equity means knowing and understanding those we're leading, eradicating barriers and policies for those who have experienced structural and systemic oppression, and partnering on a path of support that can foster each person's self-efficacy. To do this effectively, leaders have to begin with their own reflection of how they show up in their leadership context.

While it can sound redundant, leaders must start with themselves. They have to model and practice their own self-reflection so others see and learn from their example. There are no shortcuts or workarounds. "Positionality," as described by James Banks (1996), asserts that our social identities are markers of our *relationship* to others as opposed to just our personal qualities. So, who we are matters because it will impact how we interact with others.

For school leaders, this means that we bring our lived experiences, opinions, values, and history to the data we gather, the issues we decide to prioritize, and the ways in which we judge what is "good" teaching or which candidate is the "right fit."

Positionality identifies power dynamics and names the way it can operate not only because of one's job title but also due to social location and relation to *others'* identities. By understanding who we are and how our leadership has been shaped by our experiences and standing in the world, we are in a stronger place to build healthy cross-cultural relationships with others. We can recognize the interrelatedness of who we are and how we show up in various contexts. Conversely, without a thorough understanding of who we are, *we will do harm*. We will act in ways that replicate unequal power dynamics and reenact bias and stereotypes in our day-to-day practice. We will appear clueless at best and discriminatory at worst. Thus, the first tenet of CRSL (Khalifa, 2016) is critical self-awareness that will enable leaders to:

- understand the context in which they lead
- interrogate personal assumptions about race and culture and their impact on the institution
- be acutely aware of inequities that negatively affect their students' potential and impact outcomes
- create a new environment of learning for children and families who have experienced marginalization

As our identities develop over time and across contexts, there is no arrival point—no box to be checked that says, "Critical self reflection? Done!" An understanding of our positionality must be embedded into each new team, instructional vision, goal for the year, and hiring committee. And leadership teams need the time and space to do this work *together* so they can serve as both models and resources. Since about 80% of leaders in educational settings identify as white (Peters, 2024), being aware of how whiteness impacts leadership becomes even more critical as we continue our work to diversify leadership teams so they are reflections of the students and families we serve:

> In coaching cross-racial teams, it's important to start with the ways race, and other salient identifiers, might be

showing up in our shared work. We consider how feedback styles are influenced by racial backgrounds; how approaches to problems and comfort with conflict can be impacted by our identity. By being clear about who we are and what we value, we can then develop authentic partnerships. But if race is unacknowledged and we aren't actively talking about how it impacts our leadership styles and strategies, we are in big trouble. Not only will we be less effective, but we will also ensure that racism will continue to operate unheeded.

(Chandler-Ward & Denevi, 2023, pp. 120–121)

This tenet of critical consciousness needs to be actively pursued as leaders seek to make conditions more equitable. So often, those of us with identities that are reflected in mainstream and majority cultures have no sense of how we may be impacting those who are regularly stereotyped and experience bias and harm. For those of us who see ourselves reflected over and over in leadership positions and teams, we have to work even harder to understand how we may be complicit even though we see ourselves as "good" people.

Putting This Notion of Critical Consciousness to the Test

An educational service district (ESD) in the Pacific Northwest was interested in developing new ways to support both teachers and aspiring leaders of color. While their cohorts of color provided critical mentoring as well as valuable racial affinity space, it was clear that without a parallel structure for white colleagues to do racial identity work, their efforts would not be as effective. So, the ESD team developed a series to focus on how leaders can build cross-racial solidarity in their efforts to address racism. The participants of color were asked to invite white colleagues to join them for an all-day workshop as well as ongoing meetings throughout the school year. This small but subtle shift in the creation of the teams made all the difference. During the initial workshop, colleagues of color entered the space filled with energy and enthusiasm. The organizing team noticed that multiracial spaces didn't often feel this inviting, and participants quickly noted, "We got to invite the white folks into the space!" When the participants of color determined who they wanted to partner with to do the cross-racial work, they were empowered in a new way.

The teams started the day together to talk about what it means when they say "in solidarity," and there was a panel of leaders who talked about how they approached cross-racial work. Then, they broke out into racial affinity groups led by facilitators who provided a much-needed structure and guidelines. For example, several of the white leaders were very uncomfortable as they transitioned to the affinity space. It was interesting to note how even though their colleagues of color saw them as important allies, they had not really considered their role in the cross-racial collaboration. They explored how folks of color *have* to be aware of their race as often they are the only or one of a few people of color on an administrative team. Yet the white folks can be blissfully ignorant of how their whiteness is showing up and affecting their relationships with colleagues of color. They explored the notion of accountability partners and the ways in which white leaders could work to support each other and ease the burden on people of color to always have to be the ones to raise issues of race and racism. They noted predictable patterns and how they could begin to disrupt some of their behaviors that were getting in the way of having productive, authentic, and positive relationships with their colleagues of color.

They then finished out the day together in their cross-racial teams to set goals for their ongoing work. The ESD would be checking in on the teams and making site visits to see how the collaborations were progressing. Finally, they all came back together at the end of the year to assess their progress. Participants noted what a valuable space had been created both to do individual identity work and to build collective action and efficacy.

The next chapter will offer specific tools to support identity development so we can build principled partnerships across race as we work collaboratively to challenge inequity and create better systems.

How Leaders Can Build Teacher Efficacy

Having a strong sense of self also enables leaders to support teachers in understanding their own positionality, identity development, and sense of their own efficacy (Chism, 2022): the ability to provide a sense of value and belief within staff that leads to greater outcomes for marginalized students. Many leaders find this challenging because they often hear from faculty who feel like they are being asked to do more for struggling students, but they don't have the time or the specific skills needed. The exhaustion and sense of defeat for these teachers are real, and these feelings can be attributed to a deficiency of "efficacy": the perception educators hold that their effort will have a positive effect on student learning. So, if a leader has a teacher with low efficacy, it means that the teacher may not believe they have what it takes to make a difference. And that belief will have a powerful impact on their expectations, behavior, and student learning—especially for our most marginalized students. Educational leader Dwayne Chism sums it up in the following way:

> The belief gap is often attributed to risk factors that teachers may associate with students of color, such as lower socio-economic status, more aggressive behaviors, family structures that are unsupportive of school and learning, or lack of focus and motivation. Some educators view these conditions as bigger than themselves; as a result they may develop a sense of helplessness regarding their ability to educate. Other well-intentioned educators embrace a savior mentality, characterized by seeking to protect students of color from harm.
> (Chism 2022, p. 63)

Both of these approaches will create low academic expectations for students: one based in deficit thinking and stereotypes, and the other in a belief that the students can't handle the level of work required and will fail if they are challenged. In the Beechwood example at the beginning of the chapter, it's clear that the math department members were not considering how their beliefs about their students might be affecting who they deemed "ready" for an advanced class. They never considered how their grading practices or recommendations might be subjective and thus riddled with bias. Students can only do better when we expect them to. So how can a leader build up a teacher's sense of efficacy?

One strategy is to be aware of the teacher behaviors that indicate high versus low expectations for marginalized students. In their seminal work *Creating the Opportunity to Learn* (2011), Wade Boykin and Pedro Noguera outline key indicators that can be observed in classrooms:

- Call on low-expectation (LE) students less often than on high-expectation (HE) students.
- Likely to give LE students less praise and more criticism for failure.
- Show less acceptance of ideas put forth by LE students.
- Provide briefer and less informative feedback to questions raised by LE students.
- Give LE students less benefit of the doubt.
- Allow LE students less time to answer questions.
- More likely to provide LE students with correct answers, whereas they are more likely to provide clues or rephrase a question for HE students.

(Boykin & Noguera, 2011, pp. 78–79)

By having specific indicators, leaders can be better positioned to engage teachers who may be struggling with their own efficacy and ability to teach students who may come from a very different background than their own. But instead of offering excuses or reasons why they can't teach those students, leaders have to hold onto their unwavering belief that teachers have the capacity to learn and grow. They have to be ready to offer specific support and strategies for how those teachers can be "warm demanders" who have high expectations for all, challenge any deficit mindsets, and demonstrate care that is empowering as opposed to operating as "saviors" for children experiencing marginalization (Bondy & Ross, 2008). In Chapter 9, we provide an observation tool to support leaders in exploring teacher–student relationship quality to help indicate where expectations and bias may intersect.

A Foundation of Equity at Beechwood

How might we apply this to the opening situation at Beechwood? How could the leadership team have engaged the math department members more directly? They could have named the deficit thinking they observed along with the data. Instead of making this only a student achievement issue, they could have stated their intent to look at ability grouping as a potentially inequitable practice that they want to explore together. They could have affirmed the teachers' commitment to the students and their belief that their system was fair while naming the disparate outcomes of that system—providing a both/and frame as opposed to an either/or stance. As long as teachers feel they are being called racist, they will defend themselves. By beginning with a belief that these teachers can effectively teach all students, they could then move to what was getting in the way and explore ways to shift current practices. And when faced with predictable resistance, the leaders could have been ready to withstand the heat and engage the pushback as opposed to folding at the first sign of conflict. By being in collaboration with the department to explore the assessment criteria, the leadership team would be better positioned to engage, reflect, and promote a shift away from tracking that was excluding the most marginalized students.

The goal of this chapter is to set the conditions for the rest of the strategies and tools we will share throughout the text. We began with the base layer of the ecosystem, the foundation we need to support a healthy ecosystem. By rooting our practice in equity, we can address unhealthy ways of being and adapt practices that will lead to a well-cultivated, flourishing organizational culture. By grounding ourselves in clear definitions and articulation of the inequitable conditions, we can then identify practices that will not only help educators to grow and thrive but also help our institutions to advance greater equity and success for all students. How might we ensure that leaders embody equitable practices for the foundation of equity to be strong? The next chapter outlines processes for ensuring that our work to make our educational settings more equitable is both effective and sustainable over time.

Summary

This chapter explored the foundational importance of equity in education, emphasizing that surface-level diversity efforts were insufficient to address systemic inequities. Through a real-world example, it examined how entrenched practices like ability grouping and biased assessment reinforced inequality. The chapter called for a shift in beliefs and actions, challenging educators and leaders to disrupt deficit thinking and embed equity in every facet of school culture. It also introduced Culturally Responsive School Leadership (CRSL) as a crucial component for creating sustainable change that promoted student success and educational justice.

For Further Reflection

1. Where have we seen surface-level equity efforts in our school, and what would it take to move toward deeper, systemic change?
2. What practical steps can we take as a team to embed equity more fully into our policies and practices?
3. How can we, as leaders and educators, develop and model culturally responsive leadership practices that support equity? What shifts in mindset or action might this require from us as a team?

References

Banks, J. (1996). *Multicultural education, transformative knowledge and action: Historical and contemporary perspectives.* Teachers College Press.

Boykin, A. W., & Noguera, P. (2011). *Creating the opportunity to learn: Moving from research to practice to close the achievement gap.* ASCD.

Bondy, E., & Ross, D. (2008). Teacher as warm demander. *Educational Leadership.* 66(1).

Chandler-Ward, J., & Denevi, E. (2023). *Learning and teaching while white: Antiracist strategies for school communities.* Routledge.

Chism, D. (2022). *Leading your school toward equity: A practical framework for walking the talk.* ASCD.

Cobb, F., & Krownapple, J. (2019). *Belonging through a culture of dignity: The keys to successful equity implementation.* Mimi & Todd Press.

Cohn-Vargas, B., Khan, A., Epstein, A., & Gogolewski, K. (2022). *Belonging and inclusion in identity safe schools: A guide for educational leaders.* Corwin.

Cohn-Vargas, B., & Steele, D. (2013). *Identity safe classrooms, grades K-5: Places to belong and learn.* Corwin.

Galloway, M., & Ishimaru, A. (2019). Leading equity teams: The role of formal leaders in building organizational capacity for equity. *Journal of Education for Students Placed at Risk (JESPAR), 25*(4), 1–19. https://doi.org/10.1080/10824669.2019.1699413

Khalifa, M. (2016). *Culturally responsive school leadership.* Harvard Education Press.

Pendharkar, E., & Sparks, S. (2023). New national data show depth of disparities in a chaotic year of schooling. Education Week. Retrieved from https://www.edweek.org/leadership/new-national-data-show-depth-of-disparities-in-a-chaotic-year-of-schooling/2023/11

Peters, H. (2024). School leaders of color face high levels of burnout. Here's what they need to thrive. Chatlkbeat. Retrieved from https://www.chalkbeat.org/2024/07/17/what-men-of-color-need-to-thrive-as-education-leaders/

Steele, C. (2011). *Whistling Vivaldi: How stereotypes affect us and what we can do.* Norton.

Stevenson, H. (2014). *Promoting racial literacy in schools: Differences that make a difference.* Teachers College Press.

3

Practices to Lay the Foundation

Here, we offer three different tools to help leaders and teachers assess and develop their equity literacy. The first resource, Creating Your Vision for Equity, will provide a framework for defining, envisioning, and enacting what equity looks, sounds, and feels like at your site. The second resource, Pre-Assessment: Are You Ready to Lead Your Vision for Equity? is intended for those who will be initiating and developing their site's equity analysis, practices, and programming. The self-reflection questions speak to a range of skills needed to bring a vision to actuality. That way, leaders can assess where they are and what they need to work on. The third tool, Social Identities Portrait, is adapted from *Anti-Bias Education for Young Children and Ourselves* (Derman-Sparks & Edwards, 2020). While there are many identity inventories out there, we like this one because it highlights how our identities develop over time and across contexts—so the work to understand who we are and how our identity impacts our work is never "done." This tool also emphasizes how our identities are socially constructed: For example, Elizabeth wasn't born knowing what it means to be a white, Italian-Catholic, woman—but how has she been carefully taught what those group identities mean and signify from interactions with her family, church, school, peers, social media, etc.

Creating Your Vision for Equity

Developing a school's vision for equity is a complex and critical undertaking, one that demands a commitment to disrupting entrenched inequities and reimagining a school's foundational values. It is not enough for equity to consist of surface-level initiatives or performative gestures; equity must be embedded into the very fabric of a school's culture, policies, and daily interactions. This process entails examining beliefs, biases, and practices, and invites community members to co-create actionable steps for equitable outcomes. Consider using opening meetings at the start of the school year, or the initial staff meetings early in the school year to do this work. When leaders frame this process, it can be helpful to approach these conversations with humility and openness. Leaders might frame this conversation by saying something like the following:

> As we begin this work I want to acknowledge that developing a school's vision for equity is complex and necessary. This isn't about quick fixes or performative gestures. It's about reimagining how equity is embedded into the foundation of our school's culture, policies, and daily interactions. I invite all of us to approach this process with humility and curiosity, recognizing that examining our beliefs, biases, and practices can feel challenging but is essential for meaningful change.
>
> This is about taking shared responsibility for creating an environment where every member of our community—students, staff, and families—can flourish. I encourage us to listen deeply to one another, to hold space for different perspectives, and to recognize our judgments or biases that might come up. This process is not about shame or blame, but about ensuring we are aligned on equity and have actionable steps that will make equity a lived reality for everyone in this community.

From there, leaders can facilitate a process of reflection that involves individual exploration, small-group exploration, and whole-group synthesis of definitions for equity.

Self-Reflection
Timeframe: about 15–20 minutes

Members of the school community—teachers, administrators, staff, students, and possibly families—will begin this process by critically exploring their assumptions about equity and inequity. This reflection is essential for identifying how individual beliefs and biases may perpetuate systemic inequities. Provide community members time to reflect on the following questions:

- What does equity look like in our school?
- What does inequity look like in our school?
- How do unconscious assumptions and implicit biases shape how we perceive students?
- Where does equity intersect with our current practices?
- What challenges or gaps can we identify in achieving equity?

You might even consider putting a graphic up on a sheet of poster paper, with "equity" on one end of the spectrum and "inequity" on the other end of the spectrum, inviting community members to share specific examples of what equity and inequity look and sound like in the community.

To anchor this reflection, it also can be helpful to draw upon definitions of equity as a guide, such as the one we propose in Chapter 2 by Drs. Galloway and Ishimaru (2019); this definition emphasizes fairness in processes and outcomes and the redistribution of resources to address structural disparities. It shifts the focus from intentions to impact, challenging participants to move beyond superficial commitments to equity. Providing a range of definitions of equity might prompt deeper thinking about what your school values and what they want to be true for their vision for equity.

Share Perspectives to Build Collective Understanding

Once individuals have completed their reflections, then it's time for folks to gather in groups, most ideally role-alike ones of some kind. These discussions can provide an opportunity to surface diverse perspectives and experiences, allowing the community to identify shared values and places of dissonance. Choose a facilitator to keep time and ensure all voices are included. The facilitator can encourage participants to share their reflections openly while identifying patterns and themes that emerge. Using visual tools such as sticky notes or digital collaboration platforms can help organize ideas and highlight areas of commonality.

Recognize that resistance may surface, often rooted in defensiveness, someone feeling attacked, or fear of change. Address this resistance by reaffirming the purpose of this exercise while thoughtfully challenging assumptions that uphold inequitable systems. For example, instead of framing discussions around "what's wrong" with the current practices or locating the issues with specific individuals, invite participants to consider "what possibilities exist" for creating more equitable outcomes.

Co-Create a Vision for Equity

Timeframe: 30–60 minutes, depending on the group size

With a foundation of reflection and dialogue in place, the next step is to co-create a shared vision for equity. This vision should be a living document, subject to ongoing updating, and reflective of the community's values and aspirations. Begin by drafting a working definition of equity, using sentence starters such as:

- "At [School Name], equity means..."
- "We achieve equity through..."

The goal is not to achieve perfection but to articulate a starting point that can evolve over time. Ensure that the process of drafting the vision is collaborative, with input from all stakeholders. This inclusivity not only strengthens the vision but also fosters a sense of ownership and accountability across the community.

Community members might write their definitions on sticky notes and place them on the wall. Community members can group post-its by theme. Another option is to create a T-chart with "Equity means" written in one column and "We achieve equity through…" in the other column. Group members can place their definitions on this T-chart and then take a look at the results and synthesize their findings. Samples of equity statements include the following:

- In our preschool, equity means honoring every individual and their needs by practicing our mission statement every day, and giving students differentiated educational opportunities that provide choice, autonomy, and center joy. We commit to practices that remove barriers to learning, affirm cultural and social identities, and cultivate a sense of belonging where every child feels seen, heard, and valued.
- Equity means intentionally creating a just, anti-oppressive, and inclusive curriculum, pedagogy, and school environment where all members of our community are valued, supported, and empowered to thrive. This requires disrupting inequitable systems, eliminating barriers to success, and actively redressing inequities to ensure that everyone has the resources, opportunities, and dignity to succeed.
- As a leadership team, equity means positioning each person to succeed with consideration of the broader community. We achieve equity through intentional investment in people and programs by communicating openly and transparently, practicing active listening, and taking an empathetic approach to decisions and policies.

Consolidate and Synthesize

Timeframe: 30–60 minutes, depending on the group size

After each group has developed their working definition, everyone will come back together to share and discuss their ideas. For this stage of the process, encourage community members to get to a "good enough" vision for equity. People can get caught up in wordsmithing and lose the plot of what they are trying to achieve. Leaders should frame this "good enough" stance at the outset of the process.

This step fosters a broader dialogue about areas of resonance and divergence, enabling the community to synthesize individual contributions into a unified vision. The process of consolidation should prioritize equity in both content (what it means) and process (how to achieve equity). Facilitators can guide the group in identifying common themes, addressing gaps, and ensuring that the final vision reflects the diverse needs and aspirations of the school community. This step is not just about achieving consensus but also about creating a vision that is both actionable and transformative. A synthesized definition of equity from the three examples above might look like the following:

- Equity means transforming systems, policies, and practices to ensure all individuals are valued, supported, and seen. By intentionally addressing historical inequities and centering the most marginalized voices, we create pathways to success and belonging for every member of our school community. We commit to
  - creating responsive and just learning conditions
  - designing learning experiences that remove systemic barriers and that honor the identities, backgrounds, strengths, and lived experiences of all community members

Translate Vision into Action
Timeframe: 30–60 minutes

A vision for equity is only meaningful if it leads to tangible change. To implement the vision, identify specific, measurable goals that align with the school's priorities. One way to do this is to have community members go back to their role-alike groups and set team/department-related goals, or everyone in the school community can set a goal they discuss with their supervisors. In addition to setting goals, though, community members should identify what they hope will happen in the next several months. For example, community members might set milestones for

November, January, and April to track progress and maintain momentum. These checkpoints can be embedded into staff-, department-, or grade-level meetings to assess whether the community's actions are aligned with the vision and to make adjustments as needed. It is also important to address potential barriers to implementation, such as resource limitations or resistance to change, by fostering a culture of accountability. Identify accountability partners or teams to oversee specific initiatives and ensure that equity remains at the forefront of decision-making. Sample prompts for action planning could be the following:

- Identify ways you hope to see progress toward your vision this year. Include qualitative measures (i.e., what community members will say and feel through feedback surveys) with quantitative measures (i.e., student outcome data and climate assessment data).
- What's one action step you will take by November, January, and April?
- On a scale of 1–10, how committed are you to this action step?
- What might get in the way of you achieving this action step?
- How will you address what might get in the way?
- Who will be your accountability partner to ensure you follow through?

In practice, this might look like the sample in Table 3.1.

Institutionalize Equity Practices and Maintain Accountability

Embedding equity into a school's culture requires sustained effort, which involves making the vision visible and actionable and integrating it into policies, professional development, and daily practices. For example, you might include equity vision as a standing agenda item in meetings, prominently display the vision in common areas, and/or incorporate it into the district or school's strategic plans. Regularly revisit the vision in staff meetings, professional development sessions, and leadership team meetings to assess progress and reaffirm commitments. Leaders also play a pivotal role in modeling equity-centered

TABLE 3.1 Math Department Goal Statement

Goal Statement for the Math Department:
By January, the math department will conduct an audit of the current math placement process to identify barriers that disproportionately impact marginalized students. The goal is to ensure all students, especially those from historically underrepresented groups, have equitable access to advanced coursework.

November Milestone	1. Collect and analyze disaggregated data (by race, gender, socioeconomic status, and students with IEPs/504s) to identify inequitable patterns in math placement. 2. Engage teachers, counselors, and administrators in reviewing this data to understand systemic barriers.
January Milestone	1. Redesign the placement process to reduce bias by incorporating multiple measures, such as student work samples, growth data, and teacher observations, alongside standardized assessments. 2. Provide targeted professional development for staff to recognize and disrupt deficit thinking that may influence placement decisions.
April Milestone:	1. Monitor outcomes of the new placement process to measure an increased access for marginalized students. 2. Share findings and next steps with the school community to maintain transparency and accountability.

Accountability Structures:

- Data Analysis Team: Math department lead, instructional coaches, equity leader.
- Accountability Partners: Leadership team and grade-level coordinators.
- Regular Check-Ins: Embed discussions into staff meetings in November, January, and April.

---

behaviors rooted in the vision. Developing a vision for equity is not a one-time task that gets shelved for the school year, but a continuous assessment of how the school's foundation codifies what's central in a school's values and what is possible in education. The process requires courage, humility, and an unwavering commitment to disrupting inequitable systems. Table 3.2 breaks down this process in discrete steps. While the timing will vary for each activity, we encourage leaders to take their time developing their vision, as a half-hearted or rushed effort sets the tone for how leadership might approach issues of inequity.

TABLE 3.2 Steps to Develop a Vision for Equity

Step	Description

Self-Reflection	• Define inequity: list qualities or examples of inequity experienced or observed
	• Define equity: identify qualities or examples of equity within and beyond the school
	• Consider alignment with overarching goals, such as the Portrait of a Graduate or school or district mission and values
	• Additional questions for self-reflection:
	   • What does equity look like in our school?
	   • What does inequity look like in our school?
	   • What implicit biases may shape how we perceive students?
	   • Where does equity intersect with our current practices?
	   • What challenges or gaps can we identify in achieving equity?

Share Perspectives to Build Collective Understanding	• Gather in teams divided by roles, departments, or divisions • Choose a facilitator to ensure balanced equity of voice and airtime • Share reflections on equity and inequity • Look for commonalities and differences in shared ideas • Use sticky notes to list individual points and post them collectively

Co-Create a Vision for Equity	• Collaboratively generate a "good enough" working definition of equity for the school
	• Use sentence starters like:
	   • "At [School Name], in our division/role, equity means..."
	   • "We achieve equity through..."
	• Use a large poster or shared digital document to display the group's final definition
	• Review and refine the statement collectively

Consolidate and Synthesize	• Each role-alike group selects a representative to present their equity definition • As a larger group, discuss areas of resonance and divergence • Agree on a unified vision • Merge ideas into a singular vision statement for the school, ensuring it reflects collective input

(Continued)

TABLE 3.2 Steps to Develop a Vision for Equity (*Continued*)

Step	Description
Institutionalize Equity Practices and Maintain Accountability	• Identify short-term action steps tied to the vision (e.g., November, January, and April checkpoints) • Set aspirational goals: What does success look like in a year? • Determine accountability measures (e.g., quantitative and qualitative) • Address potential barriers and plan responses • Decide where the vision statement will live (e.g., handbooks, meeting agendas, visible spaces) • Plan ongoing engagement through division and all-staff meetings • Establish follow-up protocols to revisit and assess the vision's relevance and progress • Commit to reviewing and adapting as needed to align with evolving equity needs

Pre-Assessment: Are You Ready to Lead Your Vision for Equity?

In *Leading Your School Toward Equity: A Practical Framework for Walking the Talk*, Dr. Dwayne Chism (2022) offers several assessment tools that leaders can use to both identify their own areas for growth and establish a common framework to use with teachers. Table 3.3 is an adaptation of Chism's "Leading for Equity: A Pre-Assessment" that we ask leaders to complete *before* undertaking a cycle of observation and growth. One of the frustrations of many teachers we work with is that they don't have leaders who can support them when it comes to improving instruction. At best, the feedback is general ("Good job! You're doing great. Keep up the good work") and not specific enough to help them improve. At worst, they feel like their supervisor doesn't really understand their instruction and culturally responsive teaching moves. Too often, principals and other site leaders have become so overwhelmed by management issues that they no longer serve as instructional leaders. And many have not had the kind of culturally responsive foundation and instructional leadership development they need to support their teachers. Nothing will affect morale more than allowing teachers, who

TABLE 3.3 Pre-Assessment: Are You Ready to Lead Your Vision for Equity?

Statement I have evidence to show…	1 (Strongly Agree) 2 (Agree) 3 (Disagree) 4 (Strongly Disagree)	Evidence—How do I know?
1. My ability to self-reflect regularly to uncover any hidden biases and stereotypes I may possess.		
2. I'm having conversations about conditions of inequity across constituents.		
3. My level of understanding around what signifies equity to effectively guide others within my school/district environment in *their* understanding of where inequity is operating.		
4. My ability to engage and inspire staff to examine their own beliefs and shift their practices in service of greater equity.		
5. I provide coaching and deliver feedback to support others in identifying and addressing instructional practices that are culturally unresponsive.		
6. My ability to help others gain the skills necessary to effectively advocate for equity when seeing daily circumstances associated with stereotypes or bias.		
7. I lead others in using data to disrupt inequities in my building or district and to establish effective strategies for improvement.		
8. I persist and advocate for equity in the face of resistance and challenge.		
9. My ability to engage in ongoing reflection about my beliefs and actions rooted in my identity and positionality—and to model necessary shifts towards greater equity.		

colleagues know are struggling, to flounder or to continue to do harm to marginalized students. At best, leaders are complacent and, at worst, complicit when they don't interrupt and engage teachers about bias, stereotypical, or discriminatory practices.

For example, leaders will often identify #5 as an area of growth for their own leadership practice: *I provide coaching and deliver feedback to support others in identifying and addressing instructional practices that are culturally unresponsive.* There are a number of reasons leaders find this practice challenging:

1. They may not have a strong background in instruction (generally) or in the tenets of culturally responsive strategies. So the lack of their own expertise creates a gap for them to address this effectively or confidently.
2. They fear conflict with staff and will avoid addressing it directly as it may produce defensiveness that will shut down any possibility for growth.
3. They are afraid that by mentioning it, they will only make the situation worse between the teacher and their class.
4. They know what they would like to see, but they can't quite figure out how to communicate that to the teacher.

Each of these reasons would identify a different action item. For reason 1 above, the leader may want to engage in their own professional development to learn more about culturally responsive teaching. They would need to shore up their own understanding of equity-centered instructional practices before trying to lead others.

But reason #3 would require a different kind of introspection: What's really going on when leaders think they will "make the situation worse" by naming the problem? Clearly, when a leader sees a teacher not meeting expectations, the situation is already challenging. So avoiding confrontation will only make the situation worse—most importantly for the students. What happens when educational leaders fail to interrupt teaching practices that they know are not serving students? Are they willing to preserve the comfort of the teacher at the expense of the students who are experiencing bias and/or ineffective instruction? An equity foundation would center the needs of the most impacted or marginalized, so to let the issue go unaddressed would not support a commitment to serve all students. So, how could a leader shift their approach to frame this issue for the teacher so as to effectively improve their process? What does the leader need to push through their discomfort in this situation? How could they make the issue explicit and demonstrate to the teacher that they are committed to helping them improve? By acknowledging their need for skill development in this area, a leader can establish a focus for their own growth and development.

Elizabeth used this assessment with a group of white leaders who were working on their feedback skills to counter some of the ways that dominant cultural norms will influence their management, such as fearing open conflict and maintaining comfort over the discomfort of naming racism. Rather than avoiding these patterns, they explored recent situations or current dilemmas when they had failed to confront a white colleague on problematic behavior. They spent time really analyzing what was happening for them in the moment, and with greater clarity, they could develop a plan to redress what had happened, own their actions, and make the commitment to do better next time.

By walking through some of the ways we use this preassessment as a diagnostic tool for leaders, we hope you can see how applying this to a leadership practice can increase efficacy. Often, we are not specific enough in the kinds of shifts we need to make as leaders. By identifying an observable skill you want to get better at and the reason why it may be a challenge, the more likely you are to adopt a new behavior or practice. And the better you will be when supporting and modeling for the teachers and instructors in your building.

Social Identities Portrait

This is an effective inventory for all educational personnel to be fully cognizant of their positionality and how their experiences and identities impact their values, decisions, and ways of showing up with colleagues and students. It is a tool to help ensure we are critically reflecting on who we are and how we can develop our skills as culturally responsive educators. We use this activity after describing systems of power and privilege and how they might be operating via policies, procedures, curricula, and/or pedagogical approaches. This activity then allows individuals to locate themselves and think about their own group memberships and proximity to power. Where are they in relation to larger social systems that are operating in our schools and communities? How have their own identities been forged and impacted by social norms and conventions? And how have their students been affected by these social dynamics—what are the dominant group norms that may be showing up in their classrooms? Assessment and feedback criteria? Curricular choices? Collaboration with parents/caregivers and community partners? Table 3.4 outlines the process for completing the Social Identities Portrait.

Based on your identity and lived experiences, please fill out the Descriptions of Self. In each row, read the social identity term in the first column and write in columns 2 and 3 whatever word(s) you used to describe yourself as a child and the words you use now. Then circle **or bold** the identities in columns 4 and 5 that apply to your life.

TABLE 3.4 Social Identities Portrait (adapted from Derman-Sparks & Edwards, 2020)

Social Identity	Description of self		Groups Defined as the Norm; Recipients of Societal Advantages	Groups that Are Marginalized and Targets of Institutional Prejudice and Discrimination
	Childhood	Currently		
Ethnicity or heritage			European American	All other ethnicities, including Indigenous peoples
Place of birth			Born in the country you now live in	Immigrant
Language			English	Home languages other than English
Racialized identity			White	People of Color; biracial; multiracial
Gender			Men/Male; cisgender	Women/Female; nonbinary, agender; transgender, etc.

(*Continued*)

TABLE 3.4 Social Identities Portrait (adapted from Derman-Sparks & Edwards, 2020) (*Continued*)

Social Identity	Description of self		Groups Defined as the Norm; Recipients of Societal Advantages	Groups that Are Marginalized and Targets of Institutional Prejudice and Discrimination
	Childhood	Currently		
Sexuality			Heterosexual	Asexual, bisexual, gay, lesbian, queer, polyamorous, etc.
Religious beliefs			Christian or Christian tradition	Muslim, Jewish, Buddhist, Hindu, pagan, atheist, etc.
Age			Productive adults (ages 20-50 for women, 20-60 for men)	Children, adolescents, women over 50, men over 60
Body type/ size			Slim, fit Medium height for women Tall for man	Large, overweight Very short or very tall
Able self (physical, mental, emotional health)			Healthy No apparent disability	Any form of disability: physical, mental, emotional, learning, behavioral
Economic class			Middle to upper class	Working class; living in poverty
Family structure			Male/female married parents with one to three biological children	Unmarried; single parent; gay or lesbian parents; child free; divorced; adoptive, foster, or blended family; more than three children

Note: You may not always have words to describe these identities. That's okay. Write down your best thoughts at the moment. Don't leave a section blank. You can always redo this as time goes on.

Reflection/Discussion Questions:

1. Which three identities have had the biggest impact on you? In what ways? And why do you think these three have emerged as the most salient/impactful?

2. Have different aspects of your identity been more salient (or less) during particular times of your life? For example?
3. How does your identity impact your work with students? Colleagues? Families? Are there times you notice aspects of your identity more than others?
4. How did you feel while completing this reflection? What emotions surfaced for you?

Introduction to the Self-Reflection Tool

Timeframe: about 15–20 minutes

Have participants read over the introductory directions. Together, read through the various social identity groups listed in column 1 on the far left. Ask participants if any of the terms are unfamiliar so you can clarify terms before they complete their inventory. Encourage participants to self-identify in ways that feel most authentic to them in columns 2 and 3. These help educators recognize how our understanding of our identities is not fixed and actually develops over time, especially when we reflect on different contexts. It's also important to provide a reflection back to childhood experiences because then educators can think more directly about the children they are working with and how their identities are emerging in the classroom or on campus.

The last two columns often present a challenge for some; they may never have identified themselves according to a social group, especially for locations of identity privilege. Some may not want to identify with a dominant group, so that's why we recommend talking about the larger systems of mainstreams and margins before doing the exercise. That way, they can see how these dynamics were in place before anyone in the room was born. While we did not ask for these conditions or locations of power, we are responsible for knowing how they operate and how we have been affected by our development and social group memberships. Then we can be in solidarity and work across differences to address unequal power and create more equitable educational systems.

Participants will then complete the inventory either on paper or via an electronic form. Once everyone has completed the inventory on their own, ask participants to make small groups of three or four members.

Small-Group Discussion
Timeframe: about 15–20 minutes

Working in groups of three or four, ask participants to reflect together on the four discussion questions (listed after the inventory) in "rounds," meaning everyone answers question 1 before moving on to question 2. This way all voices can be heard, and a range of experiences can be shared. We find that these smaller group discussions help participants process the inventory and make sense of both their own and their colleagues' experiences. It's also a time for participants to ask questions and clarify any misunderstandings or new learnings.

Full-Group Debrief
Timeframe: about 10–15 minutes

Bring the small groups back together and pose larger questions about the exercise, some of which might include

> What new understandings emerged?
> How might participants be thinking differently about the role of identity in their own practice?

From there, you can move the conversation toward a reflection of how we are engaging students in these kinds of conversations. How are students learning about their own identities? How are they negotiating differences in the classroom and/or on campus? Are we interrupting deficit mindsets when they emerge? The goal is to surface how patterns of identity development impact our work with each other, our students, and their families/caregivers. If we are not intentional about the ways we approach the role of identity and power in our teaching/learning, we may unintentionally replicate dominant norms and continue inequitable practices. This kind of activity helps to increase not only our awareness of bias but also our ability to successfully engage and dismantle practices that may be getting in the way of authentic and effective learning and success for all.

Summary: Practices to Lay the Foundation

This chapter emphasizes the critical importance of equity as a foundational practice for educational leaders and teachers. Through tools like Creating Your Vision for Equity, the Pre-Assessment: Are You Ready to Lead Your Vision for Equity? and the Social Identities Portrait, this chapter guides leaders in defining, reflecting on, and taking actionable steps toward equity. Leaders are encouraged to move beyond superficial or performative equity initiatives by critically assessing their biases, fostering collective reflection, and co-creating a shared vision for equitable practices. The chapter underscores that equity is an evolving, collaborative effort that requires accountability, persistence, and the courage to disrupt inequitable systems.

For Further Reflection

- What would an equitable school environment look, sound, and feel like for students, staff, and families?
- In what ways have you seen your understanding of your identity evolve, and how does this evolution impact your leadership or teaching practices?
- How do your social identities shape your approach to equity, and how might they influence your interactions with students, colleagues, and families?
- How can you build accountability structures that sustain momentum and ensure equity remains a priority?

References

Chism, D. (2022). *Leading your school toward equity: A practical framework for walking the talk*. ASCD.

Derman-Sparks, L., & Edwards, J. O. (2020). *Anti-bias education for young children and ourselves*. National Association for the Education of Young Children.

Galloway, M. K., & Ishimaru, A. M. (2019). Leading equity teams: The role of formal leaders in building organizational capacity for equity. *Journal of Education for Students Placed at Risk (JESPAR)*, 25(2), 107–125. https://doi.org/10.1080/10824669.2019.1699413

Well-Being:
Nurture the Soil

Well-being requires attention to the structural and relational conditions that allow educators and students to thrive. Like tending to rich, fertile soil, well-being moves beyond surface-level fixes to address systemic inequities, workload, and the pace of work. It prioritizes autonomy, community care, relationships, and trust while challenging norms of overwork and constant productivity. By cultivating sustainable practices rooted in dignity and care, we can create spaces where educators can rest, grow, and flourish—nurturing the soil for a thriving community.

4

Well-Being: Nurture the Soil

The superintendents at Hollyhock School District, Ernesto and Maggie, wanted to try something new for the district in-service day: play. Fall was a tough time for teachers, so they aimed to liven up a long day of literacy discussions with a little fun first. As a small rural district with just one elementary, middle, and high school, they hoped educators could socialize across roles. Keeping the idea a secret, even from presenters, they transformed the Hollyhock High School gym into a playful space.

When attendees arrived, they were greeted by blue and gold streamers, 90s hip-hop blaring from a speaker, and Ernesto and Maggie welcoming them with, "Welcome to the play zone!" Inside, the gym offered basketballs, a mini pickleball court, pastries with coffee, and tables with puzzles, board games, human-sized Jenga, sculpting clay, and painting supplies.

Reactions varied. Paulina, a new teacher overwhelmed by her workload, had hoped for literacy strategies. Harry, a middle school teacher, grumbled about money being wasted during a bargaining year. Eloise, the elementary assistant principal, worried about the staff morale and wondered if this event would further teachers' cynicism and be a distraction from the challenges facing the school. Meanwhile, literacy specialists Nancy and Stella were surprised to see games instead of prepared meeting materials. "It would've been nice to have known about this shift in schedule in advance," Stella remarked.

Ernesto addressed the group: "We wanted to treat you to something different today. You work hard, and we want you to feel cared for while connecting with colleagues. Play hard now, and we'll work hard after." A smattering of applause followed. Sitting nearby, Harry whispered to Paulina, "How about they use today's budget to pay us more?"

Maybe you've experienced this at your schools and districts, too. A seemingly well-intentioned effort to support well-being, but no real clarity about the purpose, much less any roadmap for the types of proactive practices that balance teacher well-being with the essential work schools need to be doing to support student learning.

Ernesto and Maggie wanted district educators to feel cared for, to play hard before they worked hard. Their gesture reflects a common pattern where well-intentioned leaders respond to challenging workplace conditions with isolated events rather than addressing the underlying systems creating educator stress. Not only that, Nancy and Stella had prepared to lead a workshop that day, and the playtime cut into their workshop time. How did Nancy and Stella feel about how their work was prioritized? For new teachers like Paulina, she was anxious about getting some literacy strategies to be more effective in the classroom. Harry and Eloise were cynical. What might it have looked like if Ernesto and Maggie connected with educators to determine what kind of support would allow them to feel cared for? How might they have partnered with Nancy and Stella so they could have balanced learning opportunities with connection? More than that, what was the purpose of the literacy strategies workshop? Was it to follow the latest educational trend, or was it to address inequities in literacy performance for students? How is the district supporting new teachers like Paulina so that she feels equipped in her classroom? Perhaps some might have enjoyed the treats and a couple of rounds of pickleball, but what a lot of educators want is a purposeful way for their time to be used, especially if their typical professional days have not been useful in the past.

Educators want and need a lot of other things as well: higher pay, a manageable workload, autonomy, and a voice in decision-making. While we might not be able to control every factor contributing to educator well-being, people in positions of power across schools, districts, and organizations significantly influence workplace conditions through decisions about resource allocation, equity initiatives, hiring practices, and how many initiatives to prioritize simultaneously. We can reimagine school years with a more sustainable pace. We can slow down to examine the factors that contribute to educator well-being, prioritize deeper learning, and draw upon our foundation of equity as a guide for addressing what educators need to be effective and supported in their roles. Explicitly addressing educator well-being is beneficial for the entire educational ecosystem.

For an ecosystem to thrive, healthy soil is vital. Soil stores water, supplies nutrients, provides a hospitable place for plant life to take root, and decomposes and transforms the remains of dead organisms into nourishment used by other living plants, animals, and microorganisms in their creation of new life. Soil is teeming with diverse living organisms, some of which are easily discernible, such as plant roots and animals, to small mites and insects, to microscopically tiny microorganisms such as bacteria and fungi. When creating an ecosystem, the right soil composition is essential (as is the right light, temperature, and humidity) so that all living organisms can grow and thrive. Good soil, tended to intentionally, will foster an ecosystem's well-being. Soils are the base material for homemade terrariums, gardens, forests, roads, homes, buildings, and other structures set upon them, like schools.

In this chapter, we will explore how fostering educator well-being is essential for a thriving school ecosystem—one that supports not only student success but also the sustained health and resilience of its teachers. For school communities, this means getting clarity about roles and responsibilities and developing support structures that are proactive rather than reactive. For leaders, this means balancing personal work with sustaining relationships—including building trust with intention and repairing harm with humility. For individuals, it means taking responsibility for assessing one's well-being and working to address what needs fine-tuning. It's time to shift from occasional wellness initiatives and individualized self-care approaches to embrace community care practices rooted in emotional intelligence, relationships, trust and transparency, human dignity, and loving accountability. Small, fractal changes to the soil can contribute to an ecosystem where educators can flourish.

Why Prioritize Well-Being

Schools aren't designed to consider the needs of adults. If someone signs on to be an educator, there is a tacit assumption that they'll buy into the frenzied pace and thanklessness, accept low pay, feel overworked, but reap the rewards of student learning. As students continue to take their cues from adults, they learn that one has to overextend themselves to be a teacher, sacrificing long hours, long days, good pay, and cognitive and emotional energy at the whim of leaders and policymakers who make decisions about budgets, class sizes, curriculum, what books students can read and what they can't, among a host of factors. From the first days many new teachers enter the classroom, they might be socialized into a cycle that includes anticipation and survival in the fall, disillusionment by December, rejuvenation by spring, and back to anticipation the following summer (New Teacher Center, 2023). Plenty of experienced teachers, leaders, and education officials also set their expectations to this same type of sequence, often musing annually about how all the disillusionment was well worth it. As leaders, many of us have left this cycle unattended, accepting that "this is just the way it is." In ecosystems, very little growth happens when the soil is neglected.

Leaders often experience tension between the initiatives that "have to" get done with the very real needs of teachers. When setting priorities, however, leaders often skew in favor of initiatives, leaving classroom teachers behind, particularly educators of color and LGBTQIA+ educators who perform unpaid emotional labor to address inequities, which contributes to teacher burnout and attrition. When leaders do focus on well-being efforts, they tend to overcorrect, spending an outsized amount of energy on surface-level fixes for larger systemic issues, like giving stipends for additional work without exploring how to pay teachers more, or deciding to cancel a staff meeting so teachers have time to get their grades completed but not examining how the schedule could be more conducive to teachers' workloads without competing trade-offs. In ecosystems, this is akin to overwatering, saturating the soil for a brief period but not sustainably addressing the health of the seeds. When educators don't express appreciation for these scattershot well-being efforts or acknowledge how hard leaders are working, leaders feel like these efforts are fruitless and become cynical about whether anything will ever please teachers (Mielke, 2023). There is greater urgency to address educator well-being and to be more skillful about integrating well-being into the school ecosystem. Before we get into what leaders can do, let's explore the current state of educator well-being and what's at stake if things don't change.

Neglected Soil

In recent years, educators have reported—and continue to report—a greater prevalence of anxiety, distress, and burnout (Fox et al., 2023; Kush et al., 2022). Merrimack College and EdWeek conducted a survey of teacher satisfaction and well-being and found that 42% of teachers say their mental health and wellness negatively impact their school experiences (Kurtz, 2023). In a Pew research study of US public school teachers in 2023, 77% of teachers reported feeling stressed, while 68% feel overwhelmed by their responsibilities, including student mental health crises and behavioral issues. In the same survey, only 20% of teachers reported feeling optimistic about the future of education, yet they, too, highlighted an urgent need for systemic transformation (Pew Research Center, 2024). Educators on the whole are not well.

High stress, poor working conditions, low trust, micromanagement, and burnout, especially among educators of color, have an influence on how educators teach and manage their classrooms, negatively impacting student well-being and learning outcomes (Learning Policy Institute, 2023; Simmons, 2021). Schools are navigating continuing waves of budget cuts, which affect conversations about teacher compensation and bargaining efforts with unions. Despite some states offering competitive salaries and even increasing salaries (i.e., Alabama and Vermont), teachers make 5% less than they did a decade ago, with the national average salary at $44,530, which is $4,000 below 2008–2009 levels (NEA, 2024; We Are Teachers, 2024). The Learning Policy Institute (2023) found that 36.6% of educators still owe student loans and spend close to $500 of their own money per year on classroom supplies without reimbursement.

Although all educators experience stress and burnout, educators of color and LGBTQIA+ educators often experience unique stressors. Less than 20% of classroom teachers and principals, and only 10% of superintendents, are people of color (Peters, 2024). The statistics are unclear about the percentage of educators who are LGBTQIA+, as many queer and trans educators may be uncomfortable self-reporting, but the percentage hovers somewhere between 3% and 8% (Campus Explorer, 2024). Educators from these backgrounds might be asked to translate for parents who do not speak English, stand in as disciplinarians for students experiencing behavioral challenges, or be supportive mentors for students who are questioning their sexuality or gender identities. Educators from these backgrounds might be interrupted from working with their own students or completing their other responsibilities. Additionally, when there are race- or culturally based events in their communities (e.g., the Black Lives Matter protests or any sort of a cultural heritage month), educators from marginalized backgrounds are often expected to take the lead in educating their peers while navigating their own personal experiences.

Teachers from marginalized backgrounds often serve as de facto mentors for students within their racial and/or linguistic groups, sexual orientations, and gender identities, helping to make up for their school's failures to adequately address institutional racism, xenophobia, and homophobia, thereby teaching students how to cope with an unjust system by "playing the game" and code-switching to ensure safe passage through school. Educators from these backgrounds might also be directly marginalized themselves. All the while, individuals from more privileged backgrounds who don't experience similar levels of harm might take less responsibility for addressing and correcting systemic inequities in schools.

Here's an example from one of our experiences: When Lori was an early-career teacher, she was not out in the school community because protections for LGBTQIA+ educators at the time were minimal. She felt tension being in the closet when her queer students faced daily bullying and harassment. She thought it was important to be a supportive role model, so she was selectively out to students when the conditions felt safe enough. The school had no policy to protect queer students or teachers, and when bullies of any kind were disciplined, they were suspended with no further consequences. The district had clear-cut sexual harassment policies in place, but the microaggressions Lori faced, the seemingly lighthearted jokes about Lori's sexuality that she dealt with daily, had no recourse. Like many educators who share similar identifiers, Lori had to make calculated decisions about her own safety while supporting high school students through their identity journeys, adding another layer of responsibility on a teacher workload that included 150 students and 4 different preps.

Thankfully, Lori's school had a Seeking Educational Equity and Diversity (SEED) group, where 20+ educators from all backgrounds came together monthly to learn about systems of oppression and determine each person's responsibility for eradicating injustice. As part support and part accountability group, SEED was a safe place for Lori to come out, to have supportive straight colleagues who also took shared responsibility for addressing the rampant homophobia at school. While it was still a challenge to be a queer educator, Lori felt less alone knowing she was in solidarity with SEED colleagues who played a role in asking school administrators to do more to address schoolwide bullying and harassment. At the same time, while SEED groups and affinity groups provide important healing spaces, their very necessity reflects a larger, institutional failure. Rather than addressing the underlying policies and practices that create unsafe environments, institutions place the burden of coping and survival on those already experiencing harm.

Just as ecosystems are subject to damage because of drought and storms, schools without strong policies to support all community members may not be able to weather the storms of opposition—and opposition to equity efforts is increasing. When leaders neglect to take a stand and change policy and practice in service of equity, historically marginalized educators—and, as a consequence, their students—suffer the most. In 2022, the turnover rate for Black teachers was 22% compared to white teachers at 15%, largely due to the burnout Black teachers faced from racism and outsized, hidden expectations for their roles (Lambert, 2024; National Center for Education Statistics, 2022). In the early 2020s, opponents of Diversity, Equity, and Inclusion efforts in schools began introducing sweeping legislation at federal and state levels, targeting school curriculum and critical race theory, banning books, eradicating certain words (such as "equity" and "social-emotional learning"), cutting funding for inclusionary practices, and grilling school leaders who supported these efforts, which furthered the marginalization and burnout of communities of color, LGBTQIA+, and disabled communities. Some families began rallying for parents' rights and running for school board positions so they could oust superintendents and have a say in what is taught in schools and who can play on the athletic field. Because of these targeted measures at local and national levels, educators are leaving the profession at higher rates than ever (Learning Policy Institute, 2023). Among those who stay, over half of the teachers report feeling burned out (Tamez-Robledo, 2024). Educators across all identifying markers are struggling to justify why they should stay in the profession. We need to treat educator retention with greater urgency if we want to sustain a thriving educational ecosystem that supports both teachers and students.

Healthy Soil: Dimensions of Collective Well-Being

We know a lot about why teachers leave, but there are also actionable ways to support those who stay. Findings from the past decade demonstrate how high teacher well-being is linked to strong student–teacher relationships and enhances student engagement, motivation, and academic success—which helps reduce burnout and improve teacher retention (Hanover Research, n.d.; Taylor et al., 2024). Nurturing the soil of educator well-being has many dimensions, and it is important that leaders be intentional in their efforts, to choose one or two focal areas that are at the root of supporting well-being rather than oversaturating the soil with too many half-hearted efforts that eventually fizzle out. The most impactful well-being initiatives shift the focus from random, individualized approaches to coordinated efforts for community care. As leaders consider their well-being efforts, they may begin by asking:

- How do we define well-being?
- What does it mean to be an educator at our school site?
- What conditions need to be in place to support educators' well-being?
- What do leaders need to know and practice to foster well-being?

The following pages outline essential dimensions of educator well-being. While not exhaustive, they illustrate key factors to consider. We will share brief examples for leaders and discuss more in-depth processes in the next chapter, such as the portrait of an educator. We begin with complex issues like wage satisfaction, job stability, and workload management, recognizing that addressing these topics requires a more in-depth treatment beyond the scope of this book. We then will focus on areas more directly within a leader's control, particularly emotional intelligence and the cultivation of strong, supportive relationships. These elements can nurture an environment where educators feel valued and supported throughout the school year. This approach helps leaders build the trust and relational capital necessary for the growth of the entire educational ecosystem.

Wage Satisfaction

Adequate compensation reduces financial stress, enhances job satisfaction, and motivates teachers to stay in the profession. We advocate for significantly higher base salaries as the primary solution, and we also encourage schools and districts to go beyond salary conversations alone. Leaders can increase educator well-being through advocating and working for transparent salary scales, regular equity audits to ensure fair pay, housing support, competitive starting salaries for those new to a school or district, and additional compensation for those who take on extra responsibilities, whether through monetary compensation or adequate release time.

In many high-cost-of-living areas, teachers are priced out of the housing market. An EdWeek Research Center survey in July of 2022 found that 11% of teachers said free or subsidized housing for educators would increase retention (Will, 2023). The California School Boards Association noted that 158 of the 1,000 school districts are interested in providing affordable housing for staff. Jefferson Union High School District in Daly City built 122 units on district-owned land, which is occupied by 25% of district staff; these efforts increased teacher retention in a district that had experienced significant attrition year after year (Lambert, 2024). In addition to housing support, flexible and customizable health benefits and childcare subsidies can also further support educators' sense of financial stability. For public school educators, a collaboration with teacher unions and advocacy groups has been essential to increasing teacher salaries and benefits at the district and state levels; in the past few years, state legislatures and districts have dedicated their efforts to making salaries comparable to other professions requiring similar levels of education (Johnson & Hall, 2017). School budgets could also include line items for more generous professional development funding paid directly to teachers to support their learning and growth. Teachers in licensing programs—whether in district-sponsored "grow your own" or university-level programs—could get paid while they work toward their certification. In 12 states across the U.S., teacher residency programs helped alleviate financial barriers for early-career teachers while also increasing teacher retention (Saunders et al., 2024).

Additionally, leaders can compensate those taking on additional responsibilities, such as mentors and coaches, by providing stipends and additional prep time. Educators of color and LGBTQIA+ educators deserve formal compensation for their often-invisible labor—work that schools frequently exploit while failing to address inequities systemically. At the same time, we would caution against using stipends as a catch-all for doing additional work. Instead, we advocate that leaders look at their policies and typical school workloads and determine other ways to compensate teachers for taking on additional, often unrecognized, leadership work, such as offering reduced teaching loads or paid release time.

As you consider the needs of your school community, where might you consider getting more strategic about compensation? What efforts might best support educator retention?

Job Stability

When institutional cultures have high levels of trust, and when leaders are transparent in their communication, community members feel a greater sense of belonging, less anxiety, and overall better job stability, allowing educators to focus on their teaching (Steiner et al., 2023). Leaders can foster greater trust and transparency about staffing decisions and budget, and they can provide clear, ongoing communication regarding potential changes, giving teachers enough notice to prepare in case of budget cuts or a reduction in force. Where possible, leaders might work closely with unions to consider multi-year contracts to reduce employment anxiety.

One way to increase trust is through seeking feedback. Leaders and educators alike might ask:

- ♦ How are we establishing trust and identity-safety in our community so that adults and students feel they can provide authentic feedback?
- ♦ How are we incorporating feedback, particularly from those who have been historically underserved?
- ♦ How does the feedback we gather challenge us to disrupt systemic inequities in our practices?

We advocate that feedback can be powerful to increase student and adult agency, to get data directly from students' classroom experiences, and for educators to model care and their learning and growth for students (Boykin & Noguera, 2011). Let's consider the following example from one of our experiences. In Lori's experience, when she was a teacher and a leader, she used various feedback methods. At mid- and end-of-semester, she asked for feedback using the following questions:

- What is something about my teaching or leadership that has impacted you? Is there a story you can think of?
- To what degree do you feel seen, cared for, and valued?
- What is something I can do better as a teacher/leader?
- What other feedback would you like to offer that supports your learning and growth?

Lori would prepare herself before she reviewed the feedback, reminding herself that feedback was a snapshot and a gift. She also recognized that the way she modeled how she was receiving and responding to feedback set the tone in her school community. When she reviewed the feedback, she identified themes and shared her learning with the students the following week—including ways she was planning on acting (or not acting) on the feedback. Engaging in this process was humbling and important, creating greater trust and a safer learning environment for Lori's students and colleagues. However feedback is collected, the process for seeking it needs to be intentional. If leaders are going to expect teachers to ask for feedback, they need to ask for feedback, too. Leaders can request anonymous feedback (through confidential surveys) and non-anonymous feedback (through structured listening sessions or one-on-one meetings) and report back themes and action steps publicly. These actions can go a long way to fostering communal trust and furthering a school or district's collective well-being. How does your school or district gather feedback? What practices do you use to increase trust and stability?

Another element of job stability is offering opportunities for professional growth. Not every teacher wants to leave the classroom, and there aren't often ways for teachers to expand their roles without taking an administrative path. Leaders might consider creating pathways like curriculum development, technology integration, serving as a Teacher on Special Assignment, or grade/team-level coordinators, many of which allow teachers to remain in the classroom. Leaders might compensate these efforts with stipends, salary hikes, or benefits like professional development opportunities and reduced teaching loads.

Most of all, teachers feel greater job satisfaction when they are recognized for their work; specific and sustained appreciation efforts can go a long way in supporting educator well-being. Drs. Gottman and Silver's 5:1 rule (2015) of ensuring there are at least five positive interactions to every negative interaction can help leaders balance any critique with multiple positive interactions, furthering one's job satisfaction without feeling that any meeting with an administrator is solely devoted to criticism. For example, leaders might balance critique with specific acknowledgments like, "I noticed how you engaged that reluctant student through personal connection today," rather than generic praise that might feel forced or inauthentic. This authentic recognition ensures that positive feedback is genuine, specific, and supportive rather than empty or toxically positive.

Workload Management

If you were to list out all the different responsibilities you have in a school day, what would it include? How much of that workload feels manageable? Workload management for educators refers to the deliberate structuring and distribution of responsibilities to ensure teachers can meet professional demands without undue stress or burnout. The increased demands on educators' time beyond preparation, assessment, emails, and the range of meetings, conferences, and committees educators take part in create a cycle of "time poverty" that undermines educators' ability to focus on instruction and student engagement Time poverty—the relationship between the amount of work teachers must complete and the intensity of that work—has been identified as a critical factor affecting educator well-being (Creagh et al., 2023).

Effective workload management requires school leaders to address these challenges proactively by offering clear role definitions, equitable distribution of tasks, and protected time for collaboration and planning. This intentional approach could enable educators to focus their energy on high-impact practices that benefit both teachers and students. Schools with schedules that include common prep time for teachers can reduce the work teachers take home or are expected to do in their own time; this time can be devoted to lesson planning, discussing teaching strategies, assessing student work, or receiving professional development. For schools with scheduling challenges, professional learning days can be coupled with time for teachers to meet and co-plan with colleagues. Leaders might also set clear boundaries about communication outside the school day, such as a "no email after 5:00 pm and on weekends" policy. Leaders could model these practices by not responding to any outside-of-school messages unless it's an emergency; they can also communicate these policies in employee and student handbooks to make these boundaries communal and explicit.

Leaders can make the biggest impact on workload management and expectations by providing role clarity. This means outlining exactly what is expected of teachers and proactively designing ways to support them in meeting these expectations. As we mentioned earlier, educators from historically marginalized backgrounds often end up taking on extra invisible responsibilities due to a school's lack of action in addressing inequity. We are advocating for an approach called The Portrait of an Educator, which you'll find in the next chapter. It's a collaborative process that involves the entire school community and is designed to boost transparency, accountability, and schoolwide responsibility around roles. The Portrait, and the process of creating it, invites important conversations about fairly distributing responsibilities but also ensures that everyone is held to high expectations for equity. This portrait can be used for hiring, goal-setting, determining professional development initiatives, and evaluation.

Autonomy and Self-Efficacy

Giving educators the freedom to make decisions about their teaching methods and professional learning pathways fosters a sense of ownership and empowerment, which increases motivation and prevents burnout (Mielke, 2023). Educators with high self-efficacy (mastery of, and confidence in, their subject areas, instructional practices, and skill levels) are more resilient, adaptive, and persistent in facing challenges and can contribute to the collective efficacy of a school community. With greater trust and autonomy, teachers have the freedom to design lessons that reflect their expertise and address student learning needs. Teachers are trusted to know not only what's best for their students but also what might contribute to their professional growth. To promote greater autonomy, school leaders need to intentionally foster a culture of learning (Senge, 1990), where teachers might observe and learn from one another and collectively reflect on their practice. This happens most effectively when leaders are willing to model their own learning, which includes making mistakes and sharing lessons learned.

However, more autonomy and self-efficacy doesn't mean that teachers can be free to do whatever they want if autonomy perpetuates harm or draws upon antiquated teaching methods that work for very few students. In our ecosystem framework, equity serves as a foundation for how policy is designed and the kinds of practices a school engages in to best serve all community members. Autonomy and self-efficacy are about teacher choice within a set of agreed-upon schoolwide practices.

For example, Brandywine Middle School teachers noticed that Black and Brown students and students with disabilities were often held to low expectations, and many students didn't have the opportunities to demonstrate their abilities to be independent, self-directed learners. Rather than imposing a standardized solution, leaders worked collaboratively with teachers in using Universal Design for Learning (UDL) practices and creating a framework that balanced teachers' content expertise with a schoolwide goal of improved outcomes for Black and Brown students and students with disabilities. In the staff professional development day, teachers co-designed lessons that fostered independence using

UDL practices, and they received feedback before lessons were implemented. At quarterly follow-up staff meetings, teachers brought student work samples and analyzed the successes and challenges of their approaches. This balance of a shared school commitment alongside honoring teacher autonomy increased staff collective efficacy and accountability. The process wasn't perfect, and there was some resistance to these efforts. But doing this work collectively allowed leaders to respond to the resistance directly and reinforce their commitment to equity—while also honoring teacher expertise. As you consider this example, what structures exist in your school that simultaneously honor teacher autonomy while advancing your collective aims?

Inclusion in Policymaking

Think of a recent policy change or big decision at your school or district. Who was involved? Whose voices were missing? Involving educators in decision-making processes ensures that their insights and experiences shape educational policies. This inclusion leads to more practical and effective policies, greater engagement in change-based initiatives, and enhances educators' sense of value and influence. In practice, this might look like teachers serving on school committees that shape policy around curriculum and school culture. Leadership teams might conduct regular town hall-style meetings to gather input from staff before implementing major changes.

Leaders need to seek input from those most impacted by school decisions to ensure greater equity in decision-making. This means creating spaces or focus groups where those most historically marginalized can share their experiences openly, with a commitment to act meaningfully on the feedback received rather than engaging in performative listening exercises that go nowhere. This also means that committees reflect the diversity of identities and roles within the school to ensure policies consider all community members. Finally, this means taking this input and applying it to policies and practices in a sustained way—and seeking feedback on implementation. For example, when Abundance Academy, the school we mentioned in our introduction, wanted to shift their school's practices around climate, growth, and evaluation, they first formed committees that included teachers, non-teaching staff, and administrators. These committees co-designed empathy interview questions about staff experiences. Committee members practiced interviewing one another before interviewing staff. They then analyzed interview results together and used iterative processes to design prototypes and seek feedback on these prototypes before implementing them. While leaders weren't able to act on all suggestions from the feedback, they implemented two initiatives—a monthly staff forum to share concerns and create solutions, and ongoing schoolwide professional learning on giving and receiving feedback.

Community Care

In our opening story, while Ernesto and Maggie took a fragmented approach to address mental and physical health, their efforts may have been more fruitful if they were sustained. Schools that promote ongoing wellness programs can significantly improve staff health and morale (Lever et al., 2017). Schools can offer many approaches to mental and physical well-being: on-campus fitness classes, mindfulness sessions, access to mental health resources, and affinity spaces for those who share common identifiers—particularly those who have been more historically marginalized (Harvard Kennedy School, n.d.). Any well-being effort focused on mental and physical wellness necessitates that leaders actively engage in the process, too. Their positional power means that their actions set the standard for what's expected.

If we are going to reimagine educator support, we need to advocate for practices beyond the out-of-office message after 5:00 pm or on weekends. Educators, on the whole, need better boundaries and more rest. Tricia Hersey, also known as the "Nap Bishop," is a prominent advocate for rest, emphasizing their importance as tools for liberation and resistance against systemic oppression. Hersey founded The Nap Ministry in 2016, an organization that promotes the idea of "rest as resistance" and "rest as reparations." Her work is rooted in Black radical thought, liberation theology, and a critique of capitalism and white supremacy. Hersey's approach is not just about individual self-care but about communal liberation and challenging societal norms that equate worth with productivity (The Nap Ministry, n.d.). Hersey's book, *Rest is Resistance: A Manifesto* (2022), elaborates on her philosophy, calling for a radical reimagining of our relationship with work and time. Hersey encourages people to prioritize rest as a form of resistance to the capitalist demands for constant productivity, advocating for a more just and equitable world where rest is seen as a human right, not a luxury.

For schools to embrace Hersey's philosophy, they would need to integrate practices and policies that prioritize rest and self-care for both staff and students. Schools can promote rest by offering flexible scheduling, such as time off after major events, non-homework days (or a re-evaluation of homework entirely), and creating restorative pause days with no meetings or work expectations. School schedules might include wellness breaks or no-meetings-during-lunchtime days. Leaders can model boundary-setting, provide choice-based professional development, and solicit feedback from community members about what kinds of wellness activities are most beneficial to them (Steinmann et al., 2018). For example, before designing their August professional learning, Greenleaf School District conducted a district-wide survey, asking all employees about the kinds of wellness activities they'd like to experience the following school year. These opt-in wellness opportunities included a fiction book club, a running club, a knitting group, and a mindfulness group. The district earmarked funding to purchase supplies, so educators were not paying out of pocket for these initiatives. Establishing rest spaces and fostering community care through non-work gatherings reinforces the importance of self-care and collective well-being, challenging the norms of constant productivity.

Emotional Intelligence

Imagine you're headed to a staff meeting where you need to announce impending budget cuts and a reduction in force. Your school took part in a district-sponsored teacher residency program to increase support for students with disabilities, and now that program is getting cut. Morale is already low in your school. How would you prepare yourself for this meeting? What would you say to staff? How would you tend to your emotions and the emotions of others? In moments like these, leaders need to demonstrate and foster emotional intelligence. Emotional intelligence—defined as the ability to understand and regulate one's own emotions while effectively navigating relationships through empathetic action (Salovey & Mayer, 1990)—is central to educator well-being and is essential for addressing the systemic challenges that disproportionately affect educators and students from marginalized communities (Ladson-Billings, 1995). Leaders who center emotional intelligence in their daily actions can build trust and capacity within their schools. By modeling emotional intelligence, leaders can create psychologically safe spaces that promote healthier teacher–student relationships, reduce burnout, and cultivate equity-centered practices (Khalifa, 2018).

Leaders not only must model the behaviors they wish to see in their communities but also actively build the skill and capacity of their staff (Rice-Booth, 2023). In practice, this looks like leaders and teachers engaged in practices for addressing their emotions and responding rather than reacting to difficult moments (Fox et al., 2023). Staff meetings might include moments for mindfulness and emotional check-ins. Leaders could also model vulnerability and empathy by sharing their own challenges and actively listening to staff concerns. Leaders also need to acknowledge the power dynamics that exist between themselves and staff and the fears many teachers have about their relationships with supervisors. Anything from a quick meeting with a staff member or a seemingly benign classroom walkthrough could provoke high anxiety, especially if trust and relationships aren't present. If leaders say that their meetings are safe spaces, or if they want to welcome vulnerability, they need to consider the positional power they hold in each interaction and do their part to create psychologically safe interactions by staying curious and lowering any defenses that come up when they hear of issues that they are responsible for. Table 4.1 includes ways leaders can increase their emotional intelligence and build the emotional intelligence of their communities.

Leaders will need to be skillful in their interactions, practice self-awareness, and be intentional in how they continue to foster trust with those they oversee. When Kamryn, a principal at Ridgeway High School, faced the loss of their teacher residency program, she shared this news in advance of the staff meeting so it didn't come as a surprise. She first shared her own grief as a former special education teacher and created space in the meeting

TABLE 4.1 Ways to Increase Individual and Collective Emotional Intelligence

For Self

What to Do	What This Looks Like
Pause and reflect often	Ask yourself, "Whose voices am I centering? How are my biases influencing my decisions?" Taking time to reflect on actions and assumptions builds self-awareness.
Create space for mindfulness	Use mindfulness as a way to pause and consider how your emotions and reactions might impact others.
Ask for feedback with curiosity	Go beyond your usual circle to intentionally invite feedback from those whose perspectives are overlooked, including those you don't oversee directly. Commit to act on what you learn.
Lead with vulnerability	Acknowledge mistakes and demonstrate accountability and a willingness to learn.
Interrogate power dynamics	Consider how your positional power might unintentionally silence others or reinforce inequities. Be proactive in creating spaces where all voices can be welcomed and heard.

For Community

What to Do	What This Looks Like
Do check-ins in meetings to build community and engagement	Create space for everyone to share how they are doing and assess their well-being. Encourage people to identify one action within their sphere of control to address their well-being.
Model empathy and active listening	Invite people to listen attentively through practicing non-judgement, adopting a stance of curiosity, and listening to hear without trying to respond.
Co-create solutions to challenges	Share power by inviting a range of perspectives to solve challenges.
Provide space to give and receive feedback	In low-stakes ways, practice ways to give and receive feedback that are constructive and helpful, including people sharing how they best like to receive feedback.

for people to process their reactions; many of the residency's mentors were upset by these cuts. Kamryn facilitated a discussion asking for solutions for how to honor teacher residents and how to continue supporting students with disabilities. With the leadership team, Kamryn reviewed solutions and shared potential strategies in an upcoming staff meeting. This approach didn't reverse the district's decision, nor did it change the outcome of the residency program, but it was an emotionally intelligent act of collective care that invited openness and collaboration on schoolwide approaches to supporting students and teacher residents.

Strong, Supportive Relationships

The final dimension of collective well-being is strong, supportive relationships. This dimension is so important that we'll speak to it briefly here, but address it in more depth in the following chapter, including practices to build, sustain, and repair relationships. For now, we want to acknowledge that while fair compensation, manageable workloads, and addressing the physical and mental health needs of teachers are central, relationships, like mycelial networks in healthy soil, serve as the connective tissue that makes meaningful change possible. Mycelial networks connect different plants while redistributing essential nutrients. Similarly, relationships create vital connections across a school community, with relational practices and communal care as the nutrients. When addressing systemic injustices in schools, relationship work can support leaders in navigating the complex tension between the urgency to eradicate injustice for those most historically harmed and bringing the entire community along in the process. Leaders can serve as "warm demanders" (which we address in depth in Chapter 8), holding staff members to high expectations to root out injustice and supporting them with compassion and care. A fractured system created the inequities in education. A fractal approach can allow us to reimagine the educator ecosystem with well-being as an essential component, where small, intentional changes in relationship practices create ripple effects through the entire community.

Pause and Process

As you read these dimensions of collective well-being, which areas do you want to prioritize at your school site? Which ones are most within your control and influence? With your teams, review this self-assessment and identify which areas need greater attention. For areas that score low on this assessment scale, identify one or two areas you might prioritize in your site's collective well-being efforts and plan how you might enact these efforts (Table 4.2).

TABLE 4.2 Self-assessment for collective well-being

Dimension of Well-Being	Rate each statement from 1 to 5: 1 = Strongly Disagree 2 = Disagree 3 = Neutral 4 = Agree 5 = Strongly Agree
Wage Satisfaction	1 = Strongly Disagree, 5 = Strongly Agree
Our school has transparent and easy-to-understand salary scales. We conduct regular equity audits to ensure pay fairness across roles. Educators can access financial literacy resources, such as retirement planning or housing support. Efforts are made to secure grants and/or resources that alleviate out-of-pocket teacher expenses. Compensation for additional responsibilities is fair and not used as a blanket solution for extra work.	
Job Stability	1 = Strongly Disagree 5 = Strongly Agree
Leaders communicate openly about staffing decisions and future changes. Teachers feel secure in their roles and trust the stability of their employment. There are growth pathways for teachers that do not require leaving the classroom. Specific and sustained appreciation efforts are made to acknowledge teachers' work. Leaders balance critique with multiple positive interactions to maintain job satisfaction.	
Workload Management	1 = Strongly Disagree 5 = Strongly Agree
Teachers have clearly defined roles and responsibilities. We provide common planning time or structured time for collaboration and lesson planning. Leaders model effective workload management and encourage staff to do the same. Extra responsibilities are assigned equitably, and invisible labor is addressed proactively. Roles and responsibilities are clearly articulated and are used to align expectations and goals transparently.	

(Continued)

TABLE 4.2 Self-assessment for collective well-being (*Continued*)

Dimension of Well-Being	Rate each statement from 1 to 5: 1 = Strongly Disagree 2 = Disagree 3 = Neutral 4 = Agree 5 = Strongly Agree
Autonomy and Self-Efficacy	1 = Strongly Disagree 5 = Strongly Agree
Teachers are trusted to make instructional decisions within agreed-upon school practices. Our school has a strong culture of professional growth and trust. Opportunities are available for teachers to observe and learn from one another. Leaders model continuous learning, including sharing lessons from their mistakes.	
Inclusion in Policymaking	1 = Strongly Disagree 5 = Strongly Agree
Teachers are actively involved in shaping policies that affect their work. Leadership gathers input from staff before making major decisions. Policy discussions include a diverse representation of voices and perspectives. There are spaces for marginalized staff to voice concerns safely and openly. Teachers feel their input is valued and influences school practices.	
Community Care	1 = Strongly Disagree 5 = Strongly Agree
Our school offers comprehensive wellness programs that meet staff needs. Leaders model healthy boundaries, such as not working after hours. We provide flexible scheduling and prioritize staff well-being in policy design. Wellness activities are based on staff feedback and are easily accessible. Rest and collective care practices are promoted and normalized in our culture.	

(*Continued*)

TABLE 4.2 Self-assessment for collective well-being (*Continued*)

Dimension of Well-Being	Rate each statement from 1 to 5: 1 = Strongly Disagree 2 = Disagree 3 = Neutral 4 = Agree 5 = Strongly Agree
Emotional Intelligence	1 = Strongly Disagree 5 = Strongly Agree
Leaders demonstrate awareness of their own emotions and how they impact interactions. Staff meetings include time for emotional check-ins and community building. Leaders show empathy and share their challenges openly with staff. Power dynamics are acknowledged and thoughtfully managed by leaders. Our school prioritizes relationships over task-oriented, transactional approaches.	
Strong, Supportive Relationships	1 = Strongly Disagree 5 = Strongly Agree
Relationships are prioritized and nurtured consistently. There is trust and mutual respect between staff and leadership. Leaders and staff engage in open dialogue to address conflicts constructively. Our community practices care and support, especially in challenging moments. Efforts to strengthen relationships are intentional and visible in our culture.	

Dimensions of Individual Well-Being

While leaders will do what's in their spheres of influence to shape the culture of their communities, all adults in a school community can take responsibility for how they are showing up at their sites. The Assess Your Well-Being Tool, developed by Tamisha Williams (tamishawilliams.com, 2024) and adapted for our framework, offers a practical and powerful way to evaluate personal well-being across various dimensions. This tool encourages building one's emotional intelligence to increase self-awareness and being able to identify areas that need further attention. Anyone in a school community can use this tool to assess how they are doing and develop growth-focused well-being goals based on what they find.

Leaders can encourage community members to use this tool—or make this practice a regular routine—quarterly during staff meetings, during professional development days, or at various intervals throughout the school year. Before beginning the assessment, it's essential to understand that this tool provides a high-level, informal look at your well-being across five key areas: emotional/mental, physical, resource, social, and spiritual well-being. It's not a clinical assessment but rather a reflective practice designed to guide your well-being in the workplace. By integrating it into the school culture, it becomes a practice for sustaining educators in an ongoing way so they can be more attentive to their needs, increase conversations about well-being, and shift school cultures from solely academic to ones that recognize and value human complexity.

Process

Familiarize Yourself with the Dimensions
Review the five dimensions of well-being. Take a moment to reflect on how each dimension connects to your work.

Dimension	What This Entails	How This Connects to My Work
Emotional/ mental	• Self-awareness and emotional regulation • Self-compassion and affirming self-talk • Stress management techniques and coping mechanisms	

Physical	• Exercise and physical activity • Nutritional habits • Sleep quality and patterns • Consciousness and connection to your body
Resource	• Access to wellness resources • Financial stability and management • Career development and job satisfaction
Social	• Quality of relationships with colleagues • Support network and sense of community • Communication and conflict engagement skills • Boundary-setting skills
Spiritual	• Meditation and mindfulness habits • Finding meaning or purpose in life • Connection with nature

Complete the Assessment

On the sliding scale, place a symbol for each dimension based on how satisfied you are with that area of your life, where 1 represents "needs attention" and 7 represents "thriving." This reflection should be based on recent experiences. You can complete this process in one sitting or take your time, returning to it over a few days.

Dimensions of Individual Well-Being	Rating on a scale of 1–7 *1 = I'm working on nurturing this area to increase satisfaction* *7 = I'm thriving in this area and am feeling satisfied*						
	1	2	3	4	5	6	7
Emotional/mental							
Physical							
Resource							
Social							
Spiritual							

Reflect on Your Current Well-Being

After you've rated each dimension, review your overall well-being snapshot:

- Where are you thriving? Identify areas that feel strong and satisfying.
- Where do you need more attention? Reflect on dimensions that may need more care or nurturing.

Identify What's Working

Answer the following reflection questions to gain insight into the habits and strategies that support your well-being. Ask yourself:

- What's working well in supporting your well-being?
- How can you build on what's already working?

Address Challenges

Reflect on any obstacles that might be preventing you from nurturing areas that need attention:

- What's getting in the way of improving these dimensions?
- What support or resources could help you overcome these challenges?

Set Action Steps

Identify one to two specific actions you can take in the next month to improve one or more dimensions of your well-being. These actions should be small and manageable, something like waking up 10 minutes earlier (or sleeping in 10 minutes later) each day, taking a mindful moment at the end of each day, or practicing more self-compassion, with clear outcomes you can track. It's helpful to do a weekly check or set reminders to share progress with an accountability buddy. Consider the following as you plan your action steps:

- How will you monitor your progress?
- Who can serve as an accountability partner?

Track Progress
The tool encourages you to return regularly (quarterly or semi-annually) to track your well-being over time. Use this reflection to see how far you've come and adjust your goals as needed. Progress in well-being often involves small, incremental changes.

Next Steps
Return to this tool periodically, reflect on changes in your well-being, and adjust your wellness plan accordingly. For additional support, leaders might encourage people to engage with a trusted mentor, coach, close colleagues, or affinity group to deepen the impact of this practice. Leadership teams might also use this tool to deepen their self-awareness and build support structures for one another.

The Firmament for Flourishing

Just as healthy soil is essential for thriving plant life, a nurturing environment is crucial for educators to flourish. A lot of school leaders expect positivity at the outset. Whether wearing "Be grateful" t-shirts or having an overly sunny disposition when engaging with people, leaders can perform positivity without cultivating conditions where positive emotions can be more deeply rooted in relational care, self-care, and equitable school conditions. Educators in the Hollyhock School District needed leaders who addressed well-being in more sustainable ways. When adults are well-cared for, when they feel a sense of autonomy and self-efficacy, and when they are valued for their backgrounds and expertise, they are more positive, not because they received a $5 gift card for the local coffee shop. Positive emotions, and intentional work on the part of leaders, contribute to greater self-efficacy, and greater self-efficacy contributes to collective efficacy, which increases positive emotion, engagement, and a sense of purpose and accomplishment (Seligman, 2011). All of these emotional states have a direct effect on student outcomes. By focusing on the dimensions of well-being, schools can create sustainable ecosystems where educators are not just surviving but flourishing. It is through balancing visionary goals with the daily realities of school life that we can cultivate a more equitable and healthy educational environment where teachers are motivated to do their best work and can be better models for students about what it means to be well (Harvey, 2021).

Even small shifts, like fractals, in leadership practice can significantly impact the well-being of educators, both collectively and individually. Each micro move that nurtures the soil of educator well-being provides the firmament for everyone's growth. In the next chapter, we offer specific practices you can use to nurture the soil in your communities, which includes reimagining the Portrait of an Educator and a process to build, sustain, and repair relationships.

Summary

This chapter emphasizes that creating a thriving school ecosystem starts with fostering educator well-being, likened to nurturing healthy soil for growth. Surface-level wellness efforts like one-off activities don't lead to sustained change; proactive, sustained practices that address systemic issues and collective well-being will support a school's long-term efforts. Leaders are encouraged to balance the urgency of initiatives with teachers' well-being through emotional intelligence, trust-building, and clear communication. By prioritizing these dimensions, schools can move beyond survival to cultivate environments where educators and students flourish together, supported by sustainable practices, assessing one's own well-being, and relational care.

For Further Reflection

1. How can leaders in your context move beyond surface-level wellness initiatives to implement meaningful, systemic changes that directly impact educator well-being?
2. In your context, what strategies could leaders use to balance the demands of initiatives with the personal and professional needs of teachers?
3. What small, consistent actions could you or your leadership team take to nurture trust and relationships, creating a foundation for long-term well-being within your school community?

References

Boykin, A. W., & Noguera, P. (2011). *Creating the opportunity to learn: Moving from research to practice to close the achievement gap.* ASCD.

Campus Explorer. (2024). *Guide for LGBTQ+ teachers: Statistics and resources.* Retrieved from https://www.campusexplorer.com/student-resources/lgbtq-teachers-guide/

Creagh, S., Thompson, G., Mockler, N., Stacey, M., & Hogan, A. (2023). Workload, work intensification, and time poverty for teachers and school leaders: A systematic research synthesis. *Educational Review, 77*(1), 1–20.

Fox, H. B., Hester, W. T., & Wasil, A. (2023). Can educators thrive? A pilot study of a multi-component educator well-being professional development intervention. *Journal of Interdisciplinary Studies in Education, 12*(1), 62–84.

Gottman, J., & Silver, N. (2015). *The seven principles for making marriage work: A practical guide from the country's foremost relationship expert.* Harmony.

Hanover Research. (n.d.). *Tiered approach to teacher well-being.* Washington Association of School Administrators. Retrieved from https://wasa-oly.org/WASA/images/WASA/6.0%20Resources/Hanover/Tiered-Approach-to-Teacher-Wellbeing.pdf

Harvard Kennedy School. (n.d.). *The proven impact of affinity spaces.* Retrieved from https://rrapp.hks.harvard.edu/how-to-guide/the-proven-impact-of-affinity-spaces/

Harvey, N. (2021, March 18). *The PERMA approach to staff wellbeing.* Optimus Education Blog. Retrieved from https://blog.optimus-education.com/perma-approach-staff-wellbeing

Hersey, T. (2022). *Rest is resistance: A manifesto.* Little, Brown Spark.

Johnson, D. E., & Hall, D. R. (2017). Merit pay, teacher job satisfaction, and retention: A mixed-methods study [Thesis, Concordia University, St. Paul]. Retrieved from https://digitalcommons.csp.edu/

Khalifa, M. (2018). *Culturally responsive school leadership.* Harvard Education Press.

Kurtz, H. (2023). Is teacher morale on the rise? Results of the second annual Merrimack College Teacher Survey. *Education Week.* Retrieved from https://www.edweek.org/

Kush, J.M, Baldillo-Goicoechea, E., Musci, R.J., & Stuart, E.A. (2022). Teachers' mental health during the COVID-19 pandemic. *Educational Researcher, 51*(9). https://doi.org/10.3102/0013189X221134281

Ladson-Billings, G. (1995). Toward a theory of culturally relevant pedagogy. *American Educational Research Journal, 32*(3), 465–491.

Lambert, D. (2024). California wants to accelerate schools' efforts to build 2.3 million units of housing. EdSource. Retrieved from https://edsource.org/2024/california-wants-to-accelerate-schools-efforts-to-build-2-3-million-units-of-housing/716695

Lambert, D. (2024). Disrespect, low pay, lack of support keep Black teachers out of the profession. EdSource. Retrieved from https://edsource.org/

Learning Policy Institute. (2023). The state of the teacher workforce: A state-by-state analysis of the factors influencing teacher shortages, supply, demand, and equity. Retrieved from https://learningpolicyinstitute.org/

Lever, N., Mathis, E., & Mayworm, A. (2017). School mental health is not just for students: Why teacher and school staff wellness matters. *Report on Emotional & Behavioral Disorders in Youth, 17*(1), 6–12.

Mielke, C. (2023). *Illuminate the way: A school leader's guide to addressing and preventing teacher burnout*. ASCD.

National Center for Education Statistics. (2022). Teacher turnover and retention rates. Retrieved from https://nces.ed.gov/

National Education Association. (2024). Educator pay and student spending: How does your state rank? Retrieved from https://www.nea.org/

New Teacher Center. (2023). Phases of first-year teaching. Retrieved from https://newteachercenter.org/resources/phases-of-first-year-teaching/#:~:text=This%20resource%20provides%20an%20overview,reflection%2C%20then%20back%20to%20anticipation

Peters, H. (2024). School leaders of color face high levels of burnout. Here's what they need to thrive. Retrieved from https://www.chalkbeat.org/2024/07/17/what-men-of-color-need-to-thrive-as-education-leaders/

Pew Research Center. (2024, April 4). What's it like to be a teacher in America today? Retrieved from https://www.pewresearch.org/social-trends/2024/04/04/whats-it-like-to-be-a-teacher-in-america-today/

Rice-Booth, M. (2023). *Leading within systems of inequity in education: A liberation guide for leaders of color*. ASCD.

Salovey, P., & Mayer, J. D. (1990). Emotional intelligence. *Imagination, Cognition, and Personality, 9*(3), 185–211. https://doi.org/10.2190/DUGG-P24E-52WK-6CDG

Saunders, R., Fitz, J., DiNapoli, M. A., Jr., & Kini, T. (2024). *Teacher residencies: State and federal policy to support comprehensive teacher preparation*. Learning Policy Institute & EdPrepLab. https://doi.org/10.54300/358.825

Seligman, M. E. P. (2011). *Flourish: A visionary new understanding of happiness and well-being*. Free Press.

Senge, P. M. (1990). The fifth discipline: The art and practice of the learning organization. Doubleday/Currency.

Simmons, D. (2021). Humanity, healing, and doing the work. Learning for Justice. Retrieved from https://www.learningforjustice.org/

Steiner, E. D., Woo, A., Suryavanshi, A., & Redding, C. (2023). *Working conditions related to positive teacher well-being vary across states: Findings from the 2022 Learn Together Survey*. RAND Corporation. Retrieved from https://www.rand.org/

Steinmann, B., Klug, H. J. P., & Maier, G. W. (2018). The path is the goal: How transformational leaders enhance followers' job attitudes and proactive behavior. *Frontiers in Psychology, 9*, 2338. https://doi.org/10.3389/fpsyg.2018.02338

Tamez-Robledo, N. (2024, May 9). Teacher well-being depends on workload, school climate, and feeling supported. EdSurge. Retrieved from https://www.edsurge.com/

Taylor, L., Zhou, W., Boyle, L., Funk, S., & De Neve, J.-E. (2024). Wellbeing for schoolteachers. Wellbeing Research Centre, University of Oxford. Retrieved from https://wellbeing.hmc.ox.ac.uk/news/wellbeing-for-schoolteachers/

The Nap Ministry. (n.d.). Rest is resistance. Retrieved from https://thenapministry.com/

We Are Teachers. (2024). 2024 average teacher salary: What are the top-paying states? We Are Teachers. Retrieved from https://www.weareteachers.com/average-teacher-salary

Will, M. (2023). More districts are building housing for teachers. Here's what to know. Education Week. Retrieved from https://www.edweek.org/leadership/more-districts-are-building-housing-for-teachers-heres-what-to-know/2023/11

5

Practices to Nurture the Soil

We don't just plant seeds and hope they grow; we tend to the soil, ensuring it has the right nutrients, water, and light. Without care, seeds struggle to survive, let alone thrive. Supporting educator well-being is no different. If we want our schools to be places where both students and staff have the opportunity to grow and thrive, we must cultivate a climate that nurtures every person's well-being, ensuring the soil—school culture—is healthy and sustainable. To create an environment where students can succeed, the culture and practices within a school must sustain educators.

In the previous chapter, we shared the dimensions of collective well-being and what leaders might do to address well-being within their spheres of influence, including their own well-being. In this chapter, we focus on practical tools for supporting educator well-being at the collective and individual levels: The Portrait of an Educator and a process to Build, Sustain, and Repair relationships. The Portrait of an Educator provides school community members with clear definitions of roles and responsibilities, what these responsibilities look like in practice, and the opportunities to use the Portrait for growth and evaluation efforts. The process to Build, Sustain, and Repair relationships provides leaders with specific skills to build trust, sustain rapport, and address harm in a meaningful way. These practices are essential for school leaders who aim to create environments where all educators, especially those from marginalized groups, can grow.

Supporting Collective Well-Being: The Portrait of an Educator

Overview and Purpose

One way to establish a foundation for well-being in a community is to develop a Portrait of an Educator. Many schools develop a portrait of a graduate as a way to backwards design the student experience until their matriculation. The Portrait of an Educator works somewhat similarly, with the notable exception that we're striving to retain teachers rather than have them matriculate. This portrait can be used for a range of purposes:

- to design climate and wellness assessments
- to identify characteristics of effective, culturally responsive teaching, which then can be used for evaluation
- to set goals
- to create site-based initiatives for equity and professional learning
- to determine and/or develop professional learning

The portrait, while powerful, needs to remain a dynamic part of the school's culture. Just as soil needs to be tilled, so, too, do the characteristics of a site's teachers. Times change; legislation passes; new generations of educators will push the boundaries of what it means to be an educator; and neuroscience research and AI continue to shape our understanding of how we teach, learn and what it means to be human. Thus, just as school community members are developing its portrait of an educator, there also needs to be time allocated to assess the portrait and all its components, to compost what may not be working, and to regenerate criteria that best meet the needs of the moment. So before you begin this process, leaders should make sure to block time on the calendar to create the portrait, most likely a few sessions; time to assess down the road (six months in, one year in); and also a time when they'll recreate the portrait entirely. The process for creating this portrait is outlined in detail in the following pages; Table 5.1 offers a quick guide of this process, including

TABLE 5.1 Steps to Develop a Portrait of an Educator

Step	Process for Teaching Staff	Adjustments When Including Non-Teaching Staff and External Partners
Gather the Community and Frame the Exercise	• Bring together all school staff (teachers, leaders, support staff) in a professional learning day or series of staff meetings • Establish the purpose: to create a *Portrait of an Educator* that reflects the site's commitment to equity, identity, and cultural responsiveness	• Include classified staff, counselors, support services, and administrative roles to ensure the portrait reflects all types of educators who interact with students daily • Include external partners, community-based organizations, district-level staff, or consultants who support or collaborate with schools but may not work directly in school buildings • Frame the exercise to include how non-teaching roles contribute to the school ecosystem (e.g., student services, family engagement, operations, etc.), even if they aren't interacting directly with students or staff daily
Initial Reflection	• Invite all participants to reflect individually on the ideal dispositions, knowledge, and skills educators need at the site • Encourage imagination at this stage • Encourage creativity through drawing, writing, etc.	• Provide examples that focus on relationship-building, administrative support, student and family services, or community engagement to guide reflections for non-teaching staff • Encourage reflections on how external work impacts schools, such as policy influence, resources, professional development, or partnerships that enhance school well-being

(Continued)

TABLE 5.1 Steps to Develop a Portrait of an Educator (*Continued*)

Step	Process for Teaching Staff	Adjustments When Including Non-Teaching Staff and External Partners
Small-Group Sharing and Synthesis of Ideas	• Group participants into non-role-alike teams (two to three people) • Share ideas and synthesize characteristics that educators should embody	• Include cross-role groupings (e.g., teacher aides with administrative staff) • Explore how various roles intersect and support the broader educational mission • Explore connections between school needs and external support
Combined Group Sharing	• Groups combine and refine their portrait • Identify key characteristics to keep • Consider outliers that may be less common but still important	• Encourage teams to consider how support staff characteristics complement teaching staff • Ensure all staff members and external partners see their role in the larger school vision
Gallery Share and Responses	• Display group portraits for a gallery walk • Use a coding system to indicate places of resonance, questions, or disagreements with the characteristics presented	• Ensure non-teaching staff and external partners feel included in feedback and influence well-being • Reflect on characteristics that align with their roles and contributions to the school's success
Get to "Good Enough" Alignment	• Facilitate conversations to refine the characteristics identified in the gallery walk • Ask guiding questions to foster deeper reflection and alignment	• Ensure the non-teaching staff's and external partners' contributions are integrated into the final portrait, ensuring equity in representing various roles

(*Continued*)

TABLE 5.1 Steps to Develop a Portrait of an Educator (*Continued*)

Step	Process for Teaching Staff	Adjustments When Including Non-Teaching Staff and External Partners
Draft Initial Portrait	• Work with a leadership team or committee to synthesize the key characteristics into a working draft • Review for alignment with the mission and equity vision	• Ensure representatives from support staff and other roles are involved in the final drafting process so all roles are equitably represented in the final portrait
Review Portrait Characteristics and Add Examples	• Groups review the characteristics in practice • Each group adds five specific "looks and sounds like" examples that demonstrate each characteristic in action	• Encourage groups to add specific examples from non-teaching roles, e.g., how office staff, counselors, or aides demonstrate characteristics in their daily work • Include examples that show how external staff or community partners exhibit these traits in their collaborations with schools
Finalize and Test the Portrait	• Pilot the portrait in different school settings (classroom observations, mentoring programs, and professional learning communities) • Refine as needed based on feedback	• Test the portrait across non-teaching settings, such as student services, administrative meetings, or family engagement activities, ensuring the characteristics are applicable across roles

adaptations for non-teaching staff and those who aren't working directly in a school.

Process

Ideally, this process would be completed with every member of a school community, including classified/non-teaching staff. Anyone who chooses to work in schools is an educator because students are taking their cues from every adult they interact with—whether those interactions are positive, neutral, or challenging. At the same time, there are key characteristics of the work that staff complete and that teachers complete. Office administration, student support services, operations staff, or family liaisons need a portrait that reflects the ways in which they foster the well-being of students and staff. For those working in education-adjacent roles (consultants, district-level administrators, or community-based partners), their portrait may include characteristics of how to be effective contributing members of school communities. Use your discretion at what configuration of adults would work best for this process.

Step 1: Gather the Community and Frame the Exercise

Now that we've established that the ideal scenario is one in which everyone is involved, let's get people into the room together. This process will take a full day if you have a professional learning day, or three to four staff meetings, to get a first draft of the process outlined. The first thing to remember is that you're going for a good-enough portrait on this first go-around. It's important to get the ideas down on paper without wordsmithing. As you initially frame the purpose for this activity, it's helpful to say something like:

> Today we're going to develop the portrait of an educator at our site. The purpose of this process is to identify the criteria that define what it means to work here, and what it means to be effective at one's job. This is a site that puts a primacy on equity, on identity, and on cultural responsiveness. In order for us to be culturally responsive with students, we need to consider the needs, backgrounds, abilities, and skills of the adults as well. To that end, this activity will invite you to be optimistic about what it means to work here.
>
> This process will be messy, nonlinear, and possibly challenge us to consider what matters for educators at this site. We'll take our time with this process, because getting

it right is better than rushing through it. From the portrait we develop, we then will be able to explore these core criteria in more depth. For example, we'll get more specific about what effective teaching means, consider 'look fors' and so on. Hopefully, this will make sense as we engage in the process.

Once you've framed the activity, anticipate common questions to prepare your responses. Some may dismiss it as a waste of time, so it's crucial for you and your team to align on the activity's purpose and importance. Approach planning conversations with openness rather than defensiveness, focusing on how the portrait will benefit all community members rather than justifying its necessity.

Once you get started, invite everyone to reflect individually first. Provide blank sheets of paper on tables, perhaps markers or any additional art supplies. Invite people to write, draw, or create sculptures or symbols. It can be helpful to set a timer. While some people take longer to process, timed activities have the paradoxical effect of inspiring greater creativity. Ten minutes is typically enough for idea generation to take hold, but for the purposes of this activity, 15 minutes might be better. When you start this portion of the process, make sure to name that you're seeking aspirational characteristics rather than the current reality. You will get to the current reality eventually, but for now, the focus is on what is ideal and what would enable adults to do their best and most equitable work alongside students. Post the following questions on the screen, share it verbally, or perhaps include it at the top of a handout you provide to people:

> *What is the portrait of an educator at our site?*
> *What dispositions, knowledge, and skills do educators here need to possess?*

Once again, this may be a place where you receive pushback or even a little snark—those moments of resistance that often mask deeper concerns about being included. Folks whose values are out of alignment with the school, or folks who don't feel like their identities matter, may not have anything aspirational to say. Staff members who have experienced marginalization may be skeptical because previous initiatives failed to include their perspectives; they may need to see concrete actions following the portrait development before trusting these aspirations are achievable. Take that in stride and trust the process.

Step 2: Small-Group Sharing and Synthesis of Ideas

For the next round, invite people to group up in non-role alike groups of two to three; if you can, mix people up across grade levels, roles, and subject areas. You may have these groups pre-determined, or depending on the size of the community, let people choose groups (in bigger communities, folks might not know each other well, which would be ideal). In whatever ways you choose to create groupings, keep the groups smaller at this stage to increase the level of participation in each team. Each person should have up to five minutes to share what they created and how they determined these characteristics. In total, this portion of the activity should take about 15 minutes.

Next, folks will stay in their small groups, and they will have 15 minutes to create a new portrait based on the conversation just had. They will determine which characteristics are most important and therefore keepable. At this stage, too, encourage groups to consider outlier characteristics as well. A group doesn't need consensus on all characteristics, but rather a willingness to consider characteristics they may not have considered. Once again, groups are invited to draw, write, or sculpt whatever they decide collectively. After this 15-minute segment, invite people to take a break. If this session takes place on a staff meeting day, you may invite folks to reflect on what they've learned so far and share where this process is going next.

Step 3: Combined Group Sharing

After the break, each group will combine into bigger groups of four to six people; these groups will be the core group to take this portrait a level deeper. First, each smaller group from the previous round will select a representative to share their characteristics and how they landed on these characteristics (about 10 minutes per group). Then the combined group will have 15 minutes to write, draw, sculpt, or create a revised portrait in a way the group deems best; you might want to ask groups to choose a note-taker and commit ideas to a shared large post-it paper. Whatever you decide, groups will eventually need to move from a more open form of idea generation and representation to some type of representation that would be understood by others.

Step 4: Gallery Share and Responses

When each group has completed their portrait, they'll post their portraits around the room or leave them on their tables so that others can take a look at what their colleagues have created. Everyone will then walk around the room and review what colleagues have written. Keeping their responses anonymous, people will then use the following code for responses:

- ✳ This resonates with me; this is a common characteristic in our school.
- ? I'm not sure about this one. I have more questions.
- ✗ I haven't seen this characteristic here or it doesn't align with what's ideal.

Provide about 10–15 minutes for this activity, allowing people thinking and processing time. Perhaps spontaneous conversations will ensue as well. As people are milling about and responding to each poster, leaders should listen and pay attention to themes they notice, which characteristics seem resonant and which don't. This type of observation will prepare leaders for the next portion of this work.

Step 5: Get to "Good Enough" Alignment

The next phase of this work is to get "good enough" alignment on characteristics that may comprise the portrait of an educator at your site. After everyone has completed the gallery walk and interactive activity, facilitate small- and whole-group conversations about themes. It is helpful to ask one or two people to be note-takers for the whole group so you can facilitate the dialogue while others document the process. During this alignment process, be prepared for value tensions to emerge—for instance, when some staff believe "maintaining objectivity" is essential while others see this as potentially perpetuating inequity. Rather than forcing consensus, invite staff members to explore these tensions through an equity lens, asking whose perspective might be marginalized by some of the portrait's characteristics. It's also helpful to have some questions to shape the discussion. Open-ended, non-layered questions work best. The following are examples of questions you might ask:

- What did you notice from doing this activity (in your small groups and in the gallery walk)?
- Which characteristics were most resonant for you?
- Which characteristics were you most curious about?

Begin first in pairs, asking colleagues to do a 5- to 10-minute turn and talk, sharing responses to these questions. This way, those who are more introverted or don't feel psychologically safe enough in the whole group can speak without added pressure. After the pair share, facilitate a whole-group discussion, asking folks about what came up in their conversations. Or you can guide folks through each question, devoting a certain amount of time for each question. Allocate about 15 minutes to this conversation, and once again, be prepared for any pushback you might receive. Remember to stay rooted in the purpose of the activity. At the end of the conversation, share with the group that you'll synthesize notes from this conversation, along with what's included on posters, and narrow this portrait to fewer characteristics. It's also helpful to share what your decision-making criteria are so you can be transparent about how the characteristics will be selected. After this conversation, take a longer break to give people time to digest what has transpired so far. Either return to this topic at another date or use the next staff meeting for the next portion of the work.

Step 6: Draft an Initial Portrait
This next portion, drafting an initial portrait, requires reviewing everyone's contributions and getting aligned on common

characteristics. You can do this either during lunch, with a committee that meets between sessions, or before the following staff meeting. We strongly suggest you don't do this alone, but with a leadership team or a committee of folks across a range of roles and social identifiers; this way, the process can prevent one person's biases from shaping the direction of the work. We also suggest you don't do the narrowing part with the entire community unless you work in a very small school. Once you have your group review the posters and stickers, using the decision-making criteria you've selected, narrow to a set of "good enough" characteristics (less than 10) to bring back to the community. Some of your decision-making criteria may include:

- alignment with school's mission or district learning outcomes
- alignment with the school's vision for equity and cultural responsiveness
- representative of the broad array of community members
- qualities that might not be present, but are ones the community hopes to aspire to

Once the group has narrowed the characteristics, you'll bring these characteristics back to the larger community to review and identify, specifically, what that characteristic means. This is where the work becomes more intense and granular (hence why a full day of staff development or several meetings lend themselves well to this portrait). To frame this phase of the work, it's helpful to remind people about the messy and iterative nature of this process. You may also invite colleagues to determine the disposition they want to inhabit as they engage in the next phase of this work.

Step 7: Review Portrait Characteristics and Add Examples
Get folks in groups of about five to six people. These groups don't have to be the same as the previous activities, but groups should represent different roles and identities in the school. As groups engage in this part of the process, you want to provide a generous amount of time for groups to work, between 30 and

60 minutes, with a break in between. Each group will receive one or two of the characteristics (one characteristic per large sheet of poster paper) of an educator at the site and come up with at least five examples of what this looks and sounds like in practice. After 15–20 minutes with these characteristics, in a round-robin fashion, each group will pass their list along to the next group, who will then add to the list of characteristics. For smaller communities, you may need to adjust this activity accordingly. Table 5.2 contains an example of what this might look like. When groups have explored at least three or four of the characteristics, they should take a break.

After each characteristic has been explored and examples have been added, each poster of characteristics will be placed around the room. Colleagues will have an additional 20 minutes to read through each characteristic, starting with ones they didn't get to in their small groups, and add any additional specific words and actions that demonstrate that characteristic. Once this process has been completed, you'll facilitate individual reflection and a large-group discussion about the process. The following questions could guide the discussion:

- ♦ What came up for you doing this activity?
- ♦ As you review these characteristics and specifics, what excites you? What worries you?
- ♦ How could you imagine using this portrait?

TABLE 5.2 Sample Characteristics from Portrait of an Educator

Characteristic	Looks and Sounds Like
Rapport Builder	• Takes time to develop relationships with students through intake at the beginning of the school year • Makes time at the beginning of team meetings for a quick personal check-in • Is self-aware: is aware of their identities and names their identifying markers when appropriate (i.e., I realized I'm able-bodied, which means I may not be considering accessibility as deeply as I need to) • Is socially aware (i.e., pronounces students' names correctly and asks, "Did I get that right?") • Knows at least one fun fact about all their students

Depending on the size of the group, you can once again have people share in pairs first and then the whole group (asking for two note-takers to document the discussion). This discussion should last about 15 minutes (or longer if necessary). As usual, be prepared for what questions you may receive and make sure to share the next steps. Consider saying something like the following:

> Thank you so much for your participation in this process. I realize this is just a first draft of this work, and in the following months, we'll keep refining this portrait. I'll take this portrait and these reflections from our discussion (your excitement, your worries, your suggestions for how to use this portrait) back to our team. We will take this portrait through some refinement and then share back with you the ways we'll be using it. We'll also seek your input on the refined model. Please know, though, there will come a time when we'll need to practice with this portrait, so it's important that we don't expect perfection with it.

Step 9: Finalize and Test the Portrait

After this phase, meet with the team or committee to revise the characteristics and put them in a document for use. Review the notes from the debrief conversation, particularly the ways to use the tool. Make a plan to share this tool in an upcoming staff meeting and determine the kinds of input you're seeking on it: a thumbs up/thumbs down, another round of suggestions, or whatever else would move you into the next phase of the work. Appendix A contains an example of a finalized portrait Lori and her colleagues created at her site. When she and her supervisor guided the school through this portrait process, they called the process Portrait of an Effective Educator, and they completed this process with teachers at the school. If they were to do it again, they'd guide the entire community through this process.

Finally, it is time to test out the portrait to see how it works in practice. This testing phase can look a lot of different ways. The following are examples of how this portrait can be used in the testing phase.

At Lori's former school, the portrait (Appendix A) was used to create an effective teaching rubric that was used for self-assessment, goals' conversations, and whole-staff conversations about teaching and learning. The effective teaching criteria also were developed into a one-pager for lesson observations, hiring criteria from which to develop interview questions, professional development topics (and a survey to assess which topics teachers identified they most needed), all of which were then applied to the new teacher cohort who had been hired after the tools had been developed and refined.

When Abundance Academy, the school we mentioned in the introduction, created their portrait, community members developed a tool called Elements of Effective Teaching, comprised of five domains (Planning and Preparation, Classroom Environment, Instruction, Professional Responsibilities, and Intentional Collaboration). The Instruction domain was then turned into a lesson observation for anyone observing a class; the Planning and Preparation and Intentional Collaboration domains were used to create a lesson planning template for teachers.

At El Capitan School, a comprehensive K-12 school, the site's portrait became a springboard for the site's core beliefs and assumptions about professional learning and growth. They included the following language at the top of their portrait:

> Our overarching core belief is that student-centeredness and equity are institutional priorities and that our teachers are committed to their own growth and development so they can best meet the needs of their students. Educators at El Capital believe every student is brilliant, and we co-create a community that supports students in accessing that brilliance.
>
> Educators engage in ongoing reflection on their strengths and challenges, set goals, and pursue professional growth opportunities relevant to their roles within the school so they can be engaged, intentional, healthy, whole humans who can best support students in their classrooms.

These core beliefs and assumptions were used in job opportunity statements, professional growth goals, and the school's two-year professional growth program.

Ongoing Assessment

When it's time to assess the efficacy of the tool, leaders may work with their teams or a committee to assess how the portrait holds up in reality and if it has its intended impact. This assessment process should be collaborative, transparent, and rooted in feedback from all community members. The Portrait can be assessed in the context of school-wide goals and on whether the portrait is helping move the school toward its vision of equity and supporting well-being. From these reflective processes, leaders can add new characteristics, refine existing ones, or remove aspects that are no longer relevant.

There are several ways to gather feedback on the Portrait, including the following methods:

- **Staff Surveys**: Gather feedback on how staff perceive the portrait's effectiveness. Include questions on whether the characteristics feel relevant to their roles and if they see the portrait reflected in daily school practices.
- **Focus Groups**: Hold focus groups with a cross section of school staff (teachers, non-teaching staff, support staff) to discuss their experiences with the portrait. Focus on specific examples where the characteristics have supported or hindered their work.
- **Classroom Observations and Reflections**: Use classroom or workplace observations to assess whether educators are demonstrating the characteristics outlined in the portrait. Follow up with reflection sessions where staff can provide insight into which aspects of the portrait are most helpful.
- **Goal-Setting Aligned with the Portrait**: Throughout the year, measure how staff members are setting and achieving professional goals that align with the portrait. Use their progress as a key metric for assessing the tool's efficacy.

- **Documentation of Growth:** Encourage staff to document their growth through portfolios or reflections, highlighting how they have embodied the characteristics of the portrait. Use this documentation as part of the annual review to gauge the portrait's impact on professional development.
- **Equity and Cultural Responsiveness Checkpoints:** Conduct periodic equity audits to ensure that the portrait aligns with the school's equity goals and include checkpoints where staff assess the portrait's cultural relevance. Examine whether the characteristics outlined are contributing to equitable outcomes for staff and students, particularly those from marginalized communities.

Through continuous feedback, revision, and reflection, the portrait becomes not just a static document but a living framework that supports the evolving needs of educators and the larger school ecosystem.

The health of a school ecosystem is interdependent on collective and individual well-being. School culture, the collective soil, requires intentional tending to nurture the educators within it. Supporting collective well-being is essential, but sometimes leaders can get caught up in the high-level systems and policies that preclude them from centering relationships. In the next section, we offer practices that sustain individuals. By fostering conditions that honor both the group and the unique needs of its community members through strong, supportive relationship practices, leaders can create thriving communities where educators are supported and where leaders can ensure the soil remains fertile for everyone's growth.

Supporting Individual Well-Being: Build, Sustain, and Repair Relationships

The next step in nurturing the soil of educator well-being lies in meaningful, supportive relationships. Collective well-being is stronger when individuals within a community feel valued and cared for. In the pages that follow, we will explore practices for building, sustaining, and repairing relationships—practices that not only foster trust and psychological safety, but also provide the conditions for growth.

Here's the thing: What we advocate for takes time. Leaders can put in the time on the front end to build and sustain strong relationships, or they can forego relationships in service of efficiency, which means they'll spend more time cleaning up messes on the back end. We implore leaders to practice front-loading and sustaining relationships in a fractal way as opposed to consistently being reactive. We promise the time spent will be worthwhile and much more effective.

Much of the priority of building relationships happens at the beginning of the school year—team retreats, opening meetings, and the first weeks of school. But by October, all the good capital built in those early weeks had diminished. Just as soils are rife with complex organisms that need ongoing attention, relationship-building has a lot of layers to it and requires deliberate actions over time. We need to be more intentional about how we sustain relationships year-round, from building trust, to sustaining connection, to repairing ruptures—whether significant experiences of harm or low-level conflicts that diminish trust. Leaders who prioritize relationships practice emotional intelligence, are curious to learn about others and themselves, communicate clearly, and remain reflective about their actions, making sure they align what they say with what they do. When it comes to relationships, what are your strengths? What areas do you want to improve? How might your social identities influence your relationship-building approach? In our work with leaders, we identified key behaviors that contribute to successful relationships and included them in a brief self-assessment tool (Table 5.3). Review each statement and identify how you fare. Consider, too, what you might add.

After completing this self-assessment, identify one area to prioritize for growth and develop an action plan for developing in this area. For example, if the area for growth is to follow through on commitments, an action plan might include adding "follow-up" as a final agenda item for meetings or setting

TABLE 5.3 Effective Relationships Self-Assessment

Effective Relationship Skills	I Do This Consistently	I Do This Somewhat	I Need to Do This
I prioritize time in my schedule to build trust and rapport with colleagues at the beginning of the year and at regular intervals throughout the year			
I communicate with clarity, transparency, and openness to feedback			
I actively ask what colleagues need and provide meaningful, responsive support			
I ask how others prefer to receive feedback and be appreciated, and I honor those preferences			
I take a learning stance in conversations, focusing on curiosity and collaboration rather than immediately moving toward a solutions approach			
I reflect on my interactions and leadership practices, seeking feedback from multiple sources, and act on what I learn to do better			
I model what I hope to see through my way of being and behaviors, including appreciation, celebration of successes, vulnerability, and authenticity			
I follow through on my commitments or communicate clearly if I am unable to follow through			
I collaborate and delegate responsibilities and/or partner with others to share power and responsibility			
I provide meaningful, actionable feedback and coach others toward growth			
I address moments of rupture as soon as possible and collaborate on solutions that meet the needs of the moment and those impacted			
I take responsibility for harm when it occurs and strive to repair relationships with dignity and care			
I am aware of potential power differentials in conflict and address them by centering the needs of those most historically marginalized while honoring the complexity and dignity of all involved			

calendar reminders for follow-ups where appropriate. If the area of growth is to model what you hope to see, then it may be helpful to seek feedback from a range of sources to determine how well you're doing this and what specific feedback others might offer for improvement.

Any leader can do the work of building relationships, but how do they foster trust and increase psychological safety—the conditions under which people are able to learn, be challenged, feel safe enough to grow? How do leaders sustain relationships over time? What happens when there is conflict or tension? It's easy to use a checklist of questions to get to know colleagues at the beginning of the year or to assess how someone is doing. But teachers are great at telling whether a leader's intentions are authentic. How a leader shows up to these conversations matters. Is the leader harried and checking the clock? Are they actively listening or just getting to the next question? Do leaders genuinely care about the person with whom they are interacting, or are they going through the motions?

Leaders can successfully attend to relationships in the ways they build trust and rapport, sustain relationships in an ongoing way, and repair those relationships in times of rupture (Creekmore & Creekmore, 2024). Table 5.4 outlines additional proactive practices leaders can use to improve the quality of relationships. We'll share what some of these practices might look like through the case studies on the following pages.

Listening and communication are foundational blocks for healthy relationships. We typically listen at three levels—Level 1, Internal; Level 2, Focused; Level 3, Global—and having awareness around these ways of listening is crucial so we can increase our self-awareness as listeners (Coactive Training Institute, 2017). In Level 1 listening, known as Internal Listening, a person is focused on their internal thoughts, judgments, and responses. We can't help but listen through this filter. We might think about our own experiences, formulate advice, or think of a comeback while someone else is speaking. For healthy relationship-building at this level of listening, it helps not to give advice, fix, dismiss, or solve, which can block the other person from sharing their own experiences and feeling heard. The listener might need to remind

TABLE 5.4 Practical Ways to Build, Sustain, and Repair Relationships

Trust-Building Practices	• Make time for 1:1 check-ins at the beginning of the year • Communicate your vision and expectations • Actively support teachers by asking what they need • Ask teachers how they like to receive feedback and how they like to be appreciated • Be an active listener • Take a learning stance in conversations rather than a "fix-it" stance • Prioritize collaboration and delegate leadership opportunities where possible
Practices to Sustain Relationships	• Check in with teachers at regular intervals (and set reminders on your calendar to do so) • Be flexible and adaptive to colleagues' needs and follow up when necessary • Follow through on what you've said you will do, or communicate clearly when you are unable to follow through • Partner with teachers in the classroom, in the committees, and on school-wide initiatives—be a leader beside others • Model what you hope to see through your way of being and actions • Practice appreciation in ways teachers have identified • Provide meaningful feedback and coach teachers toward growth through culturally responsive leadership • Communicate with clarity and transparency (and err on the side of overcommunication)
Restorative Practices	• Address a moment of rupture as close to when it happens as possible • Identify the root causes and address the rupture from that place • Be aware of and name potential power differentials when navigating conflict • Center the needs of those most historically marginalized and hold the dignity/complexity of all involved • Reflect on what you might do better/differently • Apologize if necessary and be ready to take responsibility • Collaborate on solutions that best meet the needs of the moment

themselves to stay curious and open when listening through this level. In Level 2 listening, known as Focused Listening, a person is listening fully to someone else's words. This type of listening can be considered "detailed" listening, as the listener strives to understand the exact words and phrases of the other person. For healthy relationship-building, the listener might paraphrase or repeat back what the other person said to make sure they understood. Or the listener might validate what the other person is saying by nodding or other forms of validation such as, "I hear you." The listener will need to be careful of not being so fixated on the details that they miss other cues in the conversation (emotions, energy levels). Level 3 listening, known as Global Listening, is where the listener not only pays attention to the other person's words but also to the underlying emotions, values, and potential meanings. This type of bigger-picture listening can be considered "whole-human" listening. The listener is attuned to the other person's context and experiences. For healthy relationship-building, the listener might ask open-ended questions (i.e., "What impact did that have on you?" or "What do you make of that?") to explore deeper aspects of the other person's thoughts, values, and beliefs. Listeners are better able to listen at this level when they have built trusting relationships with the other person.

What a leader communicates, what they say or don't say, can travel miles along the school gossip highway, and all members of the school community are taking their cues from leaders. But communication practices are also context-specific. Overcommunicating can feel like micromanaging, and undercommunicating can come across as a lack of transparency. We recommend adjusting the levels of communication situationally (Hersey et al., 2012), but to err on the side of overcommunicating rather than undercommunicating—and to be proactive as often as possible.

Building Relationships

In his mid-50s, Dr. Rodriguez left his corporate job to become a high school math teacher. After Mrs. Demir, the assistant principal, hired him, she made some quick assumptions in their first getting-to-know-you conversation. First, she assumed he spoke Spanish. When Dr. Rodriguez explained that he barely knew the language, Mrs. Demir deflected. Mrs. Demir also assumed that since Dr. Rodriguez was older, he didn't need the same level of support as some of the younger new teachers. Beyond their initial conversation, Dr. Rodriguez and Mrs. Demir had superficial interactions prior to her first classroom walkthrough.

Dr. Rodriguez was struggling, especially with his second-period Algebra class. Despite his subject-matter expertise, he struggled to connect with students and maintain their engagement. Hoping to gain control, Dr. Rodriguez resorted to stern reprimands and lengthy lectures about respect, which only alienated the students further. One afternoon, during an impromptu walkthrough, Mrs. Demir observed a particularly tense interaction: a group of students openly mocking Dr. Rodriguez's signature phrase, "If you respect me, I'll show you respect," to which Dr. Rodriguez raised his voice and retorted, "If you don't care about your future and want to waste your lives, that's not my problem!" The students fell silent. Mrs. Demir left the room without intervening, sending an email later that evening requesting a meeting to "discuss classroom management strategies." Dr. Rodriguez spent the night anxious, interpreting the email as a precursor to a reprimand rather than support.

Drawing inspiration from the practices in Table 5.4, let's assess the dynamic so far between Mrs. Demir and Dr. Rodriguez: Mrs. Demir had an initial getting-to-know-you conversation with Dr. Rodriguez, but it wasn't clear if further conversations were a priority. Mrs. Demir made some blanket assumptions about Dr. Rodriguez based on his name (she thought he could speak Spanish) and his age (she thought he would figure things out easily). From this interaction alone, she may have already caused a rift in the relationship with Dr. Rodriguez since her comments didn't sit right with him. She was making assumptions and not seeming to consider the impact of her words. Mrs. Demir's initial interactions with Dr. Rodriguez didn't center on his identity, but relied on stereotypes rather than Dr. Rodriguez's experiences. Also, how is Dr. Rodriguez feeling now that he made demeaning comments to his students, and Mrs. Demir was present for it? How is Mrs. Demir feeling about the assumptions she made about Dr. Rodriguez's knowledge and skill? From the limited information we have, it's not clear to what degree Mrs. Demir is self-aware or if she's ever received feedback on the biases she might have. Was her email about classroom management strategies rooted in compassion or serving as a reprimand?

How might this relationship have evolved differently if Mrs. Demir had been more intentional from the beginning? What specific actions could have built trust from day one? Let's imagine a successful start to this relationship and what it might have looked like if Mrs. Demir had been more intentional in how she built this relationship.

The first thing Mrs. Demir might do is look at her calendar to determine times she would have 1:1 check-ins with teachers, especially newer teachers. Then she would consider building time for formal check-ins with returning teachers as well. We call these check-ins "re-meeting" meetings so that each year leaders are sustaining rapport with those they oversee. Mrs. Demir might have sent an email before meeting Dr. Rodriguez with a brief overview and a few questions for him to reflect on in advance. In that email, she might have shared her vision for the year, some of the hopes she had for new teachers, and an invitation for a 1:1 meeting. The email could look something like this:

> Dear Dr. Rodriguez,
>
> I'm excited to get the school year started, and we're grateful you're part of our school community. Our shared goal for the year is 'bringing out the brilliance in every student,' and I'm excited to partner with you on what that will look like in your classroom. I would also love to hear some of your hopes for the year ahead. In our meeting, I will ask you the following questions. Of course, please bring your questions for me, too.
>
> - What is a pivotal moment that inspired you to be a teacher?
> - What is important for me to know about you and your identity?
> - How do you like to receive feedback?
> - How do you like to be appreciated?
> - What are two hopes you have for the year? What are two fears?

I look forward to our meeting, and I am excited to support you this year.

Thank you,

Mrs. Demir

In this meeting, Mrs. Demir could practice active listening and focus on learning more about Dr. Rodriguez's background rather than making assumptions about him. She also might be able to share some strategies for classroom rapport-building so that Dr. Rodriguez has more to go on than content knowledge and his lesson plans. She could then share how she approaches classroom drop-ins and their purpose. By the end of the meeting, Mrs. Demir could share how sometimes the drop-ins are surprises and when she will do more formal observations. She could also share about upcoming conversations as well, such as goals conversations and mid-year conversations so Dr. Rodriguez knows what to expect.

If Dr. Rodriguez is struggling, Mrs. Demir might invite him to debrief the lesson and try some new strategies. If the school has mentors or coaches, perhaps Mrs. Demir will encourage Dr. Rodriguez to share his struggles with someone who isn't his supervisor. This way, Dr. Rodriguez can share more freely without feeling like the power differential creates a situation that feels only supervisory. Each of these fractal, proactive moves can help contribute to a more meaningful relationship at the outset.

Sustaining Relationships

Once relationships have been built (or in the case of returning colleagues, renewed), it is important that leaders sustain these relationships in an ongoing way. Earlier, we shared John Gottman's 5:1 principle that there are five positive interactions to every critical one. And yet, for these interactions to be meaningful, they need to be authentic. This means leaders need to get out of their offices and make dedicated time to be in classrooms, in the hallways, checking in with colleagues, or finding opportunities to share appreciation or collaborate.

One strategy we recommend is for leaders to set dates on their calendars proactively for 1:1 check-ins, classroom drop-ins, and informal interactions. We recognize that meetings can be put on a leader's calendar at a moment's notice, and interruptions are a typical part of a leader's work, but the more leaders make relationships a priority, the more their colleagues will take notice. Even a few minutes of informal interactions or saying hello when stopping by a classroom can go a long way in making teachers feel like leaders care about them.

While it is important to set aside time for 1:1 check-ins and informal opportunities to connect, leaders will also want to consider more formal kinds of connections as well, whether it means inviting a diverse array of colleagues to sit on a committee, inviting focus groups of teachers to weekly lunches to hear how things are going, or sharing more specific kinds of appreciations in a more formal way. Here is an example from one of our experiences. At Lori's school, employees used an online platform to set goals, reflect on progress, and review feedback. This platform also had a feature called "spotlights." If someone noticed something positive about their colleague, they sent a spotlight through this feature, which supervisors could also see.

Before Lori left the school building every Friday, she practiced what she called "Five Appreciation Fridays." Using notes from her 1:1 check-ins about how teachers liked to be appreciated, she worked through the list of staff and identified five people who she wanted to spotlight. She sent them a quick note about something specific they did that week that she appreciated. She also made sure she appreciated every teacher in other ways, too, through notes in their mailboxes, face-to-face interactions, or other ways they liked to be appreciated. She took notice of when educators were being courageous, equitable, and doing their part to address inequities at a personal or systemic level, such as the staff member who raised the importance of safety for transgender and nonbinary students and for the staff member who vulnerably addressed a recent discipline issue and recognized the impact their biases had on the situation. At the end of each semester, Lori also wrote a note card to each teacher, sharing specific actions she appreciated about them from that term. While these efforts took time, when Lori asked for feedback on her leadership, a majority of colleagues appreciated the ways they felt seen and valued.

While it is important for leaders to share specific appreciations, they also need to balance these efforts with opportunities to give specific feedback for growth. The more trust there is between leaders and those they oversee, the less sting there will be when engaging in a feedback conversation. Even these conversations can be addressed proactively rather than reactively.

If we return to our case study about Mrs. Demir and Dr. Rodriguez, we can look at what a meaningful feedback conversation might look like between them. Let's say, despite the strategies Mrs. Demir shares, Dr. Rodriguez is still struggling to develop a good rapport with students. Perhaps his flare-up in the classroom indicates something deeper, such as ongoing anger challenges. Mrs. Demir can still leverage the rapport and trust she has built so far to give Dr. Rodriguez more specific feedback on what needs to change. She might schedule a feedback conversation with Dr. Rodriguez but agree to meet in his classroom to diffuse some of the power differential between them. She might share a message in advance about the feedback they'll discuss and give him an opportunity to prepare. If Mrs. Demir is approaching the conversation thinking about how Dr. Rodriguez is able to receive feedback, she can prepare for the conversation in a way that's considerate of Dr. Rodriguez.

It's also worth noting that not everyone in a school building will get along or share the same perspective or values; they might even have long-standing unresolved tensions. We're human. Given their influential position and the power they hold, though, leaders set the tone for how those relationships play out. Leaders might consider adopting the most generous perspective toward their team members, focusing on their strengths. Even those who seem challenging at times have the potential to contribute positively to the group. For example, Elizabeth was once part of a team where one member was always negative anytime she introduced a new idea. No matter what, the first response started with, "Well, that won't work because..." Knowing the pattern, Elizabeth didn't get daunted by the negativity. Instead, she took an expansive approach to how she listened, reframing resistance as a mask for something else. This approach helped her to take a more open view of what might otherwise be perceived as negativity. Lori used a similar approach in her leadership. Before entering into a tense conversation with a colleague, she asked herself, *What's the most generous view I can take of this person right now?* Taking that stance didn't necessarily erase all the built-up challenges Lori had with the other person, but this stance allowed Lori to believe that in each moment, we're doing the best we can, and a generous view will go further in maintaining the relationship with this teacher.

Repairing Relationships

The test of a relationship's health isn't in the early stages of building it or when things are humming along, but in how relationships are sustained in times of resistance or rupture, whether in minor moments of tension or larger instances of harm. All relationships, even the most positive and productive ones, are going to experience tension. How leaders repair relationships matters. Conflict among colleagues involving curriculum, student discipline, microaggressions, or any other tense topic can contribute to increased blood pressure and a few choice words exchanged among colleagues. In these moments, our brains are primed to spot threats (Barrett, 2020). We get defensive when we feel like our identities are under attack. All of us have moments that trigger us; those who historically have felt unsafe in institutions that were not created with them in mind might also experience additional stressors (Talusan, 2022).

When ruptures happen, it's rarely just about that prompting event, but the accumulated impact of our histories and prior experiences that lead up to the rupture—like when a teacher's sharp response to feedback might stem from years of having their expertise questioned. When these breakdowns happen, leaders have an opportunity to restore relationships by how they respond. Leaders can first engage in self-awareness work by pausing to breathe, scanning the body for any sensations, and identifying emotions and thoughts without judgment. These practices calm the parasympathetic nervous system, which decreases our adrenaline and cortisol levels in times of stress (Hemphill, 2024; Menakem, 2020). These practices support better brain function; they also provide a person with more ability to have compassion for others because when we breathe and feel physical sensations, we shift out of survival mode (fight, flight, freeze, or fawn) and can access the decision-making parts of our brains to make more skillful choices about how we engage with others (Barrett, 2020). Leaders can use these practices to respond more intentionally rather than reactively, while still honoring the valid emotional responses of colleagues who are responding to systemic harm.

Coupled with these practices (also known as somatic practices), restorative practices—originating in Indigenous peacemaking processes—can support leaders with a meaningful process to repair relationships (Harnetiaux et al., 2024). Think about a time when trust was broken in one of your relationships—or in your school community. What approaches helped repair the relationship? And what might you have done differently? When ruptures happen, the following steps can serve as a guide for repair:

- ◆ Step 1: Look within. Self-reflection is a crucial component of repairing relationships. A person can take time to notice their emotions and physical sensations and consider what they might need by asking, "What am I noticing here? What might be outside my awareness that I need some support on?"
- ◆ Step 2: Keep dignity intact. Creating space for healing requires acknowledging painful experiences while still finding ways to engage that don't perpetuate harm. While maintaining everyone's fundamental humanity, prioritize the needs of those who have experienced harm, especially when interactions involve racism, xenophobia, homophobia, transphobia, or other forms of oppression. This approach recognizes that genuine repair cannot

happen without centering those most impacted while still holding the complexity of all involved.

- Step 3: Stay proximate. When harm happens, it is important to work closely with those directly affected, soliciting solutions from those most impacted.
- Step 4: Get to the root of the harm. All parties can dig deeper to understand and change the systemic factors that allowed harm to happen, such as how leadership practices might inadvertently silence particular voices or implicit systemic factors like the "hidden curriculum" of a school, whereby a person doesn't realize they have caused harm because expectations could have been made more explicit.
- Step 5: Hold complexity. While quick fixes are tempting and temporarily satisfying in moments of rupture, real, lasting change comes from examining and embracing the complexity of a situation and finding short-, medium-, and long-term solutions that address the moment and prevent further harm.

A slower, more embodied approach to repairing relationships is countercultural and will feel unsatisfying for those who want to move on quickly. But the slower work of repair can have better results. Schools that implemented restorative justice programs for students have seen a reduction in suspensions and absenteeism. In one study conducted by the Chicago Education Lab, researchers found that in Chicago Public Schools that had consistently used restorative practices for years, suspensions decreased by 50% and improved students' perceptions of school climate (Walker, 2023; WestEd, 2016). But intentional implementation of these practices matters, as does the training of all staff so they can model the practices they hope to see in others.

The following is an example of what repair looks like between adults. At Bayridge Middle School, Alex and Jessi had a tense relationship. Alex was a white, cisgender, heterosexual male who had taught at the school for over 20 years. He was skeptical of diversity and equity work and always justified how antiracist and antisexist his curriculum was because of his inclusion of women and people of color in the texts he used. Jessi was a south Asian trans woman in her early 20s; she had only taught for a few years and had become more confident speaking up in team meetings about the need to reimagine the entire curriculum to be more inclusive of different perspectives and knowledge systems.

In team meetings, Alex and Jessi's arguments often shut down the conversation. At times, Alex would condescend to Jessi when speaking about his curriculum, and Jessi would counter with calls that Alex's curriculum was tokenizing. Jessi was fed up with this dynamic and told her department chair, Amara, that she was no longer able to work directly with Alex. Jessi felt like Alex was being racist and transphobic, but no one was doing anything about it, giving Alex a pass for his demeaning comments. Exhausted and feeling helpless by these dynamics, Amara needed to mediate a conversation between Alex and Jessi to see if they could find a way to remedy their conflict.

Before the meeting, Amara grounded herself (Step 1: Look within). She spent two minutes in quiet meditation, getting grounded in her feet and doing a quick body scan. She noticed where she felt any tensions and allowed those tensions to be there. Through deep breaths, she worked to ease any tightness. She then thought about both Alex and Jessi and what each of their strengths were. Alex needed to do more work to examine his biases, but he was an effective teacher who cared deeply about his students. Jessi could be too fixed in her views, often dismissing anything anyone else said, but she pushed the department to reexamine its curriculum, something that was much needed. After getting grounded and acknowledging how she felt, Amara was still nervous, but she planned for the conversation with two hopes in mind: tensions would decrease, and each person would have a solution on the way forward. On her notepad, she wrote a brief agenda, which included

- ♦ Step 2: Keep dignity intact: Ask each person to share what they needed to feel heard and valued.
- ♦ Step 3: Stay proximate: Identify the moments where Alex and Jessi had the most conflict and the impact of these moments on one another.

- Step 4: Get to the root: Understand the bigger picture of what happened and then determine the prompting events at the root of the conflict.
- Step 5: Hold complexity: Develop an "Agreement Matrix" to identify short-, medium-, and long-term accountability for each person (Harnetiaux et al., 2024).

Amara was being realistic about outcomes while also hoping that identifying some short-, medium-, and long-term accountability measures might provide Alex and Jessi with concrete action steps and offer Amara opportunities for follow-up. Amara also hoped these action steps might ease the tensions each colleague was bringing to team meetings, something that was having an effect on the well-being of the entire department. By engaging in this process, Amara also established an approach to relationships that centered on the needs of all involved, working to keep dignity central throughout the school community.

The conversation itself was awkward and tense at times. Alex came into the conversation with his defenses up, and Jessi was exhausted from a full day of teaching. Amara began by reminding each of the department's vision for equity: "We commit to transforming systems, decentering dominance in the curriculum and in our interactions, and fostering inclusive relationships so every learner thrives." Using this vision statement as a guide, Amara stayed committed to the process, asking each person what they needed to move forward with a focus on inclusive relationships. Each person was able to agree that trust was low and that they could put more effort into working well together. Jessi shared that Alex didn't value what she had to offer, and Alex apologized for coming off like a bulldozer at times. Alex continued to defend his curricular choices but agreed to be open to new ideas. When they filled out the Agreement Matrix (Table 5.5) at the end of the conversation, Alex and Jessi were able to make some headway.

Jessi raised the idea of working on a long-term project together, and Alex thought it was a good idea. Amara worried to herself about this long-term strategy and recognized the power imbalance between Alex's established position and Jessi's more vulnerable one as a new, trans teacher of color. While she wanted solutions to

TABLE 5.5 Agreement Matrix Example

Timeframe	Action Steps	Person Responsible	Support Needed	Check-in Date
Short-term	• Avoid personal comments during team meetings • Use "I feel" statements to express concerns • Pause and listen for others' perspectives without shutting down the conversation	Both	Amara (for feedback)	Next team meeting in two weeks
Medium-term	• Meet monthly to discuss progress	Alex and Jessi	Separate scheduled check-ins w/ Amara	End of month
Long-term	• Collaborate on a shared unit project	Both	Guidance from the department chair	End of semester

emerge organically, she made a note to monitor the collaboration more carefully and provide additional support to ensure equitable collaboration. The conversation showed progress, and Amara was pleased that each person was able to offer solutions for a way forward while keeping everyone's dignity intact.

In ecosystems, the vitality of the soil determines the health of every living thing it supports and its relationships with one another. When we prioritize role clarity, include colleagues in a co-creative process to set expectations, and foster trust and relationships, we create the conditions for educators to thrive. Just as soil needs regular tending, schools must consistently assess and address their culture, ensuring it remains a fertile ground for growth. Leaders play a critical role as cultivators of this ecosystem, and nurturing the soil of educator well-being is an ongoing process, not a one-time effort. It requires continuous reflection, collaborative growth, and a commitment to centering the needs of all community members. When the soil is well cared for, growth is possible.

Summary

This chapter emphasizes the importance of intentionally cultivating school culture to support collective educator well-being, comparing it to tending soil for healthy growth. Tools like the Portrait of an Educator can guide communities in defining and sustaining equitable, effective practices that center on both individual and collective well-being. Ongoing relationship-building is a cornerstone of thriving ecosystems through trust-building, sustaining connections, and addressing conflict with humility and care. By implementing intentional relationship practices, leaders can foster environments where educators feel supported, valued, and empowered to grow.

Reflection Questions

1. How can your school community align its well-being practices with its vision for equity?
2. What specific actions can leaders take to build trust and sustain relationships in ways that feel authentic and meaningful?
3. How might adopting intentional practices for repairing relationships improve how conflicts are addressed at your school?
4. What steps can your school take to ensure that well-being initiatives remain dynamic and responsive to evolving needs over time?

References

Barrett, L. F. (2020). *Seven and a half lessons about the brain.* Houghton Mifflin Harcourt.

Coactive Training Institute (2017). *Co-active coaching: The proven framework for transformative conversations at work and in life.* Wiley.

Creekmore, J., & Creekmore, M. (2024). *Every connection matters: Building, maintaining, and restoring relationships in schools.* Educational Leadership Press.

Harnetiaux, C., Trout, S., & Wu, A. (2024). *The restorative leader: Practices for cultivating trust and collaboration in schools*. Equity Press.

Hemphill, P. (2024). *What it takes to heal: How transforming ourselves can change the world*. Random House.

Hersey, P., Blanchard, K. H., & Johnson, D. E. (2012). *Management of organizational behavior: Leading human resources* (10th ed.). Prentice Hall.

Menakem, R. (2020). *My grandmother's hands: Racialized trauma and the pathway to mending our hearts and bodies*. Central Recovery Press.

Talusan, L. (2022). *The identity-conscious educator: Building habits and skills for a more inclusive school*. Corwin Press.

Walker, T. (2023). Restorative practices and their impact on school climate: A longitudinal study. *Journal of Educational Change, 19*(4), 235–257.

WestEd (2016). *Equity coaching frameworks: Strategies for systemic change*. WestEd.

Growth:
Cultivate Continuous Learning

Growth is the ongoing process of nurturing individual and collective learning through equity-driven reflection, iterative practice, and courageous accountability. Growth-oriented cultures can be intentionally cultivated through meaningful goals, human-centered priorities, and accountability cycles. To cultivate continuous learning, leaders are encouraged to model vulnerability, confront biases, and center justice, creating conditions where educators can engage in iterative learning, celebrate successes, and build collective capacity to better serve all students.

6

Growth: Cultivate Continuous Learning

It was mid-August, and the first day back for teachers at Valley Vista High School. Renata, the school principal, and the professional development committee had been preparing to roll out their growth initiative for the beginning of the school year. The theme for this year, "Learning from one another," was posted on the opening slide of Renata's presentation to kick off the opening in-service session. After a few minutes of introductory remarks and celebrations from last school year's test score data, Renata shifted her focus for the year ahead. "It has been a hard few years. I want to thank you for all the work that you have done. I also recognize we let so much fall by the wayside in favor of just getting through. This year, I'm committed to bringing more of our growth back into the community. So with the recommendation from the professional development committee, we're introducing peer coaching this year."

Renata shared a brief definition of peer coaching, and a couple of members of the committee spoke about how this was a way that staff could best learn from one another in a non-evaluative way. There was little response from staff during the presentation, but during the question and answer portion, several hands were raised. Sheila, a longtime teacher at the school and the first to critique any new initiative, spoke first. "You keep adding things to

DOI: 10.4324/9781003531296-7

our plate, but when are you going to take something off? When are we supposed to peer coach? We can't even find subs when we're sick." Snaps could be heard around the room.

Renata responded, "Yes, we are cognizant of the schedule, and in our September faculty meeting, I'll share more about how the timing of peer coaching can work."

Tracee, sitting next to Sheila, asked, "Will everyone be doing peer coaching, like, the leaders? Or just teachers?"

"For now, this is focused on teachers," Renata responded, trying to remain neutral in her tone of voice. Tracee muttered, "Yeah, I thought so."

A few other teachers wondered about how peer coaching teams would be selected, while the union building representative wondered about the timing of coaching to make sure it didn't violate the contract.

With each question, Renata felt herself get defensive, worried the purpose of peer coaching was getting lost. Before ending this portion of the meeting, Renata said, "We say we're a culture of growth and feedback. We tell this to the students. But for the past two years, we have suspended evaluation and we haven't created any mechanisms for people to receive feedback. This is the bare minimum we are asking for this year."

The meeting ended tensely, furthering the divide between teachers and administrators.

Does this story sound familiar? Renata's story is a common one we've heard from schools around the globe. In the early 2020s, many schools suspended growth and evaluation programs in favor of survival. Coaching and mentoring roles were repurposed into student wellness coaches, substitutes, or full-time classroom teachers. Evaluations were shelved until leaders could stop the hemorrhaging of teacher attrition. The focus was on educator well-being, rightfully so, but the efforts were based on the fear of losing more teachers rather than considering the root causes of teacher attrition to begin with.

When leaders finally decided to re-engage with growth and evaluation efforts, staff members pushed back with calls of "It's too much." Leaders doubled down on mandates to move forward without whole staff engagement rather than communicating a clearly articulated purpose for why growth and evaluation matter. As we re-engage with growth and evaluation cycles, we have an opportunity to reimagine what that might look like in ways that can be responsive to individual needs, aligned with the realities teachers are facing, and, ultimately, focused on how to best meet the needs of students.

Instead of a one-size-fits-all approach, we can create flexible systems that honor the emotional and professional well-being of educators, allowing for meaningful reflection, feedback, and collaboration. This reimagining can be more co-creative rather than top-down, with growth processes that respect the expertise and capacity of each staff member—giving educators a voice in shaping their development while simultaneously fostering an environment of accountability and care.

In a thriving ecosystem, each life form gets what it needs to grow. Growth happens when the flora and fauna are diverse enough to thrive, when they have room to strike roots and complement one another's needs for light and water, and when they have clear roles to play in contributing to the health of the ecosystem. It is important to regularly check the health of the soil as well as plant and animal life; to look for signs of stress or imbalance; to water plants as needed, avoiding both overwatering and underwatering; to prune plants to promote flourishing; and to keep the ecosystem healthy through removing waste, mold, or algae.

In previous chapters, we established that equity and well-being are the foundation and soil necessary for growth. For growth to occur, leaders need to stay committed to nurturing those foundations—upholding their vision for equity, sustaining relationships, and ensuring educators are valued and held to high expectations. We also shared strategies for developing the portrait of an educator—the specific qualities educators need to possess to be effective in their work. The criteria developed from that portrait can become a roadmap by which your school can develop plans to support educator growth and accountability. Before getting into the specifics of how to support growth related to those criteria, it's important to determine what your site means by growth.

What does growth look, sound, and feel like at your site? What needs to be true at your site in order for growth to happen? What does growth *not* look like? How is growth modeled and celebrated? Who is leading these growth efforts? These kinds of questions can be a starting point for fostering a growth-oriented culture. In the next chapter, you'll receive a process for developing a growth philosophy at your school so you have a clearer rationale for the structures that support growth. In this chapter, you'll build on what you learned in previous chapters and layer growth into the ecosystem framework. We'll provide some suggestions about structures to create cultures of growth at your school site or district, beginning with planting the seeds of a growth process and ending with ways to celebrate the fruits of everyone's efforts.

Growth Cultures in a Healthy Ecosystem

What growth looks like in schools should be as varied as a thriving ecosystem. Think about that for a moment. What would you picture? In our vision for growth, some people will receive more focused support, particularly if they are new and/or struggling; more experienced educators may be called upon to support their colleagues' growth through mentoring, coaching, or leading a professional learning community. Leaders may also be modeling their own growth by sharing their goals, sharing their mistakes, and remedying their missteps—creating safer communities for those they oversee to do the same. For everyone, growth means drawing upon clearly identified practices from the school's portrait of an educator and creating a growth process centered on these practices. Growth happens when educators are exploring their beliefs about teaching and about their students, getting jostled out of their biases and a "this is the way we've always done it" mentality, and supporting colleagues into methods for teaching and learning that are healthier and more human-centered. If students are pushed to grow beyond their comfort zones, adults must be willing to do the same.

Growth is also linked to justice. We grow when we confront an unjust education system that privileges curriculum and pedagogy rooted in the dominant culture—white, cisgendered, male, heterosexual, able-bodied, neurotypical—and imagine and enact something more expansive: where every student's identity is honored; where diverse ways of knowing are celebrated; and where every member of the school community can flourish (Muhammad, 2023). Growth is evident when a math teacher encourages their students to take their time to find as many paths to the answer rather than promoting speed and accuracy, something they may have been taught to value but realize how inequitable that practice is. Growth is evident when a social science teacher using a state-mandated curriculum focused on "traditional history" is asking students to engage critically with what they're learning, asking questions like, "Whose stories aren't being told?" or "Who isn't included in this picture?" Growth is evident when a music teacher encourages her students to make clunky music rather than mimicking a song precisely right away and then inviting her students to focus on process and product with equal value. Growth is evident when a teacher shifts from a deficit mindset and low expectations for students with learning differences to a belief in the capacity of every student, designing lessons with high expectations (Love, 2019). Equity-driven growth does not leave anyone behind. It invites educators to unpack their own socializations, biases, and privileges, allowing for honest reflection and shifts in teaching practice (Milner, 2012). This kind of reflection requires a community of trust and rapport, where the emphasis is not on "getting it right" but on engaging in the continuous practice of doing better with those who believe in their ability to grow—and who imagine a more just world for students to inherit.

While many educators might be willing to grow, there can be barriers to entry, particularly perfectionist school cultures or a school or district that promotes one-size-fits-all approaches to what growth looks like (Okun & Jones, 2021). Teachers face constant pressure to perform flawlessly—to arrive each day at the peak of their abilities with no room for error or experimentation.

While we encourage students to embrace mistakes as learning opportunities, we create environments where adults cannot do the same. In perfectionist cultures, staff meetings revolve around dissecting test score data and blaming students and teachers for underperformance rather than practicing dynamic instructional methods that dismantle inequities—leaving teachers without the practical skills, courage, or community support needed to transform their classrooms. In one-size-fits-all cultures, leaders outsource their professional development to outside organizations that swoop in for one-and-done workshops tangentially connected to a school's initiatives without providing ongoing practice opportunities, signaling that growth is transactional, not transformational. Without intentional cultivation of growth-oriented cultures, teachers inevitably stagnate or treat professional learning at best as optional, at worst as a nuisance rather than the lifeblood of effective teaching.

Growth-oriented cultures need to be places where educators can be messy, have conversations that are clunky and iterative, show vulnerability, and learn ways to increase competence, knowledge, and skill. Neuroscience researchers have debunked the mythologies that it's solely the number of hours one practices new skills, but it's also the iterative nature of growth, the mistakes and redos and revisions that more greatly contribute to one's growth (Paul, 2021). Educators need time to practice, to do more "reps" with tools like choice boards or strategies to address microaggressions in the classroom. A single training day won't solve inequities; the follow-up and time to practice is where we develop the neural pathways to make change. Educators also need safe enough conditions to mess up and be accountable for making change. This is why we encourage reparative practices (see Chapter 5) as part of a school's culture, where there are intentional and structured opportunities for repair. We need leaders who have done their own personal work and who hold teachers responsible for doing their own work, too. We need schools to be places where adults recognize that the journey to make lasting change is not a one-time event nor a linear one; growth-oriented cultures value mistake-making but also hold everyone accountable for doing better the next time around.

A Leader's Role in Cultivating Growth

To support educator growth, leaders might consider deriving wisdom from Culturally Responsive and Sustaining Pedagogies (Paris, 2012) to counter these notions of perfectionism, of there being only one right way of doing things. Lessons from these pedagogies encourage both students and adults to take risks, embrace vulnerability, and explore the richness of diverse identities and ways of knowing (Gay, 2018; Yosso, 2005). Leaders might cultivate consistent opportunities where educators' cultural experiences are valued and leveraged, where high expectations—and the path to meet these expectations—are front and center, and where joy is an outcropping of productive struggle (Muhammad, 2023). Imagine a staff meeting that looked like the following: Teachers conduct empathy interviews with one another, learn more about their colleagues' backgrounds and motivations, and then co-design a classroom culture-building activity to try in their classrooms. Or imagine a staff meeting where teachers are invited to bring a lesson that was a total flop and invite their colleagues to give feedback on how to make it better. Perhaps staff might do an activity that we call, "Paper Plane Problems," inspired by organizations like Ideo. It goes something like this:

1. Each person writes a brief summary of a challenge they are having in the classroom with a request for help from their colleagues. Examples might include:

    - "How can I better differentiate this lesson for students with disabilities?"
    - "Does my opening activity effectively engage students in the topic?"
    - "What are creative ways I can ask students to show what they learned?"

2. Everyone folds their feedback request sheets into paper airplanes; the more creative, the better.
3. Everyone stands in a circle or spreads out in the room. On the facilitator's signal, they throw their paper planes

across the room. The randomness ensures anonymity and makes the activity lively.
4. Each person picks up a new paper plane. They read the lesson plan dilemma and write constructive, specific, and actionable feedback directly on the paper.
5. Planes are then placed on tables where the original creators can find them. Everyone reviews the feedback and can use it to refine their lesson plans.

An activity like this one can break down the silos between subject areas, invite diverse perspectives, honor everyone's background and experiences, and invite more play into professional learning (Aguilar & Cohen, 2022). It's possible that people might not give the best feedback to one another at first, but an activity like this one can be used to catalyze deeper conversations about effective practice, how to give and receive feedback, and how to expand our perspectives. When leaders design and consistently employ activities that encourage a diversity of learning opportunities and knowledge systems, growth is possible.

Ecosystems are interdependent on all the life within them. Similarly, growth-oriented cultures are communal, where it's not about one or two shining stars who stand out, but the ways leaders can encourage everyone to challenge one another to grow. Here, we can take a lesson from redwood trees. Redwoods grow in circles, with interconnected root systems joining trees together. Rather than competing for light, each tree ensures there is space for everyone to grow. If we apply that way of working together to our school sites, we can then recognize that our collective efficacy and success are bound in our relationships with one another—that care for one another is at the center of the learning conditions we want to create for students.

Leaders can model that collective care by soliciting feedback, sharing their learning journeys, demonstrating mistake-making and resilience, and being accountable to those they serve. If leaders can model this kind of learning and vulnerability, they establish conditions for teachers to do it as well. When leaders say "I don't know" and "I'm sorry" (something each of us has had to do in our leadership), they show they aren't above those they lead and supervise. Leaders also need to commit to doing better when they mess up, and implementing changes at the speed that those who have historically been harmed are demanding. When leaders show that it's safe to take risks and share how they learned from these risks, they challenge the notions of perfectionism that pervade school cultures.

While we promote communal forms of growth, when there is a toxic element that threatens the safety of the ecosystem, leaders need to be ready to remove elements that compromise the health of the community. For example, when Lori was a school leader, one of the teachers she supervised was accused of sexism. When Lori first met with this teacher, he was defensive and angry. The teacher shared that he didn't want to be perceived as sexist, and if anything, he wanted female students to feel safe in his class. Even though he was defensive, his sincerity seemed clear, and he had a desire to do better. Lori and the teacher explored his beliefs, developed strategies to eliminate bias, and identified action steps that would indicate this teacher's growth within a predetermined timeframe. Lori balanced being a warm demander, holding this teacher to high expectations for eradicating the sexism he exhibited while also believing in this teacher's ability to grow. Unfortunately, the teacher continued to be accused of sexism, not only by students but also by his colleagues. While the teacher noticed his actions, he apologized after the fact and didn't stop being sexist. Eventually, the teacher was put on an improvement plan to address these harmful behaviors, and after a three-month timeframe with little tangible improvement, he was not given a contract to return the following year. Letting go of teachers is hard; sometimes, though, we give people too many chances to improve without considering the impact of their actions on the health of the community.

Leaders need to model what it looks like to center the health of the community even in the face of resistance. There will be those who resist any change, such as Sheila and Tracee in our opening story. We imagine you know some members of your community who push back on just about anything. Unfortunately, school leaders typically design professional growth opportunities by considering those who are least willing or most resistant to change.

In other words, leaders design on the defensive, fearful that those who are most resistant will get in the way of change. In the Diffusion of Innovation (DOI) theory, this group is known as "the Laggards" (Rogers, 1983). DOI is a theory that posits that any intentional change effort "diffuses" through various groups over time, beginning with Innovators, the ones most excited to try new ideas, to the Laggards, those most resistant to change, like Sheila and Tracee. We advocate that rather than targeting growth efforts toward the Laggards, we instead design for those most historically on the margins and those most willing to learn and grow.

Table 6.1 draws upon the DOI theory and provides approaches leaders might take to lead growth initiatives from a stance of proactivity over defensiveness. If we return to our opening story, Renata might have chosen to pilot peer coaching with a smaller group of excited people first rather than bring the entire staff along. Through a pilot, she could gather data to determine peer

TABLE 6.1 Using Diffusion of Innovation Theory to Lead Growth Efforts

Category	*Description*	*Approach for Leaders*
Innovators	Innovators are the first to adopt new ideas They are willing to take risks and are eager to experiment with new ways	• Involve innovators in the design and pilot phase of new growth initiatives • Provide autonomy and support for experimentation • Seek feedback on ways to improve new ideas
Early Adopters	Early adopters are respected by peers and are key to the adoption of new ideas. They bring credibility to new ideas	• Engage early adopters as advocates for new initiatives • Provide leadership opportunities in growth initiatives, such as leading professional learning or mentoring
Early Majority	Early majority are pragmatic and will adopt new ideas once they see proven benefits from others	• Highlight successful examples and case studies of growth as data for early majority to consider • Provide structured opportunities for collaboration and reflection between early adopters and early majority

(Continued)

TABLE 6.1 Using Diffusion of Innovation Theory to Lead Growth Efforts (*Continued*)

Category	Description	Approach for Leaders
Late Majority	Late majority are skeptical and will adopt new ideas only after the majority has embraced them	• Emphasize practical benefits of the change initiative • Provide research and data to support the need for these growth efforts • Offer clear expectations about the change that is about to occur, and scaffolded support to engage the late majority
Laggards	Laggards are the last to adopt new ideas. They resist change and prefer traditional methods	• Provide research and data to support the need for these growth efforts. Offer clear expectations about the change that is about to occur, and scaffolded support to engage the late majority • Be willing to accept that this group might not come along and determine when it's time to move on

coaching's impact. Peer coaching efforts might then be scaled for the early majority with small-scale coaching cycles. Through practice and feedback data, Renata and the professional development committee could then revise the peer coaching program and present their findings at an upcoming staff meeting. Renata could focus her efforts on those eager for change, fostering a supportive community for growth rather than waiting for the resistant voices to join in. In the sections that follow, we'll provide a guide for what it looks like to design for what we hope to see rather than designing on the defensive, operating from the belief that in a healthy ecosystem, continuous growth is possible.

Cultivating a Growth Cycle

When working on this book, we built a terrarium. We ordered a terrarium kit online, which came with a rocky base layer, soil, moss, and tiny plastic dinosaurs. The terrarium contained no plant or animal life, so after we laid the foundation, the soil, the moss, and the dinosaurs, we took a step back to admire our creation. We congratulated ourselves and then asked, "Now what?" Our ecosystem was primed for growth, but there wasn't anything planted. The kit came with all the necessary foundations, but nurturing growth was up to us.

We took a cutting from a succulent and planted it in the soil. We set up a watering schedule and ensured the plant had enough light exposure. Eventually, after enough dedicated time and attention, the succulent struck roots. Soon after that, buds began to form as offshoots of the original plant. Currently, the plant is getting bigger, and, eventually, with careful cultivation, we'll make room for more plants, giving each one time to strike roots and go through the process of growth.

School leaders might put a lot of time and effort into creating visions for equity. They might have clearly defined roles and qualities of effective instruction that look amazing on paper. They might have learned how to navigate resistance and center the needs of those most marginalized, regardless of pushback. But to what end? Like our terrarium, school leaders need to test the foundations they have established through developing processes and structures for growth.

We often hear leaders say things like, "We want a mentoring program," "This year everyone is going to take part in a PLC," or "We adopted this new curriculum because research says this promotes a better way of learning." Or even worse, leaders saturate the community with initiatives and make everything as important as everything else. In our ecosystem framework, this is where a fractal approach to growth is essential, taking more intentional and incremental steps to make sustainable change that best serves students. Doing less creates greater opportunities for growth.

Leaders need to consider which growth structures align with their initiatives, mission, and values and how to ensure those structures are rooted in equity and center the well-being of the educators whose growth they're responsible for. To cultivate continuous learning, leaders need to ask:

- How will educators grow?
- How might leaders support educator growth in ways that are equitable, differentiated, and personalized in support of well-being?
- Which structures will support growth?
- How do leaders model their own growth and promote a culture of learning?

In the next chapter, we'll provide an array of structures—what we call "gardening tools"—leaders might use to promote ongoing growth at their sites, whether through self-directed approaches, small-group efforts, or 1:1 approaches like coaching and mentoring. For now, though, we'd like to outline the process for growth that any school leader can facilitate, regardless of whether a school has abundant resources to support coaches and mentors or whether they are working with limited budgets and need everyone to be full-time in classrooms. At this point, we assume the soil is rife for planting, that collective and individual well-being have been addressed, and now it's time to plant the seeds for growth.

Gardening with a Growth Orientation

Putting on the Gardening Gloves for Equity and Justice

At the beginning stages of the growth process, we encourage educators to develop an equity and justice lens. Developing an equity and justice lens allows us to enter into the growth process with a recognition that we all hold biases and beliefs and that our openness to investigating these beliefs will create more room for change. Oftentimes, when we raise issues of inequity in our school communities or talk about structural forms of oppression, those who have had more advantages can feel like this work is a waste of time, and that those with privilege are on the receiving end of a shame and blame fest. Leaders should be conscious of how they present growth opportunities and the environment they create to foster them. Leaders might share about their own equity journeys or missteps as an example of how this work is clunky; or they might begin by acknowledging that we all hold biases—that it's part of our wiring—and that if we can learn something through socialization, we can unlearn something, rewiring our brains with new beliefs and practices. Or they might begin a meeting with a visioning session, asking staff what justice would look like for all students, listing that somewhere visible, identifying the barriers in the way, and discussing what needs to be removed to achieve justice. This kind of framing allows the rest of the growth path to unfold in all its messiness and challenge, struggle and success, with everyone having a part to play in the process.

Core Criteria for an Equity and Justice Lens

We filter all our experiences through our socialization, the beliefs and values we formed at an early age, and what has been reinforced in our communities. This cycle of socialization (Harro, 2000) creates the biases we hold and can inhibit us from recognizing how the dominant culture might be operating—the values, beliefs, norms, and practices that are widely accepted and considered "normal" and institutionalized within a society, often reflecting the perspectives and interests of the group in power. When we develop an equity and justice lens, we expand our perspective beyond our socialization and envision justice as creating outcomes where students can learn in their full dignity. We develop an equity lens by doing the following:

- ♦ Understand systems of oppression: Explore how society has been organized to give structural advantages to a small subset of the population, thus reinforcing the dominant culture; we can examine this in how (and for whom) schools were designed, and the opportunity gaps that exist for Black and Brown students, students in poverty, LGBTQIA+ students, and students with disabilities, among other historically marginalized groups; we work instead to eradicate inequities and design systems that serve all students.
- ♦ Interrogate our beliefs: Rather than accept our beliefs about the world and about others as true, we work to

understand where those beliefs come from and shift our beliefs and actions to be more inclusive and expansive.
- ♦ Acknowledge complexity and hold lightly to views: We learn to recognize that the path to equity is messy, non-linear, and manifold. There are multiple perspectives at play, and those perspectives are rooted in others' identities, socialization, and values. Our truth is not everyone's truth, so we remain open to learning and holding loosely the beliefs we have, especially ones that cause harm.
- ♦ Practice cultural humility and identify what more we need to learn: We recognize that there is a lot we don't know; through listening attentively and being curious over defensive, we remain open to learning about others and consider how we might, in an ongoing way, continue to eliminate bias and harm and develop new systems and supports for our communities (Chávez, 2012).
- ♦ Define what justice looks and sounds like: Determine what outcomes are necessary and what barriers need to be removed so all students can learn fully and outcomes are not predictable by identity.

Before we continue, take a moment to review the key features of an equity lens and think about what justice looks like in your community. Which beliefs or biases do you want to shift or confront on the path to a healthy ecosystem? What is the support you need to learn and be challenged?

Planting Seeds for Growth

Identify Growth Areas and Analyze Data Sources
The seeds for growth are varied. Sometimes schools have sitewide (or district-mandated) initiatives based on quantitative and qualitative data that guide the growth of an entire community. Some schools will draw on the portrait of an educator and invite individual teachers to set growth goals based on the criteria for effective teaching. For example, at Mosaic School, a small K-8 suburban school, the principal created a rubric based on her school's qualities of effective teaching and invited teachers

to self-assess based on those qualities. Teachers came to their fall goals conversations with rubrics in hand, as well as any data sources (i.e., student work samples, test score data) that revealed why this was an area for growth. Together, the leader and teacher determined the area for teacher growth, which then became the focus point for the school year.

Whether growth areas are determined by districts or individuals, we advocate that the process be collaborative or self-directed where possible, as collaboration decentralizes the role of a leader as the arbiter of a teacher's growth, and self-direction invites the teacher to have agency in their growth process. At the same time, we recognize that some teachers' growth areas need to be leader-directed to ensure students have an equitable learning experience. If that's the case, our hope is that the process can be empowering for the teacher, that their learning leads to long-term change rather than resentment, humility rather than resistance. In this instance, a leader will need to communicate care for the teachers, acknowledge their strengths and their commitment to students, and demonstrate commitment to teachers' growth.

This is where the portrait of an educator can play an important role. Clear criteria for effectiveness set a collective expectation for the community. In the absence of these criteria, growth can become a free-for-all that is either determined by those in power or by individuals who might have ideas of what they want to improve upon, but that might miss the mark for what's most needed or important. One activity we like to do is invite educators to review the criteria for educator effectiveness and put a star next to five possible areas for growth. At a staff or department meeting, teachers get into pairs or groups of three to discuss the areas they selected initially. Colleagues are given the opportunity to ask probing questions to help clarify the teacher's thinking. After this conversation, teachers are then asked to prioritize one or two areas for growth and put a star next to those areas. From there, a teacher then digs into what data sources say about this area for growth to further determine if these areas should be a priority.

When assessing data sources to determine growth, we advocate that qualitative data sources play a crucial role in the early stages of the process. This data, known as "street data" (Safir & Dugan, 2021), emphasizes the importance of educators gathering qualitative, narrative-rich data from the experiences of students, educators, and community members. Street data complements quantitative measures like test scores and grades by offering a more complex portrait of the student and teacher learning experience. Table 6.2 offers some examples of street data and its purpose.

Analyze the Data and Determine a Priority

With whatever data sources a teacher has gathered, they can analyze this data for patterns so they can narrow their focus and

TABLE 6.2 Types of Street Data and Purpose

Type of Street Data	Purpose
Equity participation tracker	To track who participates in classrooms—by demographics and engagement types—to uncover equity patterns in teacher–student interactions (Boykin & Noguera, 2011)
Equity classroom scan	To examine student demographics across course types (e.g., AP, remedial) to identify inequities in access and participation
Student interviews	To host audio-recorded focus groups with a diverse range of students or conduct a more in-depth ethnography of one particular student group through interviews to learn about student experiences in classrooms Categorize findings by theme and share the findings with the school community
Shadow a student	To identify a student historically on the margins and follow them around for the day; debrief the experience with the student and share insights with colleagues
Home visits	To meet with families in their homes or community spaces to build trust and learn about their backgrounds, cultural wealth—the knowledge and skills they possess from their backgrounds—and aspirations (Yosso, 2005)
Classroom walkthroughs (also known as instructional rounds)	To observe classrooms with a small group without evaluating or critiquing, but instead focus on observation and notice what the students are doing: Who is holding the cognitive load—the onus of learning—during instruction; how students are interacting; whether smiles, laughter, and joy are present; what productive struggle looks like; debrief observations and identify patterns and next steps (Hammond, 2014; Muhammad, 2023; Teitel, 2013)
Artifact analysis	To examine student work from a range of learners, identify patterns of performance and ways students express their learning, and identify gaps and opportunities that inform instruction

prioritize an area for growth. A data analysis protocol might look like the following:

- Prepare yourself to review data. Remember to practice cultural humility. Consider the students for whom you do this work and hold them in your mind as you review the data.
- Review data sources and analyze them. Pay attention to outliers and hold lightly to these outliers. We tend to get fixated on one negative outlier rather than identifying general patterns. Be careful of falling into this trap and focus on "right spotting" over "wrong spotting." Use the following questions as a guide for analysis:
  - What do I notice?
  - What patterns can I find?
  - What are the top two or three patterns I see?
  - What do I interpret about what I notice?
  - What conclusions can I draw from these patterns?
  - What are the implications of these conclusions for students?
- Encapsulate the data: If you were to come up with two or three headlines based on this data, what would they be?
- Make room for emotions: In reviewing data, both pleasant and unpleasant emotions may surface. Emotions that arise in data conversations are often connected to our identity, sense of self, and the impact we hope to have on those we serve. In moments where difficult emotions arise, it's helpful to notice emotions, name them, and investigate where they come from. Naming and investigating emotions diminishes their power over us and gives us more information about how to address them.

Examples of findings might include something like the following:

- A teacher wants to hold all their students to high expectations but has come to recognize—through looking at student–teacher interactions in the classroom—that

they hold their Black male students to low expectations compared to their white and Asian students.
- A teacher values differentiated instruction and equitable participation but notices that during class discussions and small-group activities, multilingual students are less engaged than their peers.
- A teacher wants to create an inclusive environment and has repeatedly called the classroom a "safe space," but learns several LGBTQIA+ students feel uncomfortable when the school counselor shares that these students have been coming to her with concerns about other students in that class making hurtful, microaggressive comments.
- The math department wants to center racial equity in the math curriculum and has realized the existing math curriculum is outdated and perpetuates inequities by failing to reflect the diverse cultural contributions to mathematics, instead relying heavily on standardized assessments that disproportionately disadvantage students of color. Department members are piloting the new curriculum and set of assessments, but they are resisting the implementation of this new curriculum because it's just "easier" to do what they always have done.

When you have analyzed the patterns you notice, it's time to finalize a priority for growth. This priority could be differentiated by department, individuals, and or be a schoolwide plan for growth. We encourage leaders to be courageous advocates for those least supported in classrooms, the students most in need of justice, and prioritize their growth initiative from there. This focal area is the seed that, ideally, with time and care, will strike roots that lead to buds and blooms for all students.

Watering Seeds

Plants don't get watered once and grow. They grow with careful, ongoing tending, with the right amount of water, light, and air quality; they grow with a recognition that external forces may make growing conditions more challenging, and they persist through those forces by staying creative and adaptive on their way to meeting more just outcomes.

Set a Stretch Goal

We advocate that educators set a "stretch goal," something that addresses the gap between the priority for growth and their reality—and challenges each of us to grow beyond our comfort zones (Vygotsky, 1978). This goal also needs to be personally meaningful and compelling and should come directly from teachers themselves rather than top-down. Sometimes grade-level teams might set a shared goal, or teachers working on the same team can set a goal. Regardless, each person needs to be invested in this area for growth. This goal should also be measurable, with tangible evidence of growth. Setting a goal might take the form of an outcome statement, something an educator hopes to be true by the end of the timeframe in which they'd like to demonstrate growth, or it might be in the form of an inquiry question. Samples of goals might look like the following:

- Statement: *I want to hold all students to high expectations and eliminate the disparity of holding Black male students to low expectations.*
- Statement: *I want to thoughtfully implement a math curriculum that centers racial equity and equip teachers with the skills for its implementation.*
- Inquiry question: *How might I solicit feedback from those I serve and act on it in ways that are equitable?*
- Inquiry question: *How might I ensure my classroom is an affirming space for LGBTQIA+ students?*

Identify What Success Will Look Like and Determine a Timeframe to Achieve This Goal

In this part of the process, educators will need to be clear about what, specifically, will happen as a result of achieving this goal, being specific about how they will address this goal with interim benchmarks along the way. These benchmarks should include what success will look and sound like for educators and students, along with specific artifacts that determine success. One approach is to create a growth plan or schedule moments for reflection on whatever calendar tool a school is using. For example, North Creek School District uses a growth plan form (Figure 6.1). Grade-level

NCSD 2nd Grade School-Year Goals Plan

Data sources	• Student focus groups • Student shadow day notes • Spring test score data
Patterns from the Data	Focus Group Finding Headlines • Multilingual learners feel less represented in classroom discussions and instructional materials. Shadow Day Finding Headlines • Frequent disruptions in certain classrooms negatively impact instructional time, disproportionately affecting students needing additional support. • Teacher–student interactions highlight unintentional disparities in how high-expectation feedback is delivered across student groups. Test Score Data Headlines • Achievement gaps persist between Black and Latinx students and their White and Asian peers in literacy, despite schoolwide efforts to improve equity. • Grade-level proficiency in reading has decreased by 12% overall, with the most decline seen among students with disabilities.
Priority	Cultivating inclusive, culturally responsive learning environments that support the success for Black and Latinx students, students with disabilities, and multilingual learners.
2nd Grade Team Goal	Increase teacher knowledge and application of high-yield, high-impact instructional practices, including Hattie's "Hi-5" strategies, by embedding equity as a foundational lens in lesson planning, classroom instruction, and student engagement. These practices will create inclusive, culturally responsible learning environments that support the success of all students.

Growth Time-frame	Success Criteria	Artifacts of Success (Data Sources)
October	Teachers: • Teachers will focus on implementing two foundational Hi-5 strategies (e.g., think-pair-share and structured academic conversations) during classroom instruction to build a baseline for collaborative learning. • Teachers will participate in initial peer observation cycles where peers will observe how teachers use an implementation tool to provide targeted feedback on their use of Hi-5 strategies. • Teachers will engage in grade-level reflective discussions to analyze observation feedback and identify one specific area for improvement in their Hi-5 strategy implementation.	Teachers: • Peer observation notes using the implementation tool to document the frequency, type, and effectiveness of Hi-5 strategies in the classroom. • Annotated lesson plans showing where Hi-5 strategies are intentionally embedded.

FIGURE 6.1 NCSD goals plan (*Continued*)

	Students:	Students:
	• Students will participate in teacher-facilitated Hi-5 strategies such as small group problem-solving, think-pair-share, or turn-and-talk to build collaboration and communication skills. • Students will receive explicit instruction on how to use these strategies effectively (e.g., guidelines for group discussions or how to give meaningful peer feedback).	• Observation data documenting student participation in Hi-5 strategy activities (e.g., percentage of students actively participating in discussions). • Formative assessment data that includes student reflections or quick surveys capturing their understanding of the strategies and their perceived usefulness.
	Teachers:	Teachers:
	• Teachers will refine their use of specific Hi-5 strategies (e.g., collaborative learning structures, accountable talk) to align with students' developmental needs. • Teachers will participate in mid-cycle peer feedback sessions to discuss their progress and challenges in implementing Hi-5 strategies—and make adjustments if necessary.	• Peer feedback forms documenting specific Hi-5 strategies observed during instruction. • Classroom observation data showing the frequency and quality of Hi-5 strategy implementation. • Teacher reflections or self-assessments on their use of Hi-5 strategies.
December	Students:	Students:
	• Students will engage in structured group work that incorporates Hi-5 strategies, such as turn-and-talk, collaborative problem-solving, or peer feedback. • Students will demonstrate understanding of Hi-5 strategies through their participation in modeled activities.	• Observation notes indicating the types of Hi-5 strategies students are engaging in and their level of independence. • Student work samples or exit tickets reflecting their use of Hi-5 strategies during class activities. Grade-level team will analyze the efficacy of each strategy and determine which ones led to better student outcomes.
	Teachers:	Teachers:
	• Teachers will incorporate the most successful Hi-5 strategies into differentiated lesson plans, tailoring instruction for diverse student needs (e.g., scaffolding for multilingual learners or advanced extensions for high-achieving students). • In a final staff meeting, grade-level teachers will share evidence of Hi-5 strategy success.	• Differentiated lesson plans highlighting the integration of Hi-5 strategies for various learning needs, with plans for increasing student self-direction. • Observation data showing consistent and integrated application of Hi-5 strategies during instruction.

FIGURE 6.1 (Continued)

April	Students: • Students will actively use Hi-5 strategies independently showing increased collaboration and self-regulation. • Students will provide peer feedback as part of their engagement in Hi-5 strategy instruction, such as reviewing group work or presentations.	Students: • Recorded or written examples of peer feedback aligned with Hi-5 strategies. • Student-created products (e.g., group projects, written reflections) demonstrating their use of Hi-5 strategies to solve problems or achieve learning outcomes. • Observation data showing students' confidence and independence in using Hi-5 strategies.

FIGURE 6.1 (Continued)

teams analyze data, identify patterns and conclusions, set goals, and then determine their path for growth.

Take a moment to pause and consider what your school does to foster the growth process.

♦ What does goal-setting look like? How do educators plan their goals' process?
♦ Are there interim moments to assess progress?
♦ What might you draw upon from this process and adapt for your school site?

Establish Accountability Conversations

Once you have determined your goal and planned a path toward achieving it, then it's beneficial to be in dialogue with an accountability partner. Ideally, once someone has determined their goal, they share it in conversation with a peer or supervisor to increase responsibility for seeing this goal through. The following are some reflection questions to guide the conversation:

♦ What is your goal or inquiry question?
♦ How did you land on this goal? What did you learn from data sources?
♦ At the end of this process, what will success look like? What evidence will show you and others success?

- What steps will you take to achieve this goal or answer this question? What evidence will demonstrate progress in a [pre-determined] timeframe?
- What do you hope to learn in this process?
- How does achieving this goal ensure all students have the opportunity to learn, grow, and thrive?

During the conversation, the person sharing their goal will do most of the talking while the accountability partner listens and keeps notes of the conversation; this approach decentralizes each person's power and makes the conversation a collaboration. It's helpful for accountability partners to follow up with any action items and schedule their next meeting times throughout the process.

When asking the "what steps will you take" question, this is where the growth trajectory will have the most variance. In schools with well-established coaching or mentoring programs, this pathway might include some co-learning opportunities or some scheduled observations and feedback sessions on the teacher's practice. For schools that can afford additional professional learning, the teacher might attend a workshop, or for schoolwide growth initiatives, leaders might design workshops in-house and/or invite outside presenters to lead an ongoing workshop series. We advocate that leaders prioritize professional learning that contains continued practice so that it's not a one-and-done process. Some teachers might opt for more self-directed methods of learning, such as action research—wherein teachers identify a problem, implement a solution, and analyze the outcomes to improve practices or address issues in their classrooms. In the following chapter, we describe this variety of professional learning structures with a process for how to select the learning structure that best meets your school's needs.

Nurturing Buds and Blooms—The Midcycle Check-In

In ecosystems, seeds need time to take root; growth is not immediately visible, and much work needs to be done—ensuring life in the ecosystem is nourished—prior to the more tangible signs of growth. Leaders might want to remind teachers about what a fractal approach to growth looks like: small and intentional. Flowers don't bloom all at once. All leaves don't unfurl in a day. But close attention and little moves to remove barriers and provide opportunities for growth will eventually lead to something more beautiful. To nurture buds and blooms, it's important to reflect, celebrate successes, and course correct if necessary. If early buds are poking through the soil where a teacher's shifts in practice are having an impact on students, it's likely that one's dedicated efforts are paying off. If no buds are forming, then it may be time to consider the lessons learned, assess one's techniques, and try something different.

At least midway through a growth cycle—whether mid-semester or mid-year—an interim check-in is a crucial reflection opportunity for teachers or leaders to demonstrate progress toward their goals. It is important for leaders to model their growth and learning, and it is equally important to create conditions for teachers to do the same: to share their messy drafts, their processes, their biggest learning moments and failures, and the wisdom they gleaned through the process. Learning is a challenging endeavor, and it also is a celebratory one. Leaders have the power to make space in 1:1 meetings, professional learning sessions, or whole staff meetings to balance humility and hard work, struggle, and celebration—and see how that might, with meaningful support along the way, contribute to how teachers model that same growth process for students. If educators can see where they are experiencing success—early blooms—this will increase their motivation to continue. If educators notice that something isn't working, then they can prune their approach and make adjustments for growth.

Mid-point check-ins can be in conversation with peers, coaches, or between leaders and those they serve. This conversation can occur during staff meeting time, in a mid-year in-service day, or any other time where there is already dedicated, built-in time to support reflection. Otherwise, other priorities might override this check-in. For this reflection, it's helpful for teachers or leaders to bring artifacts that reflect progress, or the lack thereof, toward their goals. Teachers or leaders can meet with their accountability partner with the following questions as a guide for the conversation:

- ♦ How are you doing so far related to your goal or inquiry question?
- ♦ What have been some wins? What have been some learning opportunities?

- Which artifacts of practice did you select and why? What do these artifacts indicate about your progress, or where you might need to change course?
- What adjustments or considerations, if any, need to be made for you to meet your goals?
- What support do you need?

This part of the process might require increased accountability on the part of leaders to determine if progress is actually happening through identifying tangible measures, buds and blooms, of growth. Leaders may need to be warm demanders, something we address in greater depth in Chapter 8, to give hard feedback when necessary, and/or to provide more oversight if goals are not being addressed. Leaders need to be willing to give direct feedback, rooted in specific evidence, to share where a teacher is falling short of their goals. Here, too, it's helpful to remind teachers that falling short is not a failure, but rather an opportunity to reflect on what else might be possible.

Take a moment to pause and consider how your school or organization invites opportunities for reflection. Do you have dedicated time in the schedule for educators to reflect on their practice? To what degree are educators bringing artifacts of practice to the conversation? What might you do to encourage reflection, including ways to make mistake-making an important part of the learning process?

Celebrate Continuous Growth

If you have ever grown plants, flowers, or vegetables, it's exciting when things are in full bloom. And this growth is worthy of celebration. At the end of the growth cycle, accountability partners can take intentional time to reflect on their progress. One-on-one conversations, staff-wide reflections, or small-group meetings can provide space for educators to share their insights, lessons learned, and evidence of success. When possible, it's helpful if this final conversation feels celebratory. Accountability partners can share artifacts of practice—student work, lesson plans, observation notes—that demonstrate how they met their goals. The following questions can be a guide for the conversation:

- What is the story you are telling about this growth cycle?
- What did you learn, and how will you apply it to your work?
- What are you most proud of professionally in relation to this growth cycle?
- What areas of growth do you want to focus on next time?

Sharing these reflections publicly, with colleagues or teams, helps normalize vulnerability and highlights the collective effort behind individual successes.

Just as we want to celebrate successes, we need to recognize that some things take longer to bloom than a single season. Plants might need more time to strike roots or for the seeds to germinate. Sometimes, invasive species get in the way of growth, such as weeds or creatures that eat the initial outcroppings. It's easy to lose heart when something doesn't grow or fully flourish, but it's also important to assess why growth didn't happen, whether because of external factors like storms or drought or deep freezes, or because of overcrowding, or because the conditions weren't right for certain plants to grow.

As the staff at North Creek School District reflected on their goals, colleagues were invited to share a "brag and swag" success or a "fail forward" lesson (brown, 2017). For the first 10 minutes of the meeting, teachers in mixed grade-level groups presented their successes or failures using student data and shared anecdotes about how these strategies increased collaboration and engagement in the classroom. Each person also shared an action step they were planning to take to either sustain their success or address their failure. These reflection sessions reinforced an environment of trust, psychological safety, and taking responsibility for doing better, emphasizing that success and failure alike are vital to the learning process. For all growth efforts, those who are dedicated to equity and justice for all students will recognize that they may need to play the long game and recognize that the commitment to continuous learning and growth is central.

You can find a summary of this entire growth process in Table 6.3 for your reference.

TABLE 6.3 Cultivating a Growth Cycle

Phase	Description	Examples
Putting on the Gardening Gloves for Equity and Justice	Prepare for growth by developing an equity and justice lens. Understand socialization, interrogate biases, hold complexity, and practice humility	• Begin meetings by sharing leaders' equity journeys or framing growth opportunities through justice • Conduct a visioning session: "What does justice look like for all students?"
Planting Seeds	Identify growth areas collaboratively. Use data to set clear, equity-centered priorities	• Teachers self-assess using a rubric for effective teaching • Use "street data" (e.g., student interviews, shadowing) to uncover patterns
Analyzing Data	Review qualitative and quantitative data to identify patterns and prioritize focus areas	• A teacher discovers lower expectations for Black male students through classroom interaction data • The math department identifies outdated, inequitable curriculum practices
Setting Goals	Create meaningful, measurable stretch goals with evidence and timelines	• Statement: "I want to ensure my classroom is a safe space for LGBTQIA+ students" • Inquiry: "How might I solicit and act on feedback equitably?"
Establishing Accountability	Collaborate with peers or supervisors to share goals and progress Build systems for sustained dialogue and reflection	• Teachers meet in peer triads to share growth goals and discuss progress • Leaders follow up with observation feedback aligned to goals
Mid-Point Reflection	Pause to assess progress, adjust plans, and celebrate wins while identifying the next steps	• Reflection questions include: "What artifacts of practice reflect progress?" • Teachers bring evidence to discuss wins and lessons learned in staff meetings

(Continued)

TABLE 6.3 Cultivating a Growth Cycle (*Continued*)

Phase	Description	Examples
Celebrating Growth	Reflect on successes and failures, share lessons learned, and set the stage for continued growth	• Teams share "brag and swag" (successes) and "fail forwards" (lessons learned) in mixed grade-level meetings • Use student work or classroom data to highlight success stories

At each phase of the growth process, encourage reflection on the following questions:
- What beliefs or biases do I need to shift to foster equitable growth?
- How can I gather an array of data sources to inform my growth goals?
- How do I normalize mistake-making and vulnerability in the process?
- How do I remain accountable to my colleagues and students throughout the process?

Sustaining a Culture of Continuous Growth

We want to end this chapter by celebrating a successful growth effort from one of our experiences. Elizabeth joined the leadership team at a school that had a lot of tension around student feedback. The new principal had mandated that all teachers in grades 5–12 collect anonymous student feedback, and several long-serving faculty members had concerns. Previously, the school had used the term "student evaluation," and teachers had found the anonymous feedback to just be an opportunity to attack the teacher. The feedback didn't feel useful or actionable—only demoralizing. And since the feedback was anonymous, it was without context, which was both concerning and frustrating. If a student raised a particular issue, there was no way to know who had made the comment. Finally, some were anxious about student bias and worried that female teachers and teachers of color would be rated lower by students (Reinsch et al., 2020).

When Elizabeth met with students, they shared another concern: retaliation. They cited examples of teachers who had gone after students who had given critical feedback. Students expressed widespread distress that if they had to put their name on the feedback form, there would be too high a price to pay. The lack of trust between faculty and students was palpable.

As a result of this distrust, the department chair group and several student groups initiated a shared growth cycle. They collaborated on a shared priority—how to give and receive meaningful feedback—to address the concerns and to shift the previous process toward a more effective model. They first reframed the process from students evaluating teachers to students sharing their experiences in classrooms. Using research-based models like the MET Project (2012), they developed a common set of questions for all teachers to ask. They also allowed for specific questions by grade level/discipline, but agreed to keep the questionnaire brief (10–15 questions).

Elizabeth had also noted that there was no training for either students or adults on giving/receiving feedback. So, they spent time talking about what makes feedback useful and actionable before administering the questionnaires. Instead of collecting the feedback at the end of the term, students planned to submit feedback about six weeks into the grading period. That way, teachers could be aware of any issues and be able to address concerns or make a course correction before the end of the academic term. Finally, teachers agreed to share the feedback they had received and to talk with students about what they heard, what shifts they could or couldn't make, and why. After implementing a student feedback initiative, Elizabeth's school collected stories of how students felt more heard and included in the learning process. These stories helped educators see the tangible impact of their work and strengthened their commitment to asking for feedback in more sustained ways.

Just as a thriving ecosystem requires careful tending, so does a growth-oriented school culture. Imagine what an ecosystem might look like if everyone and everything got what they needed. When leaders create the right conditions—planting seeds, watering soil, making sure everyone has enough sunlight, celebrating buds, and reassessing failures with compassion and encouragement—everyone in the ecosystem has the opportunity to flourish. In the next chapter, we'll explore specific tools and structures leaders can use to sustain this culture of growth, ensuring that the systems we build today will regenerate for years to come.

Summary

This chapter emphasizes the importance of cultivating growth-oriented school cultures that prioritize a deliberate set of actions to nurture continuous growth. Growth requires personalized, responsive systems that allow educators to develop an equity and justice lens, explore biases, challenge outdated methods, and adopt practices that serve all students. Leaders play a key role in modeling vulnerability, celebrating learning and mistake-making, and designing sustainable growth structures that everyone in a school community can benefit from. By cultivating an ecosystem where reflection, accountability, and continuous learning are central, schools can foster a meaningful professional growth culture for all educators.

For Further Reflection

1. How does your school currently define and support professional growth, and what gaps exist in fostering a culture of continuous learning?
2. What process does your community use to support educator growth?
3. How do you create an environment that can nurture mistake-making and accountability for meaningful change?
4. What beliefs or biases might you need to interrogate in order to lead or participate in growth initiatives that center on equity and justice?

References

Aguilar, E., & Cohen, L. (2022). *The PD book: 7 habits that transform professional development*. Jossey-Bass.

Boykin, A. W., & Noguera, P. (2011). *Creating the opportunity to learn: Moving from research to practice to close the achievement gap*. ASCD.

Brown, A. M. (2017). *Emergent strategy: Shaping change, changing worlds*. AK Press.

Chávez, A. F. (2012). Cultural humility: Transforming institutions for intercultural and social justice. *Journal of Higher Education Outreach and Engagement, 16*(4), 197–219.

Gay, G. (2018). *Culturally responsive teaching: Theory, research, and practice* (3rd ed.). Teachers College Press.

Hammond, Z. (2014). *Culturally responsive teaching and the brain: Promoting authentic engagement and rigor among culturally and linguistically diverse students.* Corwin Press.

Harro, B. (2000). The cycle of socialization. In M. Adams, W. J. Blumenfeld, R. Castañeda, H. Hackman, M. L. Peters, & X. Zúñiga (Eds.), *Readings for diversity and social justice: An anthology on racism, sexism, anti-semitism, heterosexism, classism, and ableism* (pp. 15–21). Routledge.

Love, B. (2019). *We want to do more than survive: Abolitionist teaching and the pursuit of educational freedom.* Beacon Press.

MET Project (2012). *Asking students about teaching: Student perceptions surveys and their implementation.* Bill and Melinda Gates Foundation.

Milner, H. R. (2012). *Start where you are, but don't stay there: Understanding diversity, opportunity gaps, and teaching in today's classrooms.* Harvard Education Press.

Muhammad, G. (2023). *Cultivating genius: An equity framework for culturally and historically responsive literacy.* Scholastic.

Okun, T., Jones, K. (2021). *The characteristics of white supremacy culture.* Dismantling Racism Works Collaborative.

Paris, D. (2012). Culturally sustaining pedagogies: A needed change in stance, terminology, and practice. *Educational Researcher, 41*(3), 93–97.

Paul, A. M. (2021). *The extended mind: The power of thinking outside the brain.* Mariner Books.

Reinsch, N. L., Goltz, S. M., & Hietapelto, A. B. (2020). Overcoming bias in student evaluations of teaching. *Journal of Higher Education Policy and Management, 42*(4), 415–428.

Rogers, E. M. (1983). *Diffusion of innovations* (3rd ed.). Free Press.

Safir, S., & Dugan, J. (2021). *Street data: A next-generation model for equity, pedagogy, and school transformation.* Corwin Press.

Teitel, L. (2013). *Instructional rounds in education: A network approach to improving teaching and learning.* Harvard Education Press.

Vygotsky, L. S. (1978). *Mind in society: The development of higher psychological processes.* Harvard University Press.

Yosso, T. J. (2005). Whose culture has capital? A critical race theory discussion of community cultural wealth. *Race Ethnicity and Education, 8*(1), 69–91.

7

Practices to Cultivate Continuous Learning

Whether self-directed forms of growth, 1:1 structures like coaching or mentoring, or whole-community opportunities, educators need time, space, and support to engage in meaningful growth processes. These processes allow for relationship-building, goal-setting, reflection, and continuous learning, ensuring that the growth is both intentional and sustainable. Moreover, leaders need to model the kind of learning and growth they wish to see in their staff, fostering a culture where everyone—students and educators alike—feels able to take risks, center justice and equity in the learning process, and transform beliefs and practices for all community members.

Developing a Growth Philosophy

Overview and Purpose

In order for growth to take hold, school community members need to feel safe enough to grow. They also need to understand which measures of progress determine growth. Is growth about effort, or is it about tangible results? Is it about valuing process or solely based on outcomes? The following process will support you and your school in developing a philosophy of growth that aligns with your school's values.

Process

Defining and Visioning

Early in the school year, or perhaps in the summer time, school leaders can take time to reflect on what growth looks and sounds like for them as a leadership team and what they hope to model in the year ahead. The following reflection questions can serve as a guide for their discussion:

- When was a time you grew the most as a professional?
- What conditions were in place to support that growth?
- What does growth look, sound, and feel like for you?
- What does growth *not* look, sound, and feel like for you?
- What's important for your colleagues to know about what growth looks, sounds, and feels like for you?

Once team members have reflected on these questions, they can build in time for discussion and storytelling. It helps to have a recorder to keep a log of the conversation and share back themes they heard. After hearing these themes, leaders can identify what growth looks, sounds, and feels like for their team as a whole, culminating in a definition of growth that best supports what leaders hope to foster and model. The following are some samples of growth philosophies from teams we have worked with:

- At Springer Academy, growth for the leadership team looks like grappling with ideas, making thinking visible, asking questions of self and one another, admitting our mistakes, and determining a courageous path forward for learning.
- As the leadership team at Eagleview High School, we are a community of learners who strive to model our strengths, struggles, and courage for the work we do each day. Meetings are focused on learning, humility, inquiry, and a commitment to justice. We consider students who have been most marginalized in all our decision-making and do our part to design systems and policies that affirm all students in their identities and in their brilliance.

Co-Creation

When the leadership team has developed their philosophy of growth, it's time to bring it to the community level, posing similar questions to staff and providing space for some kind of co-creative process to develop a collective growth philosophy. One potential approach for developing a sitewide growth philosophy might look like the following:

Timeframe: two staff meetings, or two hours
Roles: facilitator, note-taker
Process: Meeting 1 or Hour 1

- 5 minutes: Leader sets the purpose and conditions for the meeting. They may begin by saying something like the following:

   At this school we value growth and all it entails—the successes and setbacks, the opportunities and challenges. As a leadership team, we developed a philosophy of growth, because we also hope to model the practices we'd like to see in our community [*leaders share their philosophy of growth as an example*]. We're going to take this time now to engage in a similar process with you so as a community we can work from a common philosophy of growth.

- 20 minutes: Leaders post reflection questions on a handout or on a screen where everyone can see:
    - When was a time you grew the most as a professional?
    - What conditions were in place to support that growth?
    - What does growth look, sound, and feel like for you?
    - What does growth *not* look like to you?
    - What's important for your colleagues to know about what growth looks, sounds, and feels like for you?

- 30 minutes: We suggest having staff work in small groups, either by similar roles, departments, grade levels, or other common identifiers, such as specialists. For departments that are larger, we suggest that groups break up into teams of three to four people so that there is equitable participation in the conversation. Each group should also select a note-taker to record the conversation.

- 20 minutes: Each person has up to 5 minutes to share their responses to the following question: *What does growth look, sound, and feel like for you? Share any insights from the reflection that you feel most comfortable sharing.*
- 10 minutes: Group discusses themes from the conversation while the note-taker documents those themes.

♦ 5 minutes: Leader brings staff back together for a brief reflection and wrap-up; note-takers place their notes in a shared folder.

Depending on how much time is left in the meeting, leaders may want to share themes they heard from conversations or ask community members for any reflections they had on the process.

Meeting 2 or Hour 2

♦ 5 minutes: Leaders set conditions for the next session. They may say something like the following:

We're going to build on our conversation by now synthesizing our grade/department themes into collective themes for the community. We'll begin by reviewing what teams came up with in their last conversation, and then identify commonalities for our whole community.

There can either be posters around the room for people to write on or a shared document for people to respond to. Whatever form this document takes, there should be two columns in "T-chart" fashion with the following headers: "What growth looks, sounds, feels like" in column 1 and "Conditions to make growth happen" in column 2.

♦ 20 minutes: Everyone reviews teams' notes in the folders, jotting down any themes they notice.
♦ 15 minutes: On posters around the room, staff members write responses to the following question: Based on what you read in the notes from the last session, what

does growth look, sound, and feel like at our site? What conditions need to be in place for growth to happen?
- 15 minutes: Leader facilitates a whole-group discussion around themes that emerge.
- 5 minutes: Leader shares next steps, which include synthesizing what people have shared and coming up with a working philosophy of growth for the school community.

After everyone has given their input on a philosophy of growth, the leadership team can gather and begin drafting statements for staff to vote on. As we shared in Chapter 5, this is a point in the process where schools and organizations tend to stall out; they might strive to seek consensus on a growth philosophy versus determining something that is safe enough to try. When sharing potential philosophy statements, leaders could consider sharing two or three statements to choose among with the following voting criteria:

- 3 = this is safe enough to try as our growth philosophy
- 2 = this is mostly safe enough to try after some revisions
- 1 = this is not safe enough to try and/or doesn't reflect our values

The goal here isn't to achieve consensus, but for a majority of people to vote in the 2–3 range. Once the votes are tallied, leaders can share a "safe enough to try" growth philosophy statement with colleagues to foster growth in the school community. The following are examples of schoolwide growth philosophies that have been developed using this process:

- At Synland Charter School, we are committed to modeling the messy learning process for our students. We believe that sharing our challenges alongside our successes is a more authentic way to grow. Through reflection on what we learned and adopting a "when we know better, we do better" stance, we can be more effective in ensuring students have equitable outcomes.

♦ Grace Lee Boggs Middle School is a place that supports ongoing growth. Every staff member is a lifelong learner committed to cultivating their own growth so that they may facilitate the growth of their students. We accept challenges as opportunities; we set challenging goals that push us; and we stay accountable in the process to demonstrate our commitment to growth.

Implementation

Just as we shared in Chapter 5, it's helpful to pilot a growth philosophy over time rather than wholesale adopting it as a community. Staff or department meetings might have the first 10 minutes devoted to teachers and leaders reflecting on something that supported their growth and assessing that learning against their school's philosophy of growth. Synland Charter School's monthly faculty meetings began with "messy moments". Staff members paired up with people outside their department or grade level and shared a challenge or misstep from the past month. This fractal approach to testing the growth philosophy allowed staff members to get used to sharing about setbacks in safe-enough conditions, which contributed to greater openness and vulnerability.

At Grace Lee Boggs Middle School, the growth philosophy fell flat. Leaders and staff created a schoolwide growth philosophy in the August in-service days before school started, but they didn't return to the philosophy until their November staff meeting. By that point, most staff members had forgotten it existed. The fall had been rough, as an unexpected snowstorm led to damages to the main building. Morale was low as collective bargaining for new contracts was going badly, animosity between teachers and district leaders was at an all-time high, and teachers were preparing to strike. With these extenuating circumstances, leaders were afraid to bring up a growth philosophy, which felt extraneous to the more pressing issues the school was facing.

While we can't control external forces like the weather, we can determine what feels feasible to address in our communities to nurture culture. Might there have been a moment for Grace

Lee Boggs' leaders to consider what growth might look like in a challenging time? Leaders often move transformative work to the back burner in favor of addressing what's right in front of them. This begs the question about what matters to leaders ultimately. Is it to keep a school running, or is it to transform conditions for students? What are the micro moves leaders might make in favor of that shift rather than shelving the equitable work that needs to happen in schools? Think about a time in your own experience that was challenging. What did you or the leaders in your school/organization do to address these challenges? Or what do you wish could have happened?

Feedback and Assessment

Any new policy or philosophy lives or dies by those who enact it and how they enact it. Sometimes collective exercises begin with a lot of good will and good energy at the beginning of the school year, but if leaders don't make time to test and implement what they develop and seek feedback throughout the school year, something like a forgotten growth philosophy ends up in the metaphorical dustbin of unfulfilled ideas, which fuels further cynicism. To counter what happened at Grace Lee Boggs Middle School, we advocate that whatever processes leaders introduce in the summer, they make the time to follow through at various intervals throughout the school year; not only that, but they connect whatever philosophy statements they create to student learning and outcomes, to a school's vision for equity, or to their portrait of an educator. The more a philosophy is embedded into existing policies, the more likely it will take hold and have meaning in the community. Table 7.1 offers a distilled version of this process, including some suggestions for ongoing assessment and revision.

Gardening Tools in Practice

There are a range of structures a school can adopt to support continuous learning, and the structure largely depends on the resources available—the people who can carry these processes

TABLE 7.1 Developing and Sustaining a Growth Philosophy

Focal Area	Suggested Approaches	Data Collection Methods
Defining and Visioning	• Leadership team reflection on growth using guided prompts and storytelling • Collaborative development of growth definitions through staff meetings	• Meeting notes capturing themes • Shared document outlining definitions of growth and the conditions for growth
Co-Creation	• Facilitate small-group discussions to gather diverse perspectives on growth • Use collaborative tools like T-charts or posters for thematic synthesis	• Group-generated artifacts from meetings (e.g., notes, charts) • Shared folder for team-generated ideas and philosophies
Implementation	• Pilot the growth philosophy in regular staff meetings through reflective practices (e.g., "messy moments" sharing) • Integrate philosophy into professional development activities • Link growth philosophy to existing frameworks like equity goals, student outcomes, or a portrait of an educator • Incorporate growth-focused check-ins during staff reviews	• Informal reflections and feedback on pilot experiences • Records of growth-focused discussions in meetings • Documentation of professional goals aligned with the growth philosophy • Evidence of growth practices in classroom or workplace observations
Feedback and Assessment	• Regular surveys and focus groups to gather feedback on the growth philosophy's impact • Structured reflection sessions for all staff • Establish checkpoints for leadership reflection and team-based review • Revise growth philosophy based on evolving community needs	• Survey data on the philosophy's relevance and implementation • Focus group transcripts and identified themes • Documented adjustments to the growth philosophy • Updated growth definitions and conditions based on input and evolving priorities

forward, the time to do it well, and, where applicable, the compensation for these efforts. In the final portion of this chapter, we provide a process to assess which structure will work best for your school, and, in the following pages, we outline the different "gardening tools"—structures—that can best support ongoing growth.

The Hand Trowel: Self-Directed Professional Learning

A hand trowel and self-directed learning are surprisingly similar. Both are tools for growth—one helping us dig, plant, and nurture a garden and the other allowing us to explore, question, and foster individual growth. Though small, a hand trowel is versatile and essential, much like the small steps of self-directed learning that can lead to significant and impactful growth over time. With a hand trowel, you decide how to wield it—whether for shallow weeding, deep digging, or planting with precision. Similarly, in self-directed learning, you tailor the process, exploring topics at your own pace and depth, following a path that feels right to you.

Self-directed learning is most useful when the teachers and staff are able to apply an equity and social justice lens to their learning process and when there are high levels of trust in a school community. Self-directed learning promotes the most autonomy and presumes that educators already have a commitment to continuous learning. By intentionally selecting learning opportunities that root out and redress systemic inequities, self-directed learning becomes a powerful tool for promoting growth, being accountable to students, and creating more inclusive educational environments. The following are some approaches educators might take when engaging in self-directed learning.

Action Research

Action research is one type of self-directed approach for promoting educator growth, especially when framed through an equity and justice lens. By engaging in systematic inquiry and reflection on their own practices, educators can identify and address the specific needs of their students, particularly those from historically marginalized groups (Ferrance, 2000). Action research invites teachers to challenge their assumptions and biases and highlight areas where traditional instructional methods may fall short in serving their students (Gay, 2018). For example, teachers can use action research to investigate how their teaching strategies affect student engagement and success, allowing them to adjust their approaches to meet the needs of students from different cultural and linguistic backgrounds. Much like the process we outlined in Chapter 6, this iterative process involves goal setting, data collection, reflection, and action planning. As educators reflect on their findings, they can actively disrupt inequities within their classrooms and create new practices that better support the needs of their students—while gathering more immediate evidence of impact along the way.

Let's explore an example of action research in practice. Lori was teaching a high school Humanities course focused on world religions. During the unit on Islam, Lori wondered whether students held deficit views of Muslim and Arab communities, given the Western media's damaging portrayal of Muslims, including often misguided notions of Muslim women in various cultures around the world. At her school, the student population consisted of white, Asian, Black, and Latine students, with less than 1% of the population identifying as Arab, Muslim, Middle Eastern, or North African. Lori, along with her colleagues, conducted an action research project to assess student perceptions of Muslim women and provide counternarratives across nonfiction, graphic novels, film, and poetry to counteract the Western culture's limited and reductive tropes of Muslims around the world.

Lori also recognized the limitations of this kind of project, both in the biases she may have held and the limited amount of counternarratives she would be able to provide in one instructional unit. Applying an equity and social justice lens, Lori and her colleagues first identified their own understandings of the Muslim religion and what they had been taught in school, if anything. They identified their learning gaps and made sure they were intentional in doing their own learning. For text selection, Lori and her colleagues focused on various genres, from academic essays to film to short stories to a graphic novel, all of which were localized at different places in the world and at different points in history.

When introducing the unit to students, Lori and her colleagues prefaced the content by naming the limitations of their own identities and the danger of a single story (Adichie, 2009) and turning those narratives into monolithic views of all Muslims. Lori collected initial student perception data anonymously, so students were neither publicly sharing harmful views nor feeling like their initial perceptions would bias their teachers. For each text, students were given the historical background as context. After engaging with each text, teachers asked students to reflect on their perceptions and what they learned throughout the process (Cohen & Peery, 2006). Students' perceptions changed significantly over the course of this unit, from recognizing the bias in US media to holding more expansive views about the hijab and the Qu'ran. Lori learned significant lessons she carried forward into her teaching practice, particularly around striving to be as intentional as possible in text selection for other instructional units, making sure that she applied an equity and justice lens across the curriculum and ensured that any prevailing texts—ones that were considered "canonical" in schools—were either complemented or replaced with counternarratives and critical questions related to authors, perspectives, biases, and multiple interpretations text.

Video Observation

Video observation is vulnerable, but it's also instructive for learning about how an educator's disposition and practices have an impact on student learning. Recording classroom interactions enables educators to analyze their instructional methods and the ways in which they engage with students from various backgrounds, helping to identify and mitigate unintentional biases (Borko et al., 2008). For example, by reviewing video recordings, teachers can reflect on how often they call on students of color, how they address their multilingual learners, how much teacher talk there is versus student talk, or how they use—or don't use—inclusive practices for all students. Video facilitates deeper insight into classroom dynamics, allowing teachers to notice patterns in student engagement and their own responses to different student populations (Sherin & van Es, 2009). While it takes a lot of vulnerability to do so, by sharing video clips with peers, educators can collectively reflect on their practices, creating a space where they can learn from one another and challenge practices that may reinforce inequities. This form of collaborative reflection can support teachers in refining their practices to create more inclusive, culturally responsive classrooms. We recommend using the TSRQ tool (Chapter 9) when reviewing video, as it gives teachers a firsthand look at their interactions with students and what steps they might take to create a more equitable learning environment.

The Cultivator: Small-Group Professional Learning

A cultivator breaks up compacted soil, allowing air, water, and nutrients to reach plant roots. Similarly, small group growth opportunities can disrupt entrenched patterns and provide space for productive and challenging conversations, healthy dialogue, and equitable solutions to take root. Professional Learning Communities (PLCs), Critical Friends Groups (CFGs), Lesson Study, and Peer Coaching are all examples of communities of practice, increasing colleagues' accountability to one another, promoting leadership from teachers, and balancing teacher-selected topics with a community centered on one another's growth. Regardless of the type, before any small-group interaction, it's helpful to establish some ways of working together to increase the efficacy of the group. We recommend setting group agreements that are geared toward the group's purpose, and that reflect observable behaviors team members can exhibit and be accountable for. The following is a suggested process for setting group agreements:

- ♦ Step 1 (5 minutes): Individually reflect (in writing or verbally) on the following question: *What do you need to feel heard, supported, challenged to grow, and productive as a member of this group?*
- ♦ Step 2 (10 minutes): Group members share their responses and determine common themes and potential triggers/sensitivities that arise for them in team dynamics (e.g., feeling like they're not pulling their weight, fear of saying the wrong thing, shaky in content knowledge, being the "only" of their identifying group).

- Step 3 (15 minutes): Group members then decide upon around five agreements that they'll adhere to for their time working and meeting together. This list is compiled and revisited at the beginning of any meeting session.

The following are some examples from a PLC of art educators:

- *Share your honest opinions with the groups and self via collegiality and compassion*
- *Think and work democratically and equitably, making sure everyone feels heard before we make a decision*
- *Rotate facilitators and incorporate agenda, wish-lists, and time-out for dreaming*
- *Incorporate student work in our discussions more often than not*
- *Stand on the shoulders of giants (check out what has been done before)*

PLCs and CFGs

A PLC is a group of educators, such as teachers, administrators, and other school staff, who collaboratively engage in ongoing learning and reflective practices to improve their teaching and enhance student outcomes. When PLCs are well-structured and engage in ongoing reflection and assessment of teaching practices, they can be a powerful model for improving teaching practice and, consequently, student achievement (DuFour et al., 2024). A Critical Friends Group (CFG), first developed by the National School Reform Faculty (National School Reform Faculty, 1994), is a learning community that brings together educators to engage in collaborative and constructive dialogue aimed at improving teaching practices and student learning outcomes. This model largely draws upon protocols—forms of structured conversations and interactions—to guide learning. These protocols provide a framework for discussing teaching practices, lesson plans, and other aspects of professional development. One popular and powerful protocol that we like to use is the Consultancy Protocol (Thompson-Grove, et al., 2003). In this protocol, colleagues bring a problem of practice to their group and, through structured dialogue, share a challenge, hear questions and solutions to the challenge, and reflect on new understandings they can apply to the situation. These types of problem-solving opportunities invite educators to be reflective about their practice, and a consultancy can be used with just about any topic. Figure 7.1 provides guidance for using a consultancy protocol.

Overview and Purpose: A Consultancy is a structured process for helping an individual or a team think more expansively about a particular, concrete dilemma.

Time: Approximately 15–20 minutes per round

Roles

- Presenter (whose work is being discussed by the group)
- Facilitator (who sometimes participates, depending on the size of the group)

Process:

1. (3 minutes) The presenter gives an overview of the dilemma with which they are struggling and what they need support on. The focus of the group's conversation is on the dilemma.
2. (3 minutes) The Consultancy group asks clarifying questions of the presenter—that is, questions that have brief, factual answers.
3. (3 minutes) The group asks probing questions of the presenter. These questions should be worded so that they help the presenter clarify and expand their thinking about the dilemma presented to the Consultancy group. The presenter may respond to the group's questions, but there is no discussion by the Consultancy group of the presenter's responses. At the end of the 3 minutes, the facilitator asks the presenter to re-state their dilemma for the group.
4. (5 minutes) The group talks with each other about the dilemma presented. Possible questions to frame the discussion:

    - What did we hear?
    - What didn't we hear that they think might be relevant?
    - What assumptions seem to be operating?
    - What questions does the dilemma raise for us?
    - What do we think about the dilemma?
    - What might we do or try if faced with a similar dilemma? What have we done in similar situations?

    Members of the group sometimes suggest actions the presenter might consider taking. Most often, however, they work to define the issues more thoroughly and objectively. The presenter doesn't speak during this discussion, but instead listens and takes notes.

5. (2 minutes) The presenter reflects on what they heard and on what they are now thinking, sharing with the group anything that particularly resonated for them during any part of the Consultancy. (5 minutes)

FIGURE 7.1 Consultancy protocol

One community of practice we worked with consisted of substitute teachers who came together in monthly meetings to discuss strategies, opportunities, and challenges of being a substitute teacher. Each month, the consultancy protocol guided the group's discussion, which increased group members' sense of connection in an otherwise isolating role in schools.

Lesson Study

Originating in Japan, Lesson Study involves a group of teachers working together to plan, observe, and analyze a lesson in order to improve their teaching practices and enhance student learning. Lesson study places a strong emphasis on teachers learning from one another through a structured and iterative process, with each cycle leading to further refinement of teaching practices. Lesson study emphasizes shared responsibility for improving teaching and learning outcomes and promotes a collaborative culture where teachers collectively contribute to the growth and development of their peers. This approach to educator growth has had great success in schools across the globe (Cheung & Wong, 2014). A full lesson study cycle typically occurs over a few weeks or months, depending on teachers' schedules and other commitments, but one cycle per academic term is typical. Inspired by the work of Education Northwest (2021), we have adapted their facilitator guide to offer some broad steps to conduct a lesson study:

1. **Establish Collaboration Expectations:** Set guidelines for communication, roles, and responsibilities to foster a trusting, supportive environment. See suggestions from earlier in this chapter to set group agreements.
2. **Develop a Research Theme**: Define long-term instructional goals for your students and identify a broad question guiding the lesson study cycle (e.g., building problem-solving confidence). These questions might also be tied to a teacher's goals for the year.
3. **Identify and Study a Topic:** Choose a specific subject area or concept to focus on. Base this choice on data like

student assessments, curriculum gaps, or challenging topics and study research-backed practices.
4. **Plan the Lesson:** Create a detailed plan addressing learning goals, student tasks, expected responses, and assessment methods. Incorporate evidence-based strategies and include contingency plans for unexpected challenges.
5. **Teach and Observe the Lesson:** One team member teaches while others observe, collecting data focused on student learning (not teacher performance).
6. **Debrief the Lesson:** Analyze observation data to assess whether student learning goals were met, share insights, and identify areas for improvement. See Chapter 9 for suggested observation tools.
7. **Revise the Lesson:** Use the data and debrief feedback to refine the lesson, focusing on a few targeted changes that address observed challenges.
8. **Reteach and Observe:** Apply the revised lesson to a new group of students and repeat the observation and data collection process.
9. **Reflect and Report:** Review the entire cycle, summarize key findings, and document lessons learned for broader application and sharing with peers.
10. **Share Knowledge:** Disseminate findings and revised lesson plans within and beyond the team to scale the impact of the learning.

An Example of a Cultivator in Practice—PLCCs

Abundance Academy, a pre-K-8 school focused on supporting neurodiverse students, uses something called Professional Learning Choice Cohorts (PLCCs) as part of their in-house professional learning. For a prescribed period of time (e.g., quarter, trimester, or semester), educators choose a topic to explore in greater depth with a community of colleagues who share similar interests. PLCCs are most effective when they are well-structured, when the facilitators are given guidance on how to facilitate meetings, and when the professional culture is growth-oriented. PLCCs meet at least three or four times to deepen their understanding of a topic, build community, and share learning. At the end of each term, Abundance Academy teachers gather together at their staff meeting and share their learning with colleagues. While the logistics of PLCCs were challenging (determining learning structures, training facilitators, and designing facilitator guides), teachers felt more autonomous and effective as a result of their experiences. Appendix B contains an example of Abundance Academy's Professional Learning Choice Cohort overview.

The Gardening Stake: Mentoring and Coaching

Just as a stake helps young or growing plants to grow with support and thrive in challenging conditions, a mentor or coach provides guidance, stability, and support to help individuals meet their growth goals. The stake doesn't do the growing for the plant but ensures it has what it needs to flourish. The most resource-intensive forms of growth—but also some of the most high-leverage approaches—are mentoring and coaching. Mentoring is a dynamic and purposeful relationship between an experienced and knowledgeable educator and a less experienced mentee, characterized by ongoing support, guidance, and constructive feedback. This collaborative partnership is designed to enhance the professional and personal development of the mentee, with a focus on fostering effective teaching practices, promoting reflective inquiry, ensuring equitable teaching and learning practices, and navigating the complexities of being an educator (Wang & Odell, 2002).

Similar to mentoring, coaching offers a non-evaluative, confidential space for educators to reflect on their practice, set equity-oriented goals, and receive critical feedback. Research conducted by the Instructional Coaching Group (2017) shows that coaching improves teaching practice because it is personalized, contextualized, and focused on collaboration. Based on foundations of trust and partnership, coaching can support educators to examine practices that reveal implicit biases and scaffold the use of culturally sustaining pedagogies in everyday teaching (National Equity Project, n.d.). Coaching and mentoring are powerful tools for fostering educator growth, and when framed through an equity lens, they become transformative mechanisms for addressing systemic inequities within schools. Effective coaching and mentoring are not simply about improving instructional practices, but about creating spaces where coaches and mentors can prompt teachers to reflect critically on their own biases, assumptions, and practices, all in the service of fostering more equitable learning environments for students.

Ideally, coaching and mentoring conversations are confidential so that there can be greater psychological safety to increase the coachee's or mentee's willingness to be vulnerable. When we share about confidentiality to school leaders, they often balk. How will they know if someone is growing if they can't find out what's happening from the coach? And most of the time, yes, coaching and mentoring conversations are confidential and should be. For the coach and mentor, confidentiality allows them to serve in non-evaluative roles that aren't tied to administrative oversight. Coaches and mentors are often the most knowledgeable about pedagogy, curriculum, and school culture, and their expertise is an asset in working educators of all backgrounds. If coachees or mentees feel like the coach or mentor is a mouthpiece for the administration, then they are less likely to seek support when they most need it. When a coach/coachee or mentor/mentee establishes their work together, they should talk about confidentiality and what can be shared. Sometimes coachees or mentees want administrators to know what they are working on. Sometimes coaches or mentors want to share something positive. Making agreements about what can be shared allows each party to feel clear about where the boundaries are.

Can a coach or mentor ever break confidentiality? Yes. If the coachee or mentee is perpetuating ongoing harm, compromising the safety of students or other adults, or is toxic to the health of a school ecosystem, then the coach or mentor should sacrifice trust and tell school leaders, and these leaders need to step in and address these issues directly. The coach or mentor needs to be transparent and explicit to their coachee/mentee about breaking confidentiality and why they are doing it. Teachers will be less trusting of coaching and mentoring overall if they feel like coaches and mentors withhold any information they share with the administration.

There are myriad approaches to coaching and mentoring and a wealth of training opportunities available for schools and districts. When developing coaching or hiring coaches, it's important to get aligned on what coaching means and what coaching looks and sounds like. It will also be important for schools and districts to get clear first about the types of coaching they practice before providing training and support for coaches. Does the school want instructional coaches? Equity coaches? Literacy or math coaches? While the methodologies for coaching are similar, the roles and the level of content knowledge a coach needs are distinct.

While coaching roles may differ, the approach to coaching conversations can be similar and include the following sequence of events.

Step 1: Conversation Preparation

Coaches and mentors need to be compassionate and skilled listeners, non-judgmental guides who facilitate the process of someone else's growth. To that end, we suggest that coaches and mentors plan before their conversation. Although many coaching conversations, in particular, are coachee-led, it's helpful for the coach or mentor to consider the type of conversation they will be having, the quality of relationship and trust between the two parties, the barriers that might be present in the conversation, and what a coach might ask. The following are conversation planning questions we often use when planning our coaching conversations:

- ♦ What will the topic of this conversation be?
- ♦ What is the quality of the relationship you have with this person/group?
- ♦ What are the levels of trust you have with this person?
- ♦ If there are low levels of trust and/or you do not have a positive relationship with this person/group, what might you do to develop/strengthen the relationship?

- What are this person's/group's strengths and/or core values?
- What is your goal for the conversation? And/or what's in your sphere of influence in this conversation?
- What disposition do you want to adopt for this conversation (e.g., open, confident, compassionate)?
- What might get in the way in this conversation? In other words, what barriers might be present in this situation (e.g., identity barriers, policies, expectations)?
- For whom might these barriers be present?
- How might those barriers be addressed?
- What additional learning or internal reflection might you need to do to prepare for this conversation?
- How will you begin this conversation? What are some possible questions you might ask?

Step 2: Have the conversation. How a coach or mentor listens in this conversation is everything. In Chapter 5, we shared about the three levels of listening, and in a coaching context, we call this expansive, integrated listening—listening that weaves together focused and global listening (Levels 2 and 3) and allows the coach or mentor to center the needs of the person they're talking to without judgment. Some common dispositions of expansive, integrated listening include compassion, connection, openness, or possibility, all of which are supportive stances that can allow a coachee to speak more freely and feel heard in the process.

The conversation itself can span anywhere from 20 minutes to a full hour. We'd love everyone to have generous time and space for coaching and mentoring conversations, but until those wishes are fulfilled, we suggest the following breakdown for the conversation itself (also included in Figure 7.2):

- **Opening** (2–3 minutes): a couple of minutes to check in with the coachee or mentee. It's important, though, to keep an eye on the clock, as this time can fly (and/or the coachee or mentee might be tempted to avoid the topic at hand if it's a trickier conversation).

Steps	Sample Ways This Could Sound
Opening	**Open with a warm, compassionate question:** • Hey, how are you? How's it going? • How did your recent…go?
Framing the Conversation	**Set an intention or goal for the conversation:** • What do you hope to be true by the end of this conversation?
Exploring	**Assess by tapping the coachee's thoughts first and then explore the topic at hand:** • Use the Coaching Stems to guide the conversation by probing, assessing, clarifying, and/or envisioning
Assessing Learning and Action-Planning	**Identify an actionable issue and next step.** • What's one thing you could do this week to contribute to your goal? • How committed are you to your next steps? • What might get in the way? How will you address what might get in the way? • What people or resources could help you with that? • How will you be accountable?
Closing	**Reflect on the conversation** • What do you know now that you didn't know before this session?

FIGURE 7.2 Sample coaching/mentoring conversation arc

♦ **Framing the conversation** (5 minutes): The mentee or coachee might have a goal in mind for the conversation, but if not, the mentor or coach should suggest the focus. When setting the focus, it's helpful for the mentee or coachee to share what they hope to achieve by the end of the conversation and how they hope to feel. This way, the mentor and coach can check in throughout the conversation to assess how close the coachee/mentee is to their goal and how they are feeling throughout the conversation.

♦ **Exploring** (the bulk of the time): Depending on the focal area for the conversation, the coach or mentor will need to choose their approach (Knight, 2017), which typically falls into one of three categories:

• *Facilitative:* The coach or mentor is guiding someone toward finding their own insights and understandings. They refrain from sharing their own expertise or suggestions with respect to what the coachee or mentee needs to do, and rather, through inquiry, guides the coachee in tapping into their experience and wisdom to achieve their goals. Facilitative approaches have the greatest long-term impact because the coachee/mentee bears the greatest cognitive load in the conversation.

- *Collaborative:* In this mode, the coach or mentor takes a more collaborative or dialogical stance with the coachee. They share strategies and options for the coachee, and/or the coach and coachee work on building knowledge and skill together. The coach or mentor serves as a thinking partner, sometimes through facilitative questioning and sometimes through being more directive. In this mode, both parties carry the cognitive load in the conversation.
- *Directive:* In this mode, the coach or mentor shares their knowledge, skill, and expertise with the coachee/mentee to support the coachee's learning and growth. Sometimes the coach or mentor is directive in order to share information or give advice. Other times, they are directive in order to interrupt a coachee's limiting beliefs and/or to interrupt potential inequities, taking a warm demander stance (which we outline in greater detail in Chapter 8). The directive approach places the cognitive load on the coach or mentor, so this practice is only used when necessary.

Sometimes a coach or mentor will shift their approach depending on the content of the conversation. A new teacher who is still learning culturally responsive teaching practices might need a more directive approach, whereas a veteran teacher who is feeling burned out and wants to process emotions might need a more facilitative conversation. It's important for the mentor or coach to listen intentionally to hear what the needs might be for the conversation.

- **Assessing learning and action-planning** (3–5 minutes): Once the coach and/or mentor have explored a topic fully enough, they can check in with the mentee/coachee about what they've learned and what their next steps are. Our favorite coaching questions at this stage of the conversation are the following:
  - What did you learn today?
  - What is your next step?
  - How committed are you to that next step?
  - What might get in the way?
  - What support do you need?
  - How will you be accountable for making change?

- **Closing** (2–3 minutes): At the end of the conversation, it's helpful to ask the mentee/coachee their biggest headline, takeaway, learning, or how they are feeling at this stage of the conversation. This prompting supports the mentee/coachee in reflecting on their learning and increasing their potential to take action.

Coaching and mentoring are effective because of how learner-centered they are. But not everyone receiving coaching and mentoring is willing to engage in the kinds of conversations that surface and address biases. It will be important to continuously foster relationships so that coaches and mentors can be trusted guides on the path to achieving equity and justice.

While a single conversation can yield a change in practice, mentoring and coaching are most effective when they are ongoing and intensive rather than episodic. It's important that coaches and mentors have time to engage in some type of cycle with their coachees of mentees. Coaching cycles are structured frameworks that guide the partnership between coaches and educators in improving instructional practices and student outcomes. In some schools, a coaching cycle could be six weeks, eight weeks, a semester, or a school year. The purpose and value of these cycles are to support educators in setting, implementing, adjusting, and measuring goals to support students and have multiple opportunities for growth. Coaching cycles typically follow these phases:

Phase 1: Relationship-Building

The foundation of any effective coaching cycle is trust and rapport between the coach and the coachee. This phase involves understanding the coachee's values, identities, teaching philosophy, pivotal moments in their career, and areas to focus on in coaching. Relationship-building may occur over one or two sessions and is crucial for setting the stage for meaningful partnership. In this phase, a coach will want to understand the coachee's identity and background to best understand what matters to the coachee and which aspects of their identities are important to them.

Phase 2: Goal/Inquiry Creation

Once a relationship is established, the coach and coachee collaboratively develop specific goals or inquiry questions that will guide the coaching cycle. In Chapter 6, we offer some guidance on setting goals, which can be applied in a coaching or mentoring framework as well. Similar to the process we outline, the coach will support the coachee in developing an equity lens, examine street data to understand classroom patterns, set a growth goal, and develop a path for learning, which Phase 3 of the coaching cycle articulates.

Phase 3: Observing, Reflecting, and Learning

This phase is characterized by active observation, data collection, and reflection. The coach may observe the coachee's classroom practice either live or through video recordings. Observations are typically aligned with the coachee's goals or inquiry questions. For example, if a teacher is focused on building relationships with students, the coach might observe nonverbal communication patterns. Additional strategies might include:

- ♦ Classroom Observations: Coaches should collaborate with coachees to determine the focus of observations and how the data will be used. This builds trust and ensures that the observation process is supportive rather than evaluative. Two tools we recommend for observations are the TSRQ Matrix and Integrated Classroom Practices for Equity (Chapter 9).

- Reviewing Student Work: Analyzing student work can provide insights into the effectiveness of teaching strategies and highlight areas for improvement. We suggest looking at samples from students across a range of identifiers to gauge how students are performing and consider the equitable, differentiated support each student needs.
- Reflecting on Learning/Growth: Mid-point reflections help the coachee assess progress and adjust strategies as needed. Coaches can use the midcycle prompts from Chapter 6 to shape the conversation.

Phase 4: End of the Cycle Conversation

At the conclusion of the coaching cycle, the coach and coachee engage in a reflective conversation to review progress toward the established goals or inquiry questions. This conversation should allow the coachee to take the lead in discussing their learning, growth, and areas for future development. Sample questions might include:

- What is the story you are telling about this cycle?
- What did you learn, and how did you learn it?
- What are you most proud of in relation to your goals or inquiry question?
- Which artifacts of practice demonstrate your progress?
- What are your areas for growth in the next cycle?

This final conversation not only closes the current cycle but also sets the stage for ongoing learning and, perhaps, an additional coaching cycle to cultivate continuous learning.

Cultivating Continuous Learning: Implementing Intentional Structures

Just as a gardener carefully selects tools to nurture the soil, protect plants, prune and compost dead leaves, and promote flourishing growth, leaders need to consider the intentional structures that support continuous learning in support of equity and justice. In Chapter 6, we outlined a process by which leaders could facilitate growth at their school site, regardless of the structures that exist. In the section that follows, we outline a process to determine and develop which structures leaders could implement at their school sites. For example, in Chapter 6, Renata and the professional development team developed peer-to-peer coaching as a structure to support growth. Abundance Academy implemented PLCCs. In each of these examples, leaders took their time to identify the structure that best meets their needs, got clear about the purpose of this structure, and engaged in deliberate implementation with support and training for those who were charged with facilitating growth.

We advocate that for any structure you consider, you also consider how you'll implement and sustain that structure. For example, rather than enthusiastically adopting coaching because you've read the latest studies on its impact, first consider what it might take to implement coaching. Or, if you are excited about action research or PLCs and want every teacher to take part in these structures, do your homework on how to best train and implement community members on these structures and the potential benefits while also ensuring these self-directed and smaller-community based structures are accountable for equitable outcomes for students.

A Process to Determine and Implement the Learning Structure

Daniel, the principal at Angel Creek High School, had received a lot of feedback from multilingual students about incidents of bias from teachers. The school counselor and assistant principal had already created a process by which students could report biases, and students who felt safe enough were coming forward. But the principal wasn't sure where the school went from there. Wanting to do right by the students and eradicate inequity quickly, Daniel decided the school needed equity coaches to work with staff when an incident of bias came up. The decision to implement equity coaching was a reaction rooted in good intentions—wanting to do something to support students—but the impact of the program had a more damaging effect on school culture.

The school had enough funding for two partial-release equity coaches, and any member of the community could apply to be an equity coach. But beyond initial enthusiasm, there weren't other considerations for coach selection. Additionally, Daniel thought that since staff had received annual training on bias and having hard conversations, coaches were already prepared for their roles. When the coaching program began, teachers reported for bias were obligated to receive equity coaching, which many viewed as punishment instead of support. Equity coaches were perceived to be an extension of the administration rather than confidants who were genuinely and nonjudgmentally vested in teachers' growth and learning. After a year, the program was dissolved because there wasn't enough funding to support release time for coaches.

Daniel's heart was in the right place, but not enough time and thought went into the development of the program. We're not saying that students who experience bias should wait on a long timeline before equity coaching is implemented, but we are saying that whatever plans are developed need to be considerate of short- and longer-term measures to ensure students can learn without barriers to entry—and that adults can confront their biases and make sustainable change. The following is a suggested approach to determine which structures work best for your school, along with some questions and considerations for implementation.

Create a Rationale and Connect It to Your School's Growth Philosophy

School and district leaders frequently contact us after implementing coaching or PLCs with much enthusiasm and little planning—often assigning people to these roles without clarity about how these structures might transform teaching and learning. The intentions for the structures are often good, but it's important to first determine why a specific structure should be in place. Is coaching effective for growth if the school doesn't invest in developing coaches or training staff on the coaching process? Is self-directed learning the best structure when there are a significant number of students who raise concerns about inequity or bias and little has been done to make sustainable change schoolwide?

Leaders will benefit from pausing to consider why a particular professional learning structure is effective for a school. When leaders take the time to pause and reflect, they can consider the following questions:

- What is the structure we're interested in implementing?
- Why is this the most effective structure to support professional growth at our school?
- How aligned is this approach with our school's culture and/or our growth philosophy?
- How will this structure help us uphold our vision for equity?

Create an Impact Map and Clear Goals for This Structure

An impact map is a form of "future-casting," identifying potential outcomes and impacts from an idea, trend, or initiative. In the case of developing a growth structure, leaders would take a big sheet of paper and place the name of the structure in the middle of the page (e.g., coaching). From there, leaders would draw three or four lines emanating from the center. From each of those lines, they would map the ideal impact of this structure on a specific group, such as teachers, students, community, and so on. From there, leaders would draw additional lines from those groups and map the impacts those groups would have as a result of the growth structure named in the middle of the page. The following questions can serve as guides for impact mapping:

- What do we hope to be true for the community as a result of this structure?
- What will be true for students if we use this structure?
- What will be true for adults?

Leaders could continue to draw lines outward to map the kinds of impact they hope to have. You can see an example of this impact map in Figure 7.3.

After completing this exercise, leaders could analyze the map to identify the goals they have for this structure. These goals

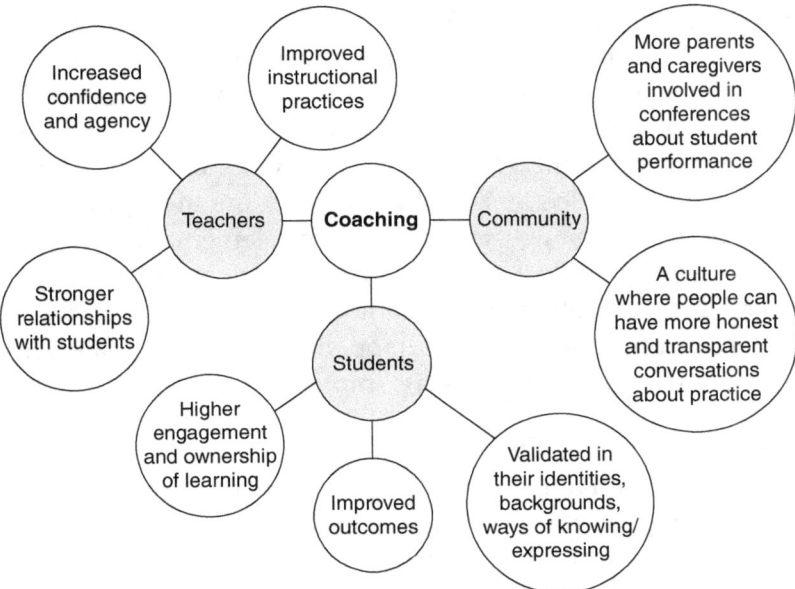

FIGURE 7.3 Sample impact map

could balance short-term goals (the next three months) with longer-term goals (one to three years). These goals will serve as a guide and allow leaders to imagine and enact what they hope to achieve when implementing this structure.

Determine the People Who Will Take Part in This Structure

Leaders also need to consider who will be the ones to lead the selected growth structures. If the structures involve group facilitation, coaching, and mentoring, who will play these roles? How will leaders ensure the folks identified are able and willing to do this work, and how will they be compensated? As we write about in Chapter 4, workload management is tied to educator well-being, so it will be important for leaders to ensure those taking on these roles aren't fulfilling these responsibilities over and above their existing roles. It helps to look for individuals with strong emotional intelligence and relational skills, with well-developed equity literacy alongside cultural humility, deep knowledge and skill in their roles, and a belief in their colleagues' capacity to learn and grow.

Create an Implementation Plan

Once the rationale and goals have been established, then it's important to create a timeline of actions for implementation. The Diffusion of Innovations theory we shared in Chapter 6 may be a good starting point when considering who the early adopters will be and how leaders might plan to bring along the school community. We suggest doing the implementation work in phases rather than in a massive shift. If there are early adopters and willing volunteers who want to pilot a program, leaders can learn from something that happens on a smaller scale before investing the energy in full-scale implementation.

Provide Training and Support

Becoming a facilitator, mentor, and/or coach also requires training and ongoing support. Time needs to be devoted to training in advance of folks taking on their new roles. Often, those who mentor or coach are thrust into the role with little training, and the school calendar is so packed that they aren't able to receive the necessary training or support to fulfill these roles. In the implementation timeline, coaches, mentors, and other professional learning leaders should first receive the skills and background to fulfill their roles rather than have the added stress of leading a group of adults before they are ready to do so successfully.

Build in Time for Assessment and Revision

Encourage all parties to engage in reflective practices throughout the process, offering feedback on how it's going and making adjustments along the way. As part of the assessment and revision process, leaders should also consider succession planning if there is a turnover in these roles. This way, the structures that get developed maintain continuity rather than become dependent on a select few people.

Table 7.2 provides a quick overview of steps, questions, and activities for determining, developing, implementing, and sustaining a growth structure.

In a world that often prioritizes efficiency and productivity, cultivating continuous learning requires a deliberate commitment to slowing down, reflecting, letting things be a little messy, and

TABLE 7.2 Determining, Developing, Implementing, and Sustaining a Growth Structure

Step	Description	Key Questions	Suggested Activities
1. Create a Rationale and Connect It to Your School's Growth Philosophy	Define why this structure (e.g., coaching, PLCs) aligns with your school's culture, values, and equity goals	• What is the structure we're interested in implementing? • Why is this the best structure to support growth? • How aligned is it with our culture? • How will this structure uphold our equity vision?	Facilitate a reflective discussion with the leadership team to articulate the "why" for this structure
2. Create an Impact Map and Clear Goals for This Structure	Visualize the potential outcomes and ripple effects of the structure for students, teachers, families, and school culture	• What do we hope to be true for the community as a result of this structure? • What will be true for students, adults, and families?	Draw an impact map with your team to identify short-term and long-term goals
3. Determine the People Who Will Take Part in This Structure	Identify who will facilitate, coach, or lead, ensuring these individuals are equipped, supported, and compensated	• Who will lead this structure? • What skills (e.g., equity literacy, cultural humility, knowledge) do they need? • How will they be supported and compensated? • How will workloads be managed?	Develop criteria for leader selection and balance workloads to prioritize well-being
4. Create an Implementation Plan	Develop a phased rollout, starting with pilots or early adopters to learn and iterate before scaling up	• What are the phases of implementation? • Who are the early adopters and early majority? • How will you measure progress and build momentum?	Create a timeline with milestones and phases for implementation

(Continued)

TABLE 7.2 Determining, Developing, Implementing, and Sustaining a Growth Structure (*Continued*)

Step	Description	Key Questions	Suggested Activities
5. Provide Training and Support	Ensure facilitators, mentors, or coaches receive adequate training before launching and offer ongoing support	• What training do these leaders need to be effective? • How will you provide ongoing support and professional development? • How can training fit into the school calendar?	Design a professional learning plan with initial training and follow-up support
6. Build in Time for Assessment and Revision	Regularly gather feedback, assess progress, and adjust the structure to improve its impact and effectiveness	• How will you gather feedback from participants? • How will you assess progress and impact?	Use surveys, observations, and reflective conversations to inform changes and refinements
7. Plan for Sustainability and Continuity	Ensure the structure remains consistent and impactful even with leadership or staff turnover	• How will you plan for turnover in facilitators or leaders? • How can the structure be embedded into school systems? • How will you ensure sustainability?	Document processes, build succession plans, and align the structure with schoolwide systems

nurturing authentic growth. Much like the gardening process, it is slow, iterative, and deeply rooted in relationships and processes. To foster continuous learning, educators need the trust and psychological safety to explore, take risks, and adapt their practices. Structures like mentoring, lesson study, or action research are powerful tools when grounded in equity and justice, but these structures require deliberate implementation and ongoing assessment to ensure they serve the needs of educators and students. Growth is not just about improving outcomes; it is about transforming the conditions in which teaching and learning occur. It's about shifting beliefs, challenging biases, and creating ecosystems where every student and educator can thrive. Like watching flowers grow, this work requires patience, collaboration, and a shared commitment to the flourishing of the entire community.

Summary

In this chapter, continuous learning is framed as an intentional process that requires time, space, and a deliberate assessment of the structures for growth. Whether through self-directed learning, small-group professional communities, or 1:1 coaching and mentoring, educators need structures that allow for reflection, goal-setting, and an ongoing commitment to learning. Leaders play a critical role by modeling the learning and equity practices they wish to see, ensuring that growth is sustainable and transformative for the entire school community. The chapter also highlights processes like developing a growth philosophy, selecting growth structures, and developing structures that align with a school's vision for equity, well-being, and growth.

Reflection Questions

1. Why is continuous learning essential for both educators and students, and how does your school currently support it?
2. What does growth look, sound, and feel like in your school community? What conditions make that growth possible?

3. How can you ensure new professional learning structures are developed intentionally and not perceived as punitive or just another thing to do?
4. What systems or processes can you put in place to ensure professional learning structures are ongoing and responsive to changing needs?

References

Adichie, C. N. (2009). *The danger of a single story* [Video]. TED. Retrieved from https://www.ted.com/talks/chimamanda_adichie_the_danger_of_a_single_story

Borko, H., Jacobs, J., Eiteljorg, E., & Pittman, M. E. (2008). Video as a tool for fostering productive discussions in mathematics professional development. *Teaching and Teacher Education, 24*(2), 417–436.

Cheung, W. M., & Wong, W. Y. (2014). Does lesson study work? A systematic review on the effects of lesson study and learning study on teachers and students. *International Journal for Lesson and Learning Studies, 3*(2), 137–149.

Cohen, L., & Peery, L. (2006). Unveiling students' perceptions about women in Islam. *English Journal, 96*(4), 18–22.

DuFour, R., DuFour, R., Eaker, R., & Many, T. (2024). *Learning by doing: A handbook for professional learning communities at work*. Solution Tree Press.

Education Northwest. (2021). *Lesson study facilitator guide*. Education Northwest. Retrieved from https://educationnorthwest.org

Ferrance, E. (2000). *Action research*. Brown University, Northeast and Islands Regional Educational Laboratory.

Gay, G. (2018). *Culturally responsive teaching: Theory, research, and practice* (3rd ed.). Teachers College Press.

Instructional Coaching Group. (2017). *Coaching conversations that make a difference*. https://instructionalcoaching.com

Knight, J. (2017). *The impact cycle: What instructional coaches should do to foster powerful improvements in teaching*. Corwin.

National Equity Project. (n.d.). *Coaching for equity*. Retrieved from https://nationalequityproject.org

National School Reform Faculty (NSRF). (1994). *Critical Friends Groups: Professional learning community protocols*. Retrieved from https://nsrfharmony.org

Sherin, M. G., & van Es, E. A. (2009). Effects of video club participation on teachers' professional vision. *Journal of Teacher Education, 60*(1), 20–37.

Thompson-Grove, G., Evans, P., & Dunne, F. (2003). *Consultancy protocol*. National School Reform Faculty. Retrieved from https://nsrfharmony.org

Wang, J., & Odell, S. J. (2002). Mentored learning to teach according to standards-based reform: A critical review. *Review of Educational Research, 72*(3), 481–546.

Evaluation:
Tend the Ecosystem

Evaluation is tending of the ecosystem through the balance of high expectations with ongoing support. Leaders must challenge existing evaluation systems to embed equity and culturally responsive teaching at the core of their practices. Schools can reimagine evaluation as a collaborative, continuous, and human-centered practice that integrates well-being, addresses systemic inequities, and supports both educators and students in flourishing in the larger educational environment.

8

Evaluation: Tend the Ecosystem

Angelica was just starting her third year as an equity director after 10 years of teaching. She was excited to move into administration and had enjoyed the beginning of her tenure as the first person of color to hold the job on their predominantly white campus. She had created substantive programming for students, and her professional development opportunities were well received. Yet she was eager to do more to address classroom strategies. She was often called in *after* something had happened: a teacher had stereotyped a student, two students got into an argument after one made a derogatory comment about their family's immigration status, or the same students of color were constantly being blamed for not paying attention, not doing their homework, showing up late, without any consideration of what might be happening to/for them in the class context. As opposed to trying to clean up the mess, so to speak, she wanted to front-load skills to help prevent or build the capacity of her peers to better address conflict and/or deficit mindsets.

She talked with her supervisor about allocating some faculty meeting time to reflect on these inequitable patterns and offer strategies to better support student learning. She enjoyed the work she was doing, but she didn't feel like it was really shifting the learning culture in service of greater equity. It was all *optional* when what she knew they needed was accountability. When she asked for faculty meeting time, her supervisor got flustered and countered, "Well, we can't change the evaluation system. It's set in stone, and it wouldn't be fair to ask teachers to suddenly meet new criteria." Angelica took a deep breath and tried to reframe the conversation, but she felt like she had just touched the third rail in a subway system. Angelica's supervisor asked her to stay in her lane and keep offering the "great programming" she had been developing. Angelica left the office deflated.

Throughout our careers, evaluation has been a hotly contested topic when it comes to assessing equitable practices in schools. For decades, we have watched as educational institutions provide equity-focused professional development via workshops, conferences, book study groups, critical friends groups, peer observations and learning walks, student feedback, and related coursework/degree programs. And yet, with all of this training, we still see persistent teacher expectation gaps and ongoing stereotype threat for minoritized students. Don't get us wrong, we know these efforts are critical to making the kinds of shifts we need. But it's clear that without an evaluation system in which equitable expectations are more firmly embedded, all the training in the world can't shift teacher practices entirely. This doesn't mean we haven't tried or that the work wasn't valuable. As noted in the previous chapters, we're a testament to the impact of professional development and to leaders who gave us the opportunity to improve and grow. But we need a bigger lever we can pull that will help to scale our efforts to impact more teachers, and we have seen how reimagining evaluation can be that lever.

We want to be specific about the *kind* of evaluation we are advocating for: similar to the range of professional development structures out there, there are myriad evaluation tools being used across the country. We have observed three key challenges with these various instruments:

1. They often do not ground the process in an equity framework. It's like there's "excellent" teaching on the one hand and then there's equitable, culturally responsive teaching (CRT), on the other hand, and never the two shall meet.

2. Those frameworks that do include references to equity are often too general, theoretical, and non-specific to really help teachers and leaders assess where they are and the kinds of changes to their practice they need to make. We see indicators like "foster respect" and "develop positive relationships" with no connections to behaviors we could observe. We call these the "mile wide and an inch deep" evaluation processes that skim the surface, but don't produce lasting results.

This then leads to our third challenge:

3. Even when we have an in-depth, specific tool that accounts for equity, it's not connected to teacher well-being and growth. It's often a stand-alone event, like an equity walkthrough, that is not truly part of a larger ecosystem. To add more fuel to the fire, teachers and leaders report that even these one-off event processes are inconsistently applied.

So how can we enhance the tools we have—and may need to accept for the time being in some districts/campuses—so that our evaluation can produce the kinds of results we need and students deserve?

In our opening story, Angelica noticed something in the school's ecosystem that impacted the student experience: teachers learning about equity, but not engaging in equitable practices in the classroom. When she requested faculty meeting time to invite a reflective conversation and greater accountability for teachers' instructional practices, her supervisor told her to stay in her lane. This notion that evaluation and accountability are separate from everything else, that only a select few supervisors are charged to engage in evaluation—or determine what teachers are to be evaluated on—is the core issue.

Here, we return to our terrarium metaphor. In this ecosystem, evaluation is the outgrowth of equity, well-being, and growth rather than something separate. Evaluation is not just an outsized process compared to everything else, but the culminating assessment of how well teachers embed equity-centered practices into teaching planning and practice, how effective teachers are in classrooms with students, how reflective and learning-oriented teachers are, and, ultimately, how students are able to learn in their full dignity. Evaluation is also a measure of how well leaders tend to the ecosystem. Tending to ecosystems requires examining how growth is happening:

- Is it healthy growth where life is flourishing?
- What needs pruning and weeding?
- How might the soil need to be regenerated?
- What needs greater care?
- How are external conditions having an impact on what is able to grow and what is stifled?
- Are these external conditions short term, or will the ecosystem need to adapt to these longer-term forces?

In terms of leadership, this kind of tending might include assessing what new growth opportunities are available, identifying ways to nurture the soil to better support educator practice, considering the components of better teacher retention, counseling out those whose values are out of alignment, and also assessing the evaluation itself to ensure it is a meaningful and useful process. This chapter will support you in thinking how you might reimagine evaluation to make it a more natural part of the school's ecosystem and, more importantly, to ensure equity is embedded within the evaluation rather than as an afterthought.

Reimagining Evaluation

Most schools and education-facing organizations prioritize teacher evaluation because it assesses the effectiveness of teaching and learning. But oftentimes schools begin and end with an evaluation system. And why wouldn't they? Evaluation models like the Danielson Model (2022), the Marzano Model (2017), and the 5D+ (University of Washington, 2012) model have all been well-researched, studied, revised, and implemented.

Why reinvent the wheel? While, yes, these models have been successful in assessing educator effectiveness, two major gaps exist: understanding the specific ecosystems we work in, and recognizing the glaring gaps to address educational inequities within those ecosystems, particularly in the ways many evaluation systems center whiteness and the culture of power, or what del Carmen Salazar and Lerner call the "whitestream" (2019). These researchers aimed to address the inequity gaps in evaluation by developing a new evaluation system, one that prioritizes those on the margins and centers CRT and learning: The Framework for Equitable and Excellent Teaching (FEET). They describe the model as follows:

> The FEET fills a gap in teacher evaluation by providing a framework for teaching that includes teaching performances that incorporate the culture of power, sustain the power of culture, and nurture critical consciousness. In contrast, generic frameworks for teaching privilege the culture of power, exclude the resources of historically marginalized Communities of Color, and negate critical stances. In generic frameworks for teaching, culturally relevant teacher performances are omitted; therefore, they are not valued or incentivized through the evaluation process. (p. 469)

Similar to how our institutions operate, well-established frameworks reinforce dominant cultures that are passing for "normal" or the way things should be done. Del Carmen Salazar and Lerner conclude by advocating that "scholars must continue to imagine, create, implement, and test approaches to teacher evaluation that transgress and promote social justice" (p. 474). Gloria Ladson-Billings underscores this point as well: "Remixing is vital to innovation in art, science, and pedagogy, and it is crucial that we are willing to remix what we created and/or inherited" (2014, p. 74). Something different needs to happen in evaluation that includes not just students on the margins, but educators who come from more historically marginalized backgrounds, which also includes ways of teaching, doing, and knowing that don't fall within the bounds of traditional, inequitable education. We need an evaluation system that remains as dynamic as the ecosystems we've created at our sites, as evolving as our understandings are of culturally responsive and sustaining pedagogies (Ladson-Billings, 2014; Paris, 2012), while at the same time, inclusive of community-based standards, and yes, well-researched approaches to how to conduct these evaluations and what to include in them.

Our framework promotes building an evaluation system that emerges from the soil of its communities and focuses on a process and set of practices that are inclusive of multiple backgrounds, experiences, ways of knowing, and educating. To that end, we advocate that leaders include the following principles to support more dynamic evaluation practices:

- **Embrace Multiple Measures of Effectiveness:** Implement a combination of qualitative (observation cycles and dialogue, student feedback surveys) and quantitative (classroom observation data, assessments) measures. This mixed-method approach provides a comprehensive, stable, and more accurate assessment of teacher quality.
- **Consider Context:** Adapt evaluation practices to fit the specific needs and contexts of different institutions and programs. Avoid one-size-fits-all models, ensuring evaluations are relevant and meaningful in varied settings. Even if you have a document you have to use, how might you add or adjust particular elements, like your classroom observation patterns, to create a more relevant experience for teachers?
- **Center Identity and Cultural Responsiveness:** Ensure the process respects and reflects the identities of evaluators, evaluees, and students. Utilize culturally responsive/sustaining tools and practices. Draw upon research-informed practices in culturally responsive and sustaining pedagogy and curriculum in assessment practices. Disaggregate data by demographics to identify and address learning gaps.

- **Collaborate:** Encourage collaboration among administrators, teachers, and students to engage all parties meaningfully in the process. Ensure evaluations include multiple evaluators and provide spaces for meaningful feedback. Incorporate teacher input and student voice to mitigate biases from a sole evaluator.
- **Train Evaluators:** Offer ongoing training for evaluators. This training should cover the evaluation model's standards, rubrics, and data collection tools, as well as effective feedback techniques.
- **Promote Continuous Learning:** Connect evaluation outcomes to specific opportunities for professional growth. Offer targeted professional learning to address identified growth areas, ensuring evaluations are not just summative but also developmental.

We will be incorporating these practices throughout our discussion of evaluation and what it can and should look like in a variety of contexts. We know that in certain districts and settings, there are very specific rules from teacher unions as well as central offices that will dictate particular parameters. Yet we also know that many of these processes are not promoting the kind of teacher development and instruction that students need. So we have to avoid the traps of "my hands are tied" or "I'm just doing what the District says I have to do." We are going to have to do a better job of meeting requirements while also considering shifts and/or additions we can make in service of better systems.

Our goal is to position evaluation as a way for teachers to know where their professional practice is compared to expectations for students and the work of their peers. It's a way to determine relative standing or relationship to one's larger educational practice: How am I doing relative to the goals we have for student success? What kind of colleague am I? And what is the quality of my relationship with families and community members? Our main objective is to help leaders become flexible and responsive in fostering a culture of continuous growth, which involves improving the evaluation process to accommodate new learning methods, practices, and changing contexts.

Addressing the Reality of External Factors

Each year when Elizabeth surveys her instructional leadership classes on the current state of teacher evaluation at their sites, the responses are both consistent and disheartening. Overwhelmingly, students in these classes—aspiring leaders, teachers, and counselors from every grade level and subject and with a range of experience levels—say current methods are at best unhelpful and at worst demoralizing. Here are the two most predictable patterns:

1. "I have not been observed or given feedback in years."
2. "I've never experienced feedback that actually helped me improve. It's usually very general, 'Keep up the good work!'"

They are frustrated by the trends they see: teacher unions that are distrustful of districts and central offices that say they can't do anything "because of the union," creating a cycle of blame and finger-pointing. For example, Elizabeth was visiting a student from her instructional leadership class at her school. At the opening of the faculty meeting, the principal was reminding teachers about a survey on student belonging that they had to complete and said, "This is mandated by the District, so we have to do it." While this may be true, it was not a productive way to introduce and evaluate the student experience, and Elizabeth watched as the teachers rolled their eyes and grumbled under their breath.

Then the principal went on to direct teachers to have a conversation about belonging with their students to make sure "they know what the word means when they do the survey." She added, "Be sure to connect what we do to the word 'belong.'" Afterward, Elizabeth asked her student what she had heard from her colleagues and learned that several faculty members had commented how useless it was to "prompt" the students—it would have been more helpful to talk about what belonging looks, sounds, and feels like, and how they could ensure that students were really feeling connected, affirmed, and known by their teachers and peers. Instead, this became another "check the box" assessment, squandering a potentially useful evaluative exercise that could have been woven into the larger picture of evaluation.

Elizabeth also has her students bring in the current evaluation documents and processes as outlined by their respective districts. This is an illuminating practice that exposes another set of important issues. In small groups, students review the various documents, compare what they see, and then talk about how these current procedures reflect the best practices we have been studying and reviewing in class. After their small group discussions, Elizabeth asks what they noticed, and the answers are usually the same:

> "It's confusing!"
> "This is the first time I have seen the official document that guides our process."
> "It was really hard to find a copy of our process."
> "It's really general, and there is no mention of specific data."

Students then begin to ask a series of important questions and make connections. Several students note that the evaluation document they found could actually be useful, but they've never seen it before. So the first takeaway is how we can make current procedures clear, explicit, and accessible to all teachers. Second, they note that there are general guidelines, but not a lot of specifics: "teacher will establish a performance goal," "evaluator will gather data," "conduct post-evaluation conference," and "prepare a written evaluation." Without details, many noted that these processes are not as effective as they could be. There's actually a lot of room for evaluators to build more effective strategies within these general parameters. This observation always creates hope, but it does mean leaders have to know how to fill in the details.

These graduate students also note some causes for concern: some districts are replacing specific classroom observations with walk-throughs or learning walks conducted by district personnel. While we know how helpful these kinds of "rounds" can be to get a more holistic understanding and appraisal of instruction across a grade level or site, they should not take the place of a leader's presence in a teacher's classroom and dialogue about their specific growth and development. Another issue they noted is that some of the teacher evaluation documents are over 30 pages long. They talked about how hard it would be for a new teacher to try to focus on their own development—let alone get the "big picture" of the process. And they said most would be overwhelmed and would not even read through the entire document.

Although there are specific realities we have to take into account when reimaging evaluation, there is far more room for improvement, enhancement, and creativity than we assume. In collaboration with unions and district offices, leaders have to be willing to engage, push, and challenge existing procedures that are not as effective as they could be. We can't continue to default to "this is the way we have to do it" and offer shifts in practice that are not only doable but also necessary.

Finding an Effective Observation Structure and Process

A great place to begin is to rethink classroom observation because it is included (or should be) in most evaluation cycles. Tending to the ecosystem means prioritizing what's happening in classrooms and making the assessment of teaching and learning a priority among the competing demands of school. In order to promote CRT, leaders have to be knowledgeable about culturally responsive school leadership and be present in classrooms in order to support teachers' growth and development. So, we need to be sure that leaders have a clear understanding of what it means to be "culturally responsive." We appreciate Zarretta Hammond's (2014) description of CRT as an important starting point:

> An educator's ability to recognize students' cultural displays of learning and meaning making and respond positively and constructively with teaching moves that

use cultural knowledge as a scaffold to connect what the students know to new concepts and content in order to promote effective information processing. All the while, the educator understands the importance of being in relationship and having a social-emotional connection to the student in order to create a safe space for learning. (p. 15)

We have to start by knowing who students are and how who they are impacts their learning. We can't tell you the number of times we ask a teacher or a leader to tell us about the racial and ethnic makeup of a classroom (not just school-wide demographic data), and they are unsure—"hmm, I think that student identifies as Latino, but I'm not sure." As we noted earlier, a critical understanding of one's identity is the first step to being an effective educator. The next step is being aware of the identities of those we teach, and this includes not only the young people but also their families and caregivers.

Next, do students get to see themselves in the learning they are doing? Can they offer their experiences and wisdom to make the learning more valuable for themselves and others? Do they have any agency, and is the learning co-constructed with their teacher? By connecting what they know already to the new skills/content the teacher has identified, students will be better positioned to develop and succeed. This knowledge will allow teachers to be in genuine relationships with their students. Teachers can note if they have high expectations for all students, or if they are making assumptions about who can learn and why. What kinds of feedback do students receive? Does the teacher solicit their feedback? Breaking cultural responsiveness down piece by piece can help evaluators be more intentional in the observation cycle. In the following chapter, we have included an adaptation of the FEET model (2019) and Chism's "Guide to Culturally Responsive Strategy Patterns" (2022) to help both leaders and teachers get better at observing and adapting practices for greater cultural responsiveness. We can no longer silo diversity and inclusion efforts or disconnect them from the academic program. We must lead teacher growth cycles with the recognition that academic success is predicated upon our understanding of and utilization of equity-based pedagogies.

And it's critical to rethink how we do those observations in terms of purpose, frequency, collaboration with teachers, and collection of actionable data. In "Let's Cancel the Dog and Pony Show," Kim Marshall (2012) called for educational leaders to take a more critical look at the way they were conducting formal classroom observations. As opposed to a one-time, announced class visit that often results in teachers putting on a show for their supervisor, Marshall describes the value of more frequent, shorter, and unannounced observations to create sustained, authentic, and more effective dialogues about instruction and pedagogy. We have seen the value of this shift. In general, the idea that a supervisor could really get a complete picture of a teacher's practice in one 45-minute observation is problematic. There is just too much to see and learn, and without a focus for the visit, there can be all kinds of general data gathered—but nothing specific enough to impact instruction. One can see so much in a 15- to 20-minute observation! By focusing the visits on specific goals developed in collaboration, the feedback can be implemented immediately. There is a real-time aspect when there is a series of observations, creating a sustained dialogue about practice that evolves over time. Evaluators and teachers are working together to improve instruction, creating a greater sense of purpose and accuracy for the evaluation.

As we noted earlier, one refrain we hear persistently from leaders is, "I just don't have the time to do evaluations. I'm too busy doing…" When we hear this, we have to be willing to engage leaders on how their time is being allocated. It's important to figure out the root cause of the time crunch, determining whether it is an organizational problem or a technical problem. We might ask, how are they planning for their evaluation cycles? We have found it helpful to create observational rounds with focal teachers, similar to the way teachers have focal students. By clustering teachers into small groups, leaders can complete a series of observations over a six- to eight-week period. Teachers can be grouped in different ways: those who are new to the profession or those with a similar focus. Sometimes leaders prefer mixed groups, pairing two more veteran teachers with effective practices with two new teachers who are just starting their careers. These groups can then be spread out throughout the year, and time for observations can be blocked into a supervisor's schedule for the year.

In our leadership roles, we approached observation similarly. We always started with new teachers so we could be sure they were off to a strong start. Then we would move on to anyone who was struggling or who was on a specific plan for improvement. These were teachers we identified at the end of the *prior* school year, and they would have developed strategies that could be implemented right as the year was getting started. In our own ways, we generally created three time blocks a week for observations and had four observation cycles (eight weeks per cycle). The length of the blocks during the week was generally 90 minutes. If you are reading this and thinking, "How is that possible?" we really want you to take a hard and long look at your time allocation. Remembering that supporting equitable instruction is one of the key tenets of culturally responsive leadership, how can we *not* allocate the time?

Our goal here is to disrupt current patterns. We can't say we want a better evaluation process, but not be willing to shift some things to get there. We worked with a group of building principals who together talked with their district office supervisor about the need to prioritize their time in classrooms. They were constantly being asked to attend meetings outside of their buildings, and these demands were getting in the way. Together, they could be much more effective in seeking change. So, if your time issue is coming from something external to your locus of control, how will you address it with your supervisor? Who could you partner with to help advocate for what you need?

The other key factor for these kinds of cyclical, multi-observation schedules is not letting other things take over the time allotted for evaluation. Leaders often report a strong start, but by November, calendar creep has started, and their observations become inconsistent. Some leaders organize their own calendars, but others rely on administrative support. In either case, the observation time has to be protected. Of course, emergencies will happen. But by making observation time a regularly scheduled event, just like your weekly meeting with your boss, you will have a much better chance of success.

The Need for Differentiation

It is important for supervisors to develop the capacities of teachers by being a visible presence in classrooms and engaging in conversations about teaching and learning (Zepeda et al., 2024). And just like instruction, supervision has to be both differentiated and developmental. At different points in their careers, teachers will need different kinds of feedback, and most evaluation cycles don't evolve after the first 1–4 years. While new teachers may be observed every year, those who have gained some kind of tenure often report never being observed after their initial years. We hear from so many mid-career teachers (5–15 years) who are starving for actionable feedback. They are typically left to their own devices, which will impact both their work with students and their relationships with colleagues. In two schools Lori worked with, committees of educators across a range of roles and years of experience designed different approaches to evaluation for more experienced teachers; even at her own school, evaluation had three tracks: a new teacher evaluation, an experienced teacher evaluation, and an improvement phase—a process by which teachers who were underperforming were taken out of the yearlong evaluation cycle and placed on a three-month improvement track. Each of these models included a differentiated observation schedule that best supported what teachers needed.

By using observation as a strategy for engagement, growth, and development, leaders can partner with teachers to design a cycle that will best improve their work based on what they need at a particular point in their careers. A differentiated approach helps teachers better meet the learning goals they have set for their students. It is also the foundation for a productive and effective observation cycle (Figure 8.1).

Since data really drives this last step, it's critical that the teacher be able to deconstruct their practice. They must identify appropriate changes so that together the supervisor and teacher can name both the next steps and a timeframe for the

> 1. **The Pre-Observation Conference:** This opening conversation identifies a specific instructional practice that will serve as the focus for the observation. Together, the supervisor and instructor identify possible aspects of culturally responsive teaching and what types of data would be collected to best illuminate the area of interest. This conversation helps to promote critical self-reflection and identify differences in experiences, identities, and prior engagement with students.
>
> 2. **The Classroom Observation:** Following the pre-observation conference, this time in the classroom allows both supervisor and instructor to apply a culturally responsive lens in the following ways:
>
>   - Content is connected to students and their backgrounds and needs.
>   - Strengths-based instruction, activities, and assessments are used.
>   - The classroom is a learning community fostering a sense of belonging.
>   - Instruction is differentiated to meet the specific needs and interests of the students.
>   - All students are held to high expectations.
>
>   The data collected will provide evidence of the ways these practices were present in the classroom based on the decided-upon focus for the observation. And the tool selected will allow for synthesis, reflection, and shifts in practice.
>
> 3. **The Post-Observation Conference:** Together the supervisor and instructor make sense of the data that was gathered. Then they can identify the types of professional learning that will lead to growth and better outcomes for students.

FIGURE 8.1 Culturally responsive framework for classroom observations (Zepeda et al., 2024)

supervisor to return to the classroom and continue the conversation. Thus, it's important that this cycle happens in a timely fashion and that the feedback is *specific* so the teacher is clear on the challenge and knows where to focus their effort. Ideally, there are not huge time gaps between the three steps. This is why we would cluster observations to focus on a set of teachers and complete their observation cycles in the span of a few weeks. Ideally, there should be very little time—hopefully just days—between the three steps.

Another note about time: these pre- and post-observation meetings don't need to be long. 15–20 minutes is usually enough time to review what you saw and talk about implications and shifts in practice. We are huge fans of voice memos, so when walking out of the classroom, grab your phone and take a couple of minutes to capture your overall impressions. For our teachers who like immediate feedback, we might even share the recording with them before our debrief. Hearing your voice communicates so much more than an email. There may be teachers who prefer your feedback first come in writing so they can process it before meeting face to face. So, you can dictate an email message with your immediate impressions and send it soon after the observation. It's not a formal evaluation letter you are writing—just your gratitude for the visit, how you felt in class, one or two things you noticed, or just how you are looking forward to talking more. The goal of this kind of feedback is a sustained, informed conversation that allows for reflection on the priorities set and strategies for enhanced practice.

Make Observation Collaborative

Having multiple observers also can benefit a classroom teacher and allow for multiple perspectives. When Lori was a supervisor, teachers were evaluated by a collaborative team that included the department chair, an experienced colleague within that teacher's department, and Lori. Logistically, finding a timeframe for the evaluation team to observe the teacher was challenging, so in their first meeting of the year, the team scheduled all components of the observation cycle for the school year and worked to get substitutes at the outset. Additionally, scheduling these meetings in advance allowed for the post-observation meeting to be timely. Logistics aside, having a team of evaluators was powerful because of the different lenses each person brought to the class observation.

It's an important reminder that observations need to be a two-way street where the leader and instructor are working collaboratively to meet the vision and instructional goals of the school. Additionally, faculty meetings should be utilized as critical sites for discussion of observation and feedback practices and be sure that the teachers are doing the majority of the talking. Taking the coaching approach we advocate for in Chapter 7, the leader's primary job is to ask questions that will engage teachers and help them to figure out the moves *they* need to make. Consider having observation meetings take place in the teacher's classroom as opposed to your office. We want to highlight these dialogues as being aspirational and even extend this notion to the need for inspiration. Typically, when we ask a teacher about evaluation, the first reaction is a heavy sigh, a dead stare, or a simple statement like "waste of time." Our current approach to most observations is at best lackluster, and at worst demoralizing. Since they are such an essential part of ensuring that all children get the instruction they deserve, we need to capitalize on these professional opportunities and see them as the gold mine they are.

Draw from a Range of Data Sources

The next challenge is having an evaluation tool that will allow leaders to capture relevant data that will form the basis for the work with the teacher. We would suggest having a range of tools as opposed to trying to squeeze everything into one. This aligns with what we know about adult learning and the value of choice. It also moves us away from the notion that there is one way, typically the dominant culture way, to conduct an observation. A range of tools better represents all the kinds of ways that learning happens in a classroom and the range of responses an instructor needs to have at the ready. The following chapter offers a number of options for your consideration. Since there needs to be dialogue prior to the observation to set the expectations and determine the focus, this is an opportune time to decide on a tool. What kind of data would be most important to gather given what the teacher is working on? Together, you can decide on the best instrument. This not only helps to focus the observation but also can allay fears from teachers who have not had a positive experience with supervisory feedback.

Identity Matters

We also cannot underscore enough how important it is to consider identity in relation to observation and evaluation. Who is the teacher being evaluated? How do their age, their racial/ethnic identifiers, their experiences of education, and other identifying factors have an impact on how the observation cycle happens? What might identity-conscious (Talusan, 2022) dialogue look like as part of the evaluation process? Just as we hope teachers will consider the values, identities, and backgrounds of their students when creating the opportunity to learn, so, too, must evaluators reflect on how identity plays a role in observation. We'll explore this topic further in the following section. We'll also take a look at challenges that speak more to a leader's ability to provide technical feedback that is both culturally responsive and equity-based.

Adopting a Warm Demander Stance

Working with Native Alaskan children in the 1970s, Judith Kleinfeld from the University of Alaska noticed that effective teachers took a very particular stance when working with students. Not only did these teachers demonstrate great connection to and care for the students, but they also had an unrelenting belief in their abilities and potential for success. Kleinfeld referred to this instructional style as "active demandingness" and coined the phrase "warm demander" (Bondy & Ross, 2008). To be clear, this does not just mean teachers care about their students. It's much bigger than that. They insist on mutual respect consistent in a caring relationship along with high expectations for meaningful work. Students are expected to do their best, and they know that their teacher is deeply invested in their success.

The warm demander stance has been found to be particularly impactful for students who are experiencing poverty and other challenges that could create low expectations for them as a result of teacher bias. Despite the challenges that these students may face or the presence of systemic discrimination, such as racism or classism, teachers who act as warm demanders will not lower standards or allow students to get away with not doing their work. They will stay engaged, working hard to understand what is actually going on and creating differing, yet equitable, pathways of success based on high expectations. Teachers position themselves as collaborators dedicated to supporting students via a positive relationship based on trust and respect that goes both ways.

Building on the concept of culturally responsive teachers as warm demanders for their students, instructional leaders also need to be warm demanders "who expect a great deal of their colleagues, convince them of their own capacity to improve, and support them with a range of resources" (Safir, 2019). Too often we work with leaders who know a teacher is not serving all their students, but who struggle to share critical feedback and specific steps for improvement. This generally happens for three reasons: First, leaders aren't sure what to suggest, meaning they don't have the technical knowledge to help a teacher improve. Secondly, leaders don't offer the kind of warm encouragement that teachers need. This is directly connected to the topics of well-being and growth we have addressed as critical components for healthy, equity-minded teachers. Finally, and perhaps most strikingly, they are not willing to move through their own discomfort and hold teachers to high expectations. This is especially true for white leaders, who make up 77% of all leaders, with the number being even higher for leaders in private schools at 83% (National Center for Education Statistics, 2020–2021). So, when it's a question of will as opposed to skill, how can white leaders hold themselves accountable?

Racialized Considerations

When we interview white leaders, too often they are focusing on what might happen if they confront a white teacher on an issue of racial bias. They offer a litany of excuses. Instead of focusing on all the reasons why they don't interrupt the behavior, leaders need to consider what's at stake when they *don't* interrupt:

> We may believe our silence in these moments is neutral, respectful, or even polite. Yet, we are prioritizing our own comfort and the comfort of other white people. It is a choice. Most often, what is at stake for white people when we interrupt are the risks of being disliked, engaging in a conflict, ruining a family gathering, being perceived as a troublemaker, or being perceived as thinking we are better than others. At times there are real consequences, such as a relationship ending or a job being at stake, but usually we are avoiding some form of social discomfort, often something to do with our ego. But what is at stake if we *don't* interrupt racist comments and behaviors? We are allowing

and signing off on harm to People of Color, supporting the status quo, not living the values we espouse, and jeopardizing our integrity.

(Chandler-Ward & Denevi, 2023, p. 49)

We have to envision a kind of antiracist leadership that allows white leaders to model discomfort and make mistakes. By beginning with humility, we are much better positioned to be true to the antiracist and equity values we espouse *and* engage white colleagues when their behavior is racially problematic. This is one way to dismantle the whitestream that del Carmen Salazar and Lerner write about. One of the most consistent themes we hear from teachers is that they know when a colleague is struggling with culturally responsive instruction or has deficit views of students or families of color. The failure to interrupt those patterns and insist on more equitable strategies will breed dissent and lower morale. While some white leaders think that confrontation will make the situation worse, as discussed in the well-being chapters, it's clear that the failure to address racial inequity—among all forms of inequity—makes everything worse—most acutely for the students, families, and colleagues of color who have to bear the brunt of the racism.

In working with white teachers and colleagues, leaders of color echo the patterns we have detailed here. But there is an additional burden on leaders of color who have to supervise white teachers who may be unwilling to acknowledge racial stereotypes and bias in their classrooms. Not only are they on the receiving end of racism, but they often have a different level of accountability to families of color for the care of their children. Those families often rely on leaders of color to protect and advocate for their children in a system that was not designed for them. While we know the value when students of color have teachers who reflect their identity (Egalite, 2024), we don't often address the added expectations for educators of color who have to stand in the breach. When delivering constructive feedback to white teachers, they often have to navigate defensiveness, assertion of intentions over impact, tears and upset, and confessions of guilt. Often, their feedback is tolerated, but not acted upon.

We have even seen white teachers unable to manage their own racial stress and discomfort (Stevenson, 2014) and challenge the feedback from a colleague of color as inaccurate or inappropriate.

In an effort to increase cross-racial collaboration and support leaders of color, white leaders can work on their own racial literacy and understand the impact of their race on their supervision, especially when it comes to feedback (Chandler-Ward & Denevi, 2023). They can support professional growth that addresses healthy racial identity development. If they notice white colleagues who are unable to navigate conversations around race or who are practicing color-evasiveness (Annamma et al., 2017) and avoiding the topic of race, they can offer to support and engage them—and not leave it to colleagues of color to pick up the slack. White supervisors can advocate for mentors for their colleagues of color if they are one of the few people of color on a leadership team, staff, or faculty. Finally, leaders can pay close attention to evaluation teams, consider diverse compositions as essential, and note the range of identities represented.

Of course, there will be times when leaders of all racial backgrounds are faced with challenging personnel issues and teachers who are struggling to meet expectations. Systems of oppression, in particular white supremacy and patriarchy, are infused into how educational systems operate and will impact all of us. Unfortunately, instructional leaders often take one of these four unhelpful approaches when handling concerns with a teacher's performance (Hall, 2019):

1. Say it's "not my problem" and send in a coach to "fix" the teacher.
2. Avoid rocking the boat and look the other way: "If I call people out, word will get around and no one will trust me."
3. Engage in a passive-aggressive sneak attack by putting "it all in writing," avoiding direct confrontation and face-to-face conversations.
4. Complete the "dance of the lemons" by reassigning the teacher rather than counseling them out.

A warm-demander approach is the most effective strategy for handling these situations. The remedy comes via in-person dialogue that is direct, clear, and articulates high expectations: "Here's what great instruction here looks, sounds, and feels like." Leaders need to offer frequent and detailed feedback that's specific and actionable. If there's a concern, name it and offer support and resources, remembering that we can't have high expectations without high levels of support. Overall, leaders have to be able to trust the process of growth and remember that there is no single intervention that will "fix" a teacher. It requires multiple interventions and work over time. Yet, when all else fails, leaders are most effective when they are honest and authentic: name the consequences, detail the next steps, and partner with human resources to ensure a fair process that will provide mutual accountability. The good news is that we can re-center our equity focus and reframe these stressful conversations as necessary steps toward more inclusive classrooms.

In his short essay "We Are All Flowers" (1992) Buddhist practitioner Thich Nhat Hanh writes about how beauty and decay are part of the same cycle. Flowers need the right conditions to bloom. Flowers also need to be pruned; sometimes cutting back a garden (a process known as "deadheading") is what contributes to more collective flourishing. In any conditions, flowers will eventually wither and turn into compost, which then nourishes the soil, allowing for new growth. Composting holds the potential for something new and beautiful to emerge. Connected to our ecosystem metaphor, leaders have the opportunity to create the conditions for growth; similarly, though, they must interrupt harmful practices, weed out those who are unable to support student learning, and be intentional in ensuring the ecosystem contributes to the health of all its members. Leaders also need to make time to evaluate the effectiveness of the evaluation itself, to cut back on what's not working, and to create opportunities for something more beneficial to grow in its place (Killion, 2018). Being a warm demander allows us to set high expectations and be a careful steward of those expectations. Being a warm demander isn't the job of a single leader though; community members can share collective care for the ecosystem by being involved in the process of co-creating it, nurturing it, holding one another accountable, composting what needs to be transformed, pruning what needs to be refined, and encouraging ongoing growth.

While we understand why there are a range of frameworks to support schools and educators, we need to do more than just graft the frameworks onto our existing practices. As a professional community, we need to engage in critical questions about whether the framework we've adopted best advances equity, addresses the well-being of adults, and leads to more equitable forms of growth. How can we pivot from the transactional approaches of checkboxes to the transformational practices of dismantling the whitestream and considering the human beings who carry out the essential work of educating—and being models for—all students? Rather than just calling on leaders to be technocrats who check boxes, let's value them as gardeners who take a loving accountability stance to ensure that the ecosystems they are cultivating are healthy. Every intentional act a leader takes to tend to the ecosystem, like fractals, contributes to the culture and health of the organization. Not only is this necessary to reimagine education, but it is also courageous and visionary in service of designing a better world for young people to inherit.

Summary

This chapter reimagined evaluation, calling for systems that were deeply integrated with equity, well-being, and growth. It critiqued traditional evaluation frameworks for being disconnected from classroom inequities and teacher well-being. Through the metaphor of tending an ecosystem, the chapter emphasized that evaluation should have been a continuous, collaborative process that nurtured both teacher and student growth. By centering Culturally Responsive Teaching (CRT) and creating meaningful, dynamic evaluation systems, schools are able to build environments where equitable practices were upheld and supported across all levels of the educational ecosystem.

For Further Reflection

1. How can we reimagine our school's evaluation system to center equity and well-being? What would that look like in practice?
2. In what ways does our current evaluation process support or hinder equitable teaching? What shifts can we explore together?
3. How can we use evaluation as a tool for growth and reflection rather than as a punitive measure? What changes would that require?
4. What would it mean to truly "tend the ecosystem" of our school through evaluation? How can we ensure that evaluation fosters both student and teacher growth?

References

Annamma, S., Jackson, D. D., & Morrison, D. (2017). Conceptualizing color-evasiveness: using dis/ability critical race theory to expand a colorblind racial ideology in education and society. *Race Ethnicity and Education*, 20(2), 147–162. https://doi.org/10.1080/13613324.2016.1248837

Bondy, E. & Ross, D. (2008). Teacher as warm demander. *Educational Leadership*, 66(1).

Chandler-Ward, J., & Denevi, E. (2023). *Learning and teaching while white: Antiracist strategies for school communities*. Routledge.

del Carmen Salazar, M., & Lerner, J. (2019). *Teacher evaluation as cultural practice: A framework for equitable and effective teaching*. Routledge.

Egalite, A. (2024). What we know about teacher race and student outcomes: A review of the evidence to date. *Education Next*, 24(1), 42–49.

Hall, P. (2019). *The instructional leader's most difficult job*. Ed Leadership. ASCD, 76(6).

Hammond, Z. (2014). *Culturally responsive teaching and the brain: promoting authentic engagement and rigor among culturally and linguistically diverse students*. Corwin.

Hanh, T. N. (1992). *Touching peace: Practicing the art of mindful living*. Parallax Press.

Killion, J. (2018). *Assessing impact: Evaluating professional learning* (3rd ed.). Corwin.

Ladson-Billings, G. (2014). Culturally relevant pedagogy 2.0: a.k.a. the remix. *Harvard Educational Review*, 84(1), 74–84.

Marshall, K. (2012). *Let's cancel the dog and pony show*. Kappan.

National Center for Education Statistics. (2020–2021). Retrieved from https://nces.ed.gov/programs/coe/indicator/cls/public-school-principals

Paris, D. (2012). Culturally sustaining pedagogy: a needed change in stance, terminology, and practice. *Educational Researcher*, 41(3), 93–97.

Safir, S. (2019). *Becoming a warm demander*. Ed Leadership. ASCD.

Stevenson, H. (2014). *Promoting racial literacy in school: differences that make a difference*. Teachers College Press.

Talusan, L. (2022). *The identity-conscious educator*. Solution Tree Press.

Washington, J. (n.d.). The Washington Consulting Group: leadership & diversity work. Retrieved from http://washingtonconsultinggroup.net

Zepeda, S., Yildirim, S., and Cevik, S. (2024). "Using classroom observation and schoolwide supervision data to facilitate culturally responsive conversations about diversity, equity, inclusion, and belonging." In Cormier, D. R., Mette, I. M., & Y. Oliveras, Y., eds. *Culturally Responsive instructional supervision: leadership for equitable and emancipatory outcomes* (pp. 166–187). Teachers College Press.

9

Practices to Tend to the Ecosystem

During the early months of the COVID-19 pandemic, Lori's partner spent her time planting a garden in their front and backyard. She first made a map of the yard and its dimensions, identified what existed, and then determined what could be planted. She chose a range of plants, some of which bore fruit and some of which were drought-tolerant to weather the impact of climate change. She selected each plant carefully. Over the next several years, she assessed the efficacy of the ecosystem she had developed. Going back to the map she developed and the notes she kept, she assessed how plants, vegetables, fruits, trees, and flowers grew in their conditions; what was needed by trellises and gardening stakes to guide growth; what drew invasive species and rodents; what to be moved and weeded out; and how everything stood in relation to everything else. On an ongoing basis, Lori's partner tends to the ecosystem and assesses how everything interacts. Based on how she developed this ecosystem, she created her own assessment tools specific to what exists within the environment.

By this time, you may have noticed that we give you a lot of choice and flexibility with the tools we offer. Keep equity at the foundation, but adapt these tools to meet the needs of your community and ensure teachers are providing equitable instruction that allows students to flourish. For this final chapter, we are sharing tools we have used to enhance the evaluation process: the Transformative Equity Practices (TEP) Assessment Framework,

Teacher Student Relationship Quality (TSRQ) Matrix, and Integrated Classroom Practices for Equity (ICPE). They are tools that assess the quality of the classroom environment, relationships between teachers and students, student engagement, and instructional practice. Use them as you see fit—whether adopting them or adapting them. We conclude this chapter by providing you with a process to reimagine evaluation, weaving all you have learned from this book to locate where educators stand, and to uphold a vision for equity in your community.

Transformative Equity Practices (TEP) Assessment Framework

Elizabeth was fortunate to work with a group of equity directors to bring together a wide variety of educators in various stages of their careers to create a teacher assessment tool that was both efficient and comprehensive. The group after a process they could design and utilize, and that collaboration yielded the TEP Assessment Framework. The Transformative Equity Practices Framework (TEP) builds on the foundational research connected to culturally responsive, affirming, and/or sustaining teaching pedagogies. We wanted to root our practice in transformative equity in order to directly challenge deficit ideologies about who is capable of learning and succeeding in our schools and on our campuses, and instead focus on strengths-based approaches to difference. We also had seen the term "culture" be co-opted in two ways: either it was used too broadly and generally to be effective, or it was just an indirect stand-in for Black and Latine students and families. Either way, these approaches did not create the kind of platform we needed to squarely address inequitable practices and their impact on students whose difference has been labeled as a deficit, not an asset. It also allowed us to consider multiple forms of difference and deficit thinking that together require an intersectional analysis (Crenshaw, 1991) in order to accurately name the issue and develop approaches to address *multiple* minoritized systems of harm. For example, a Black second grade student recently diagnosed with dyslexia will have to navigate both racism and ableism to ensure they get the transformative support they need and deserve. Ultimately, we wanted a collective tool that would help teachers more accurately self-assess their practice and establish common, observable data points. We worked to name key areas that teachers could focus on with supervisors to create an accurate picture of where they were in their professional development.

We designed the TEP assessment tool to support a commitment to faculty growth, and the process creates opportunities for evaluative feedback in five key areas:

1. Classroom environment
2. Instructional strategies
3. Classroom resources and materials
4. Relationship building
5. Professional growth

For each of five areas, you will see bulleted statements to support educators in assessing their relative standing and effectiveness and to identify areas for learning, shifts in practice, and development of new skills. Teachers and leaders provide evidence to support agreement or disagreement with their efficacy in these areas, and that evidence can be shared in a variety of ways: student work, student feedback, collegial observations, video recordings, and/or assessments. This process creates accountability for the teacher and provides important collaboration with a supervisor and/or peers as well as students.

1. **Classroom Environment**
    - I ensure an equitable classroom in which all students have a voice, are empowered, and are valued.
    - I organize my classroom so that the physical landscape includes images, materials, and resources that reflect a wide range of people and perspectives.
    - I create a classroom climate in which biased remarks are addressed and discussed and where students are encouraged to share and examine their perspectives and beliefs.

- ♦ I believe all students can experience academic success in classrooms that help them build positive identities as learners.
- ♦ I provide a classroom environment where interactions are mutually respectful and characterized by the willingness to acknowledge differences and gain knowledge and critical insight through the sharing of different perspectives.

2. **Instructional strategies**

    - ♦ I develop and use a variety of instructional strategies to encourage students' development of critical thinking and problem-solving.
    - ♦ I teach each lesson/unit using the students' experiences and prior knowledge to allow them to be a part of the knowledge-construction process.
    - ♦ I determine the success of my instructional strategies by noting whether each student has participated and whether a range of viewpoints has been considered.
    - ♦ I use a variety of assessment strategies to allow students to demonstrate an understanding of content and mastery of skills.
    - ♦ I initiate and facilitate discussions with students about topics related to community engagement, difference, and equitable outcomes.
    - ♦ I engage students in the analysis of key concepts and facts through activities and questions that consider multiple perspectives within and across subject matters.
    - ♦ I employ the elements of "wise feedback" (Hammond, 2014): holding high expectations while believing the student is capable and can improve with effort and offering specific, actionable steps to work on.

3. **Classroom resources and materials**

    - ♦ I provide opportunities for all students to see themselves reflected in the curriculum as well as to have perspectives into the experiences of others.
    - ♦ I address biases, stereotypes, inaccuracies, and marginalization in curricular content.

- I encourage students to compare, critique, evaluate, and use their own experiences as reference points for understanding and action.
- I choose materials and resources that expose students to a variety of perspectives that may or may not be part of their daily life experience.
- I employ a variety of developmentally appropriate media to stimulate student discussion and inquiry.
- I seek information about useful texts and materials from fellow faculty members and collaborate with colleagues to enhance curriculum resources.

4. **Relationship building**

   - I know my students' strengths and challenges and provide opportunities for each child to be successful in an environment of high expectations for all.
   - I am able to recognize how racism, ableism, sexism, economic injustice, and other forms of oppression may be operating around me, and how to disrupt them.
   - I build relationships with my students based on mutual trust and respect and enable my students to build similar relationships among themselves.
   - I attend to the social, emotional, and psychological health of all students to support and strengthen academic skill development.
   - I value both listening and speaking as integral parts of relational dialogue in my interactions with families and colleagues.
   - I initiate and sustain connections with all families in my classroom, and I provide equitable access to information.

5. **Professional growth**

   - I educate myself in an ongoing way about people who are leading practitioners, thinkers, and creators of resources that relate to my content area/level and transformative equity practices.
   - I value a professional environment in which active inquiry, diverse perspectives, and authentic feedback support my practice.

- I strive to be fully effective in my teaching by revitalizing my learning, adjusting and growing my practice, and revisiting my curriculum to be responsive to my students and their communities.
- I understand that in order to increase the learning opportunities for all students, I must be knowledgeable about the social and cultural contexts of teaching and learning.
- I identify assumptions and biases—both explicit and implicit—that affect my ability to provide all students with an equal opportunity to attain academic and social success.
- I commit to a process for professional feedback and expect to have authentic conversations regarding the institution's expectations and implementation of this assessment.

Using the TEP Tool

Our general approach involves scaffolding of the five areas (1. classroom environment, 2. instructional strategies, 3. classroom resources and materials, 4. relationship building, 5. professional growth) based on where a teacher is in their career. For example, a new teacher would be working on all five areas during the first years of their tenure, and they would work with their supervisor and/or mentor to identify priorities from year to year—as opposed to trying to do everything at once. A more veteran teacher would partner with their supervisor to focus on one or two areas during their evaluation process, ensuring more focused and in-depth development based on what that particular teacher needs to improve. For a struggling teacher, this tool can help pinpoint *specific* areas needed for improvement. A leader could identify a particular focus or a few statements within one area to build out an improvement plan. Observations and feedback would center on that teacher's discrete needs.

Most districts and schools have cycles for evaluation, typically based on years served, so the TEP tool could be integrated into an existing program. For example, Elizabeth worked with a school to develop a three-year cycle for experienced teachers in years 4–15 of their career. In the first year of the cycle, they identified key areas for growth after completing an assessment of their work to date in the five areas. After looking over student feedback and work samples as well as classroom observation data from both a peer and their supervisor, the teacher would decide on two to three goals to focus on for the following year. One teacher really wanted to improve his assessment strategies and see if he really had high expectations for all of his students. So, in year 2 of his cycle, he attended a professional development series on equitable grading practices and invited peers into his classroom to use the TSRQ matrix and give him feedback. He then compared that feedback with patterns of achievement in his classes. In year three, he focused on revamping his assessment strategies based on what he had learned via professional development. Then it was time for him to return to the TEP tool to do a bigger scan and to identify new areas for development. For his next cycle, he decided to focus on collegial relationships. Reflections in area 5 (professional growth) had highlighted some conflicts with his peers, especially around curricular choices, and so he wanted to work on his collaboration skills as well as giving/receiving feedback to/from adults, including parents and caregivers.

The TEP assessment tool helps educators to avoid overwhelm and provide focused and concrete areas for improvement. By having one or two goals a year, a teacher can experience growth and success. When the goals are specific and there is relevant data that can be gathered and analyzed, teachers can be empowered to make critical shifts in practice. And by having five areas to focus on, as opposed to 20 or 40 as some tools have, it is digestible and can really identify important inflection points to improve teaching/learning across the board.

Classroom Observation Tools

In many growth and evaluation structures, observation is a key feature of determining what shifts in practice look like. Witnessing a teacher's practice is essential in the growth and evaluation process because it creates an important dialogue where teachers can reflect on their own practice with a collaborator. The two observation tools we're most drawn to are the Teacher–Student Relationship Quality Matrix (TSRQ) (Boykin & Noguera, 2011) and Integrated Classroom Practices for Equity (ICPE).

Teacher–Student Relationship Quality Matrix

The TSRQ identifies the degree to which teachers display empathy, support, encouragement, and optimism in their interactions with students. Classroom observers can assess visible signs of student engagement and the efforts a teacher is making to support student learning and growth and to have high expectations for all. TSRQ also takes into account the degree to which teachers are perceived to be fair, genuine, and non-patronizing not only in their praise but also with their feedback.

How it works: The observer will first create a map of the classroom so they can indicate where students and the teacher are located. Observers then would determine the location of the teacher and students in the classroom, also indicating identifiers such as race, gender identity/expression, multilingual learners, and so on. It's helpful if observers are already aware of classroom demographics *before* observing to ensure that they are accurately indicating student identifiers and classroom patterns. Examples of proximity to particular students are important to consider, especially for those students who experience marginalization/bias: Is the teacher avoiding some students? Only working with certain groups of students or particular areas of the room? The following are some examples of identifiers:

Racial/ethnic identifiers

- Black/African American (B)
- Latine (L)
- Indigenous (I)
- Asian (A)
- White (W)
- Middle Eastern/North African (ME)
- Multiracial (M)

Gender identifiers:

- Girl (G)
- Boy (B)
- Non-binary/non-conforming (N)
- Transgender (Tr)

The observer then will fill in the classroom map so they can observe interactions. They'll locate the teacher's position in the classroom, indicating the teacher with the letter T, and then fill in where the students are located.

Once the observer has identified student demographics and teacher location, they'll monitor patterns of the student–teacher interaction by identifying how many times the teacher engages with a particular student. They'll indicate these interactions by keeping a tally underneath where the student is located. Observers will also track teacher movements during the lesson and what they say and do. The following are some examples of what observers might observe:

Track teacher interactions as positive/negative/neutral and note how often and for whom the teacher:

- greets students as they enter the classroom
- praises students specifically and authentically
- provides criticism
- redirects behaviors publicly/privately
- uses wait time when facilitating conversations
- extends student learning via inquiry (vs giving students the correct answer)
- gives the benefit of the doubt consistently
- bridges learning/comments to other students and/or connects new concepts/ideas to prior knowledge
- promotes productive struggle via encouragement, empathy, and support

When observing, it's helpful to focus on a snapshot of classroom practice. Focusing on a shorter timeframe could yield a rich discussion. Sometimes if observers spend an hour in a classroom and tally all the different kinds of teacher–student interactions, it can feel overwhelming to know what to focus on. We advocate that observers focus on a segment of the lesson—the beginning, middle, or ending—observing at least one transition from one activity to the next. We also advocate for observers to ask the teacher which time of class they should observe (ideally an area the teacher could use some support with). It's also hard to focus on all the elements of TSRQ at one time, so we often select two to three key things we are going to look for. For the observation itself, an example of this might look like the following (Figure 9.1):

	Front of classroom			
		T		
B-B III	G-L I	N-M 0	G-B III	G-B 0
B-L II	G-W II	G-W II	B-M I	G-L 0
G-B 0	B-A 0	G-A I	G-W 0	B-W II
B-B	B-L	B-L	G-L	G-A
	Back of classroom			

Timestamp	Examples of Teacher Actions	Examples of Student Actions
8:10	Greeted students at the door	Each student could choose high five, fist bump, handshake, salute
8:15	Praised student for sitting correctly at morning meeting	
	Redirected B-B for off-task behavior publicly	B-B shared they weren't off-task
	Praised G-B for the right answer	G-B smiled
8:20	Asked for volunteer to read board	G-W volunteered and read
	Teacher praised G-W student	

FIGURE 9.1 Sample classroom figure for TSRQ matrix

After the lesson, the observer and teacher can reflect on this tool together. It's important for the observers to focus on what they noticed without interpretation, but, instead, invite the teacher into the conversation to observe what they noticed. The observer may want to preface the discussion by sharing their methodology and what they were looking for. The observer should allow more time for the teacher to share their perceptions and reflections rather than the observer sharing what they noticed first. Some sample questions the observer might ask when sharing the TSRQ could be:

- How do you feel that segment of the lesson went?
- What did you notice about your interactions with students?
- How did your observations align/misalign with the TSRQ matrix data?
- What does the TSRQ matrix spark for you regarding learning and growth?
- What do you want to stop doing, start doing, or continue doing with students?
- What's your next step to make that happen?
- What might get in the way?
- How will you address what might get in the way?
- What support do you need?
- How will you be accountable?

Integrated Classroom Practices for Equity

While observing teacher–student interactions is one approach to supporting teacher growth, another way is through looking for patterns related to instruction, engagement, and environment. We have found that observation rubrics can be quite cumbersome, and when observers are watching teachers practice, they spend more time looking down at the checklist of items than they do at what's happening in the classroom. As we have noted previously, many evaluation systems don't embed culturally responsive teaching patterns into their evaluation rubrics. Or, if culturally responsive teaching is embedded in the evaluation framework, it's typically an add-on that teachers haven't received enough support and training on. Inspired by the work of Chism (2022) and del Carmen Salazar and Lerner (2019), we created the ICPE and observation guide (Table 9.1 & Figure 9.2) that support

TABLE 9.1 Integrated Classroom Practices for Equity Rubric

Competency	Instruction		
	High Pattern ←—————	— Some Pattern —————	→ Low Pattern
Learning Objectives Learning objectives are clear and communicated effectively. Outcomes align with content standards and appropriately challenge students' current abilities.	• All students understand the learning goals and can explain them in their own words. • Outcomes are challenging and achievable.	• Learning goals are unclear or could be communicated more effectively. • Outcomes are only challenging or are age-appropriate for a few students.	• Learning goals are not communicated or are very low in expectation. • Outcomes are not challenging or relevant to most students.
Lesson Design Lessons align with clear objectives, engaging activities, and relevant feedback and formative assessments. Content is connected to students' lives and incorporates diverse perspectives and experiences.	• Lessons are well-designed, aligned with objectives, and contain engaging activities • Lessons contain formative assessments and opportunities for feedback that allow the teacher to adjust and students to understand progress • Content consistently connects to students' lives and draws from students' perspectives and experiences.	• Lessons contain somewhat clear objectives and engaging activities • Lessons somewhat contain formative assessments and opportunities for feedback, but these efforts are cursory • Content somewhat considers diverse perspectives and experiences, but in a more stereotypical or tokenized fashion.	• Lessons are poorly designed and lack clear goals, and/or engaging activities • Lessons lack formative assessment and feedback opportunities • Content is irrelevant to students' lives and does not include or consider diverse perspectives and experiences; or the perspectives and experiences perpetuate harmful stereotypes.

(Continued)

TABLE 9.1 Integrated Classroom Practices for Equity Rubric (Continued)

Competency	Instruction		
	High Pattern ←———	——— Some Pattern ———	———→ Low Pattern
Complex Tasks Teacher uses a variety of complex questions and tasks to promote critical thinking, productive struggle, and student independence through appropriate scaffolding. Questions integrate diverse perspectives and experiences.	• Teacher offers challenging, complex questions and tasks; varies them effectively; promotes student independence through appropriate scaffolding; and integrates diverse perspectives and experiences.	• Teacher somewhat offers complex questions and tasks, or questions/tasks focus on recall rather than analysis or evaluation. • Students are somewhat independent, with many still relying on the teacher. • Diverse perspectives and experiences are superficially integrated.	• Teacher does not offer complex questions or tasks and/or questions and tasks focus on factual recall and replication of a teacher model. • Students remain dependent learners, either through overly scaffolded tasks or direct instruction. • Teacher relies on traditional representations of information rather than bringing in diverse perspectives and experiences.
High-Leverage Instructional Practices Teacher uses a variety of instructional practices that support student learning and are differentiated to meet the needs of diverse learners.	• Teacher draws upon an appropriate variety of instructional strategies to increase student learning. • Differentiation is evident through the ways diverse learners' needs are addressed.	• Teacher draws upon generic or overused instructional strategies so student learning is inconsistent. • Differentiation is somewhat evident to meet the needs of most learners.	• Teacher uses direct instruction and/or misaligned methods that fail to meet students' learning needs. • Differentiation is mildly evident or not evident, or only meets the needs of a few learners.

(Continued)

TABLE 9.1 Integrated Classroom Practices for Equity Rubric (Continued)

Competency	Engagement		
	High Pattern ←—————	————— Some Pattern —————	—————→ Low Pattern
Student Participation All students are actively participating and engaged in learning that is explicit and visible. Students are carrying the cognitive load and co-constructing their learning.	• Students are actively participating and their learning is visible. • Students feel affirmed and experience joy as part of the learning process. • Students are performing and expressing learning with teacher as facilitator.	• Half or fewer students are actively participating, and their learning is somewhat visible. • Some students feel affirmed or experience joy as part of the learning process. • Students are somewhat performing and expressing learning with teacher, but rely on teacher direction.	• Students are not actively participating and/or learning is not visible. • The learning environment is not positive or inclusive for most students. • Students are passive learners and/or disruptions are having an impact on learning.
Perseverance All students are encouraged to persist, and they work through challenges. Teacher serves as a warm demander, demonstrating care and encouragement while holding students to high expectations.	• Students are actively encouraged to persist and they work through challenges. • Teacher provides specific feedback, support, steps for improvement and independence. • Teacher consistently holds high expectations and encourages students to meet those expectations.	• Some students are encouraged to persist and most work through challenges. • Teacher is somewhat consistent in supporting all learners and provides feedback that creates dependence on the teacher. • Teacher somewhat holds high expectations, but these expectations may be uneven.	• Students are not encouraged to persist and/or may be discouraged from trying. • Teacher easily gives up on students who struggle, and does not provide support for learning. • Teacher lowers expectations, particularly for those from marginalized backgrounds.

(Continued)

TABLE 9.1 Integrated Classroom Practices for Equity Rubric (Continued)

Competency	Environment		
	High Pattern ← — — — —	— — — Some Pattern — — —	— — — → Low Pattern
Strong, Supportive Relationships Teacher and students demonstrate mutual respect through trust building, clear communication, and active listening. Teacher and students are adaptive and flexible when necessary, especially in times of harm; they engage in practices that address harm and repair relationships, centering the dignity of those impacted. Teacher and students practice appreciation and celebration for learning and growth.	• Teacher and students consistently demonstrate mutual respect through trust building, clear communication, and active listening. • Teacher and students remain adaptive and flexible when necessary, especially in times of harm. • Teacher and students engage actively and willingly in practices that address harm and repair relationships. • Teacher and students consistently practice appreciation and celebration for learning and growth.	• Teacher and students somewhat demonstrate respect through trust building, communication, or active listening, but could improve in one or more of these areas. • Teacher and students are somewhat adaptive and flexible when necessary, sometimes in times of harm. • Teacher and students engage reluctantly in practices that address harm and repair relationships. • Teacher and students sometimes practice appreciation and celebration for learning and growth.	• There are evident breakdowns in mutual respect, trust, communication, or active listening. • Teacher and/or students are not adaptive and/or flexible when necessary, especially in times of harm. • Teacher uses teacher-directed practices to address harm without considering impact on relationships. • Appreciation and/or celebration are not apparent for learning and growth.
Classroom Climate The classroom climate is positive, physically and psychologically safe, and conducive to learning. Students feel confident to take risks, make mistakes, and ask questions.	• The classroom climate is positive, safe, and conducive to learning for all students. • Students are actively taking risks, making mistakes, and asking questions.	• The classroom climate is uneven and is somewhat positive, safe, or conducive to learning. • Students feel somewhat confident to take risks, make mistakes, and ask questions.	• The classroom climate is not positive, safe, or conducive to learning for most students. • Students are not taking risks, making mistakes or asking questions.

Practices to Tend to the Ecosystem ◆ 239

observers in identifying equitable patterns of instruction. We break down the rubric (Table 9.1) into three core elements of classroom practice: instruction, engagement, and environment. Within each broad category, we offer a series of competencies and their definitions, along with examples of what high, some, and low patterns of practice might look like. The observation guide (Figure 9.2) is a blank document that observers can use when

Instruction			
Competency	High Pattern ← Some Pattern → Low Pattern		Questions/Comments
Learning Objectives			
Lesson Design			
Complex Tasks			
High-Leverage Teaching Strategies			
Engagement			
Competency	High Pattern ← Some Pattern → Low Pattern		Questions/Comments
Student Participation			
Perseverance			
Environment			
Competency	High Pattern ← Some Pattern → Low Pattern		Questions/Comments
Strong, Supportive Relationships			
Classroom Climate			

FIGURE 9.2 Integrated classroom practices for equity observation guide

they observe classes. There is space to indicate where a teacher falls in relation to each pattern and a place for comments and questions. Your school may already have a rubric that can serve this same purpose, though we advocate you assess to what degree cultural responsiveness is embedded into the categories of effectiveness. Are there specific examples of what cultural responsiveness looks and sounds like? If not, this may be a good time to invite a conversation about what else needs to be included.

How to use it: Whether in a whole staff meeting, a one-on-one coaching or mentoring conversation, or in a supervisor-supervisee conversation, invite teachers to familiarize themselves with the rubric. Teachers might self-assess where they fall in relation to the rubric categories and compare the observation data to their self-assessment. Before the observation, ask teachers to consider one area they want to be observed for. Even though we've broken down this rubric into three broad categories, a focus on a single area would be more useful than addressing too many factors at once. For the observation itself, use the blank guide (Figure 9.2) to assess roughly where the teacher falls in relation to the category they identified. Share at least two questions or insights based on what you observed and share these insights with the teacher in advance of the conversation so they have some time to reflect and process.

Process to Reimagine Evaluation

Imagine a terrarium. Each layer—the rocks, the soil, the plants—depends on the others for balance and health. Evaluation, in this metaphor, isn't an afterthought or an add-on; it's a way to check how the terrarium is holding up. Are the roots getting what they need? Are the plants growing as they should? Are there weeds or pests that need attention? If the terrarium starts to falter, it's a signal to adjust the conditions for everything to flourish. Evaluation helps us understand what's thriving, what's struggling, and what needs extra care. Evaluation can't be separated from equity, well-being, or growth. It's the culmination of those practices—an ongoing part of the school's culture rather than an isolated, high-stakes event.

A Process to Reimagine Evaluation

Step 1: Establish a Collaborative Design Team
Start by forming a diverse team of teachers, administrators, instructional coaches, and additional community members. This team ensures multiple perspectives inform the process and fosters ownership across the school or district. Establish agreements for how you'll work together, and create room for productive struggle. Also consider forms of compensation should this work take place outside of community members' existing workloads. Reimagining evaluation is about breaking out of traditional methods, so make sure the team you compile wants to envision something bolder than what has been done, something that weaves equity more thoroughly in the process.

Step 2: Conduct Research and Explore Best Practices
Investigate what's out there: effective evaluation models that align with equity-centered approaches. Grounding the process in proven strategies helps balance imagination with practicality. Many districts have already adopted evaluation models, such as the Danielson framework, and may be unable to overhaul everything. However, the team can consider augmenting existing tools with essential practices in equity-centered evaluation tools. For example, consider how the ICPE rubric might be a tool for teacher observation and feedback.

Step 3: Gather Input from Community Members Along the Way
Use surveys, focus groups, or listening sessions to understand educators' experiences with past evaluations and their aspirations for a reimagined process. Invite them to share challenges, successes, and practical suggestions. Educators' insights ensure the evaluation system is relevant and inclusive of community input.

Step 4: Develop Core Components of the System
Design the evaluation in ways that are dynamic, some of which include the following elements:

- **Multiple Measures**: Incorporate classroom observations, peer feedback, self-assessments, and student surveys.

- **Equity-Focused Tools**: Use street data gathering methods, the TSRQ tool, ICPE rubric, and observation guide alongside quantitative measures to identify and address inequities.
- **Collaborative Feedback**: Structure protocols for collaborative dialogue about teacher performance.
- **Reflective Practices**: Embed opportunities for ongoing reflection in the process.

A system consisting of these components can make evaluation feel less static, more dynamic, and more human-centered.

Step 5: Pilot the System and Iterate
Test the redesigned evaluation system with a small group of educators. A pilot phase helps identify gaps and adjust for what needs revision. Gather feedback, refine the tools, and adjust timelines or processes as needed before full implementation.

Step 6: Implement and Monitor
Roll out the refined evaluation system school- or districtwide. Provide training and professional development for evaluators to ensure consistent, equitable application. Continuous monitoring ensures that the evaluation process evolves to meet new challenges. Regular focus groups might highlight emerging needs for professional development in culturally sustaining pedagogy. Use ongoing surveys and focus groups to monitor its effectiveness and make adjustments.

Let's explore an example of what this looks like in practice. Abundance Academy had spent two years revising its equity and growth structures, ensuring teachers, particularly new ones, were trained in practices that best-supported students with learning differences. After dedicated time and a fractal approach to addressing these needs in their community, they took on the challenge of reimagining its teacher evaluation system to make the process meaningful, equitable, and growth-oriented.

The redesign process kicked off with a committee of teachers and leaders from across the school, a range of people with different experiences and perspectives. The committee conducted research on existing models of evaluation and what these approaches had in common. They also conducted empathy interviews with their school's community members who had undergone the existing evaluation to better understand what worked and what the pain points were. Balancing research with empathy interviews, the committee brainstormed what their evaluation model might look, sound, and feel like. The administrator facilitating the group encouraged committee members to get imaginative about evaluation and consider metaphors, symbols, and nontraditional ways evaluations could be designed and conducted. After a summer of brainstorming and imagining, the committee came up with a roadmap for an evaluation they hoped would be dynamic and empowering.

Over the next year, as administrators continued with the existing evaluation model, committee members completed small experiments as they designed: They piloted ideas like new classroom observation tools and individualized pathways for growth. One big hurdle in the process was finding the balance between the creative ideas they generated in the summer and the realities of time and resources once the school year was underway. The committee addressed this challenge by designing team-based evaluations, spreading out the workload, and training evaluators to align on how they assessed teacher practice and provided feedback. Another challenge in the design process was how to address the natural fear and skepticism teachers had about evaluation. Some teachers worried it might feel punitive. The team worked hard to shift people's perceptions, focusing on building relationships and trust while maintaining high expectations for performance.

After a year of design, the committee entered its pilot phase: They invited two groups of educators, those early in their careers and those with a longer tenure, to be part of the pilot cohort using these new structures, which included team-based approaches, common assessment methods, and differentiated approaches that took into account teachers' years of experience and backgrounds. The results of the pilot were promising but not without areas to address. Teachers who underwent evaluation appreciated the supportive approach and actionable feedback that came from multiple evaluators. It wasn't about one person's perspective but a combination of voices helping them see different aspects of their teaching. Teachers even described it as feeling more like a partnership by the end of the pilot year.

Many teachers noticed real growth in their practice, and some even found it exciting to reflect on their progress. That said, the evaluation committee also learned what needed tweaking—like clearer protocols for observations and better support for more experienced teachers. At the time of writing this book, Abundance Academy has moved toward full implementation. To maintain a dynamic approach, school leaders have set aside time each year to make adjustments to the system, ensuring it continues to reflect the school's values and equity objectives. Additionally, they have planned a comprehensive review of the system every five years. The school's redesign process is a testament to what's possible when schools take their time and stay open in the process of reimagining evaluation.

Tending the ecosystem, just as with gardening, requires ongoing reflection and adaptation, recognizing that "the way we've always done it" isn't necessarily meeting the needs of the moment. Rather than doing something efficient for the sake of checking a box, our ecosystem metaphor reminds us that growth takes time and care. Schools are interdependent places, where every element—from students and teachers to curriculum and pedagogy and beyond—relies on careful oversight to ensure the ecosystem remains healthy for all its community members. By drawing upon tools like the TEP Assessment Framework, the TSRQ Matrix, and ICPE, we can tend to the ecosystem in ways where growth is not only measured but also nurtured through practices that center on community care and human dignity. We can be accountable for cultivating classroom cultures that center justice, possibility, and transformation—and ensure schools can be places where all community members can flourish and thrive.

Summary

This chapter emphasizes the processes leaders can use to tend the ecosystem—using tools to center human dignity in evaluation and reimagining evaluation processes. Key tools like the Transformative Equity Practices (TEP) Assessment Framework, Teacher Student Relationship Quality (TSRQ) Matrix, and Integrated Classroom Practices for Equity (ICPE) rubric focus on assessing classroom environments, instructional strategies, and equitable teacher–student interactions that are learner centered and promote high expectations. The chapter also outlines a collaborative, six-step process for redesigning evaluation systems, emphasizing community input, piloting, and equity-focused tools. Ultimately, tending the ecosystem of education requires ongoing reflection and adaptation to create schools where all community members can thrive.

For Further Reflection

1. How can evaluation systems be designed to prioritize equity and growth while addressing the specific needs of diverse educators and students?
2. In what ways can tools like the TEP Framework, TSRQ Matrix, and the ICPE be adapted to reflect the unique contexts and values of your school community?
3. What strategies can be implemented to shift the perception of evaluation from a punitive process to one centered on trust, collaboration, and continuous growth?
4. How can schools ensure that evaluation systems remain dynamic and responsive to changing needs while maintaining their commitment to equity and justice?

References

Boykin, A. W., & Noguera, P. (2011). *Creating the opportunity to learn: Moving from research to practice to close the achievement gap.* ASCD.

Chism, D. (2022). *Leading your school toward equity: A practical framework for walking the talk.* ASCD.

Crenshaw, K. (1991). "Mapping the margins: Intersectionality, identity politics, and violence against women of color." *Stanford Law Review*, 43(6).

del Carmen Salazar, M., & Lerner, J. (2019). *Teacher evaluation as cultural practice: A framework for equitable and effective teaching.* Routledge.

Hammond, Z. (2014). *Culturally responsive teaching and the brain: Promoting authentic engagement and rigor among culturally and linguistically diverse students.* Corwin.

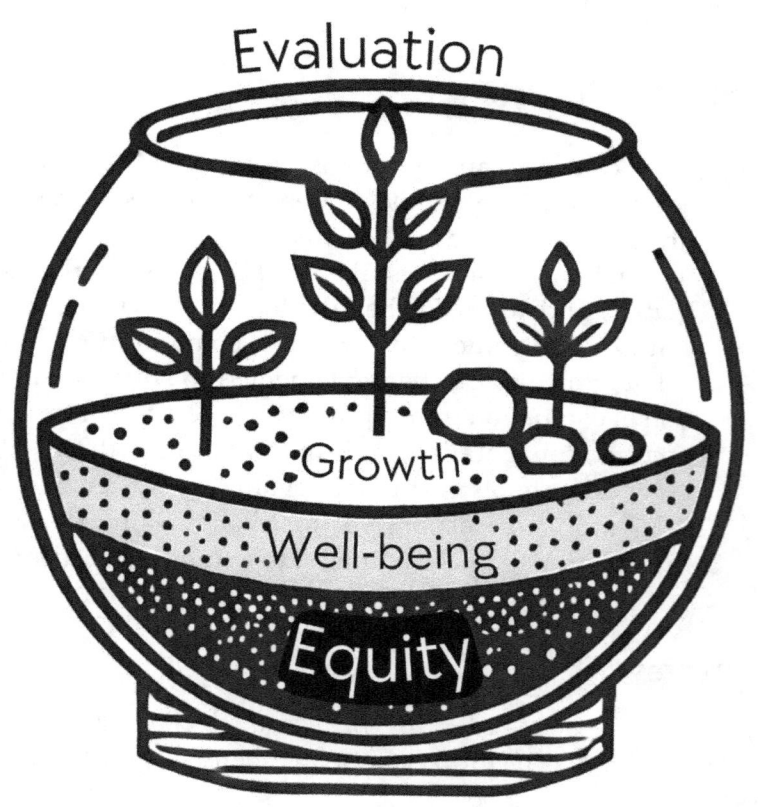

10

Conclusion

A Transformative Perspective

When writing the final pages of this book, we took a writing retreat outside Portland, Oregon, where we both currently live, and met at a cabin in the evergreen forests in the state of Washington. To get there, we drove a 65-mile stretch of highway in the Columbia Gorge, the Columbia River to our left, enormous rock faces dotted with evergreen trees and waterfalls to our right. The landscape is nothing short of dramatic and sublime: The Columbia River is a mile across at its widest points; the rock faces, some of which reach heights of 4,000 feet, have been sculpted over millions of years by volcanic eruptions, floods, and landslides. The Gorge is a biodiverse haven, with ecosystems ranging from grasslands to alpine crags, supporting over 800 plant species and 200 bird species. For thousands of years, Indigenous communities were stewards of the almost 3,000 acres of land—the Confederated Tribes of Warm Springs, the Confederated Tribes and Bands of the Yakama Nation, the Confederated Tribes of the Umatilla Indian Reservation, the Nez Perce Tribe, the Confederated Tribes of Grand Ronde, and the Cowlitz Indian Tribe.

As we traveled to the cabin, we thought about this planet, these rock formations, the river, the abundance of trees, the ecosystems, the weight of the history of colonialism and its ensuing systems: Systems, created by people, that have displaced communities, forced assimilation, put an already fragile planet into the throes of climate collapse, created narrow definitions of privilege and power that those with more historical advantage have access to, leaving so many on the margins believing that success is a scarce resource only available to a small few.

There's a lot to see about what's wrong with the world when the daily reality for so many is injustice. When those who were the original caretakers of the land have experienced so much harm. When the planet warms and human activity is the main driver for climate chaos. When the system of education is designed for assimilation, giving those with the most historical advantage greater access to silos of privilege and power. At the same time, the Indigenous communities who were the original caretakers of this land are still here, often advising local officials how to better tend to the Gorge's fragile ecosystems. While wildfires are more prevalent in this region, the evergreens demonstrate their resilience through regenerating after decimation. While schools continue to perpetuate inequities, there are visionaries like you, the ones reading this book, who imagine a different reality for our students—one that is possible through intentional, fractal steps—who believe success is not a scarce resource and every student has the opportunity to demonstrate their brilliance.

When astronauts travel to space and orbit the earth, some of them experience what is known as the Overview Effect (NASA). The Overview Effect, a term first coined by author Frank White after interviewing numerous astronauts, is a cognitive shift characterized by a sense of awe, beauty, and a profound realization of the planet's fragility and interconnectedness. This phenomenon often leads to a heightened sense of responsibility toward environmental stewardship and a deeper connection to humanity as a whole. Many of us won't have the good fortune to experience the planet at such a distance, but at the same time, a shift from a transactional perspective to a transformative one at any scale can be the catalyst we need to reimagine what's possible on this blue dot we call planet Earth.

When we first embarked on the drive through the Columbia Gorge to our retreat cabin, we both had much on our minds.

For Elizabeth, her graduate students were doing their final presentations, and she was assessing their work from the term. One of her children was coming home from college soon and another had final exams to study for. For Lori, she was winding down a busy autumn of work, preparing for the holiday season consisting of elder care and travel, she and her partner supporting aging and ailing parents. We also had an impending book deadline, the time when we handed our year's worth of work into the hands of editors and eventually into the hands of leaders like you. In the weeds of lives and work, we were too enmeshed in the busyness of our days to pause and take perspective. Thus, we decided to get away to review our final manuscript, to be out in the natural world for some perspective-taking. The natural world has been a grounding force and our greatest teacher when writing this book. Neither of us is versed in ecosystems, but we are experienced in the world of schools and addressing inequities. In writing this book, we took a step back from the world we knew and explored a world outside our daily reality; the lessons we learned from ecosystems, from what has existed long before us and will likely outlive us, has been an invaluable guide for how we might reimagine what's possible for educators in schools.

It would be egotistical for us to think that your experience of this book might yield you something similar to the Overview Effect. But we do hope something in this book sparked your imagination on a more fractal level. Perhaps as you read this book, you thought differently about how to engage your community around equity. Perhaps you thought of how you might systematize well-being efforts to be inclusive of educators, particularly those most historically on the margins. Perhaps you have a method for setting goals or implementing growth structures that is aligned with your school or district's values. Perhaps you are eschewing the more favored approaches to teacher evaluation for something more co-creative and organic. Whatever perspective you've gained from reading this book, from fractal to universal, we hope you feel equipped to build the "terrarium" of educator support at your site that has a transformative impact on the students, educators, and broader community.

Digging In

As you begin to dig into the details of this work, we offer some final advice for the journey.

Advice for Schools

- Prioritize: Pick one initiative, make a substantive shift, and then move to the next priority. Remember that less is often more, and focus builds efficacy in our busy, complicated school systems.
- Focus on your sphere of influence and control: The quickest route to burnout comes when we try to change things that are not within our control. Try not to bang your head against brick walls, and don't do anything alone. Collaboration will win the day.
- Stay fractal: Small, incremental actions make a difference. Avoid addressing all dimensions of well-being when taking on one dimension in depth may impact the others. Try out one classroom observation tool and adapt it. Invite community members to set one equity action in service of the school's vision.
- Persevere, don't perseverate: Ecosystems don't flourish in a day. Making some of these changes won't be easy. Laying a foundation, nurturing the soil, cultivating growth, and tending the ecosystem all require persistence and intentionality. Go easy on yourselves when you hit setbacks and rely on the innovators and early adopters to keep you motivated. Think about the students for whom you do this work and hold them in mind as you build an ecosystem that best supports their learning.

Advice for Districts

- Get proximate: Be on the ground with principals; they need more support. Really think about the times you are asking them to leave their buildings. Could you go to them instead? How can you help them serve as instructional leaders by doing more to support the management of their buildings?

- Practice collaboration: Work with, not over or even away from, building leaders. Build coalitions and leverage the power of the group. Ask schools what they need versus what you have been told or think they need.
- Do less and do it better: Identify the one thing that could have the greatest impact. In other words, what might you do that could have an impact on how schools address equity? Or how educators are compensated? Or how support structures look at schools? Do you want to invest the time and energy into a coaching program? Do you want to bring together school leaders to reimagine district evaluation? One initiative will gain more traction than a saturation of surface-level ideas.
- Place people over projects: It's easy to get lost in test score data and feel pressure from state legislatures. It's easy to fall prey to the latest trends and adopt curricula that promise instant results. Amidst the analytics, remember the people and how you can best support them in reimagining what's possible at their school sites.

Advice for Education Partners

- Value being the outsider: You can see things schools/districts can't because they are too in the weeds. How can you leverage perspective-taking? Provide new insights and possibilities?
- Provide transformative professional learning: What training and support can you offer for districts and schools to increase their skill and capacity in supporting equity, well-being, growth, and evaluation? How might you partner with districts and schools in designing learning opportunities that are specific to schools' needs and populations? How might you co-create the conditions for productive struggle, visioning, and joy? As a community partner, be bold in how you design the supports that transform schools in your region.
- Advocate for change at the state level: You have more proximity to state departments of education. School and district leaders are often too busy to try to push upwards.

You are in a great position to put pressure on state/government officials to make necessary changes.
- Think outside the box: Be the incubator for visionary ideas. Tend to the ecosystems of your region and model more courageous leadership by taking risks. Try not to repeat well-worn paths that may not be leading to more equitable outcomes.

Anticipate, Embrace, and Engage Resistance to Change

You may be enthusiastic leaders who are excited about transforming your communities. You may also have those innovators and early adopters who are already engaged in what's possible. And yet leaders need to develop their ability to both anticipate resistance and be prepared to address it once it comes. Too often equity advocates are derailed when opposition to a new policy or procedure emerges. They will blame themselves, saying they should have done more to ensure success, "If only our communication had been better!" Or they will demonize the resistors and laggards: "Can you believe they are going to challenge all of our hard work!" Either way, leaders of change can fall into an either/or trap that will pit them firmly against colleagues, board members, students, and families. Instead of viewing resistance as an opponent to be defeated, what would it mean to embrace and engage resistance when it comes?

Jamie Washington's (n.d.) "Enemy vs Energy" model is a framework used in organizational development to help people navigate resistance in conversations about change, particularly in discussions around diversity and equity. Resistance to shifting the status quo can come from individuals or groups who may feel threatened, uncomfortable, or defensive about the changes being proposed. Instead of being surprised or horrified by those who are resistant, equity advocates can anticipate what concerns may be raised during implementation and be strategic about how, not if, they can embrace resistance when it comes. Reframing resistance as engagement, Washington asserts that "resistance provides the energy needed to transform the current culture to a more desired state." Below are the core concepts for the two mental models, the Enemy Model and the Energy Model, for managing resistance.

In the **Enemy** Model, resistance:

- is something to be overcome, conquered, and controlled
- creates a fight or flight and win or lose contest
- positions some to seek to destroy while others feel they have lost the battle
- goes underground or becomes covert; we often get compliance, not change

In the **Energy** Model, resistance:

- is a set of positive, necessary disturbances
- creates energy for transformation
- is an indicator that real change is ahead
- acts as a protector of core values, rather than those espoused, and defines key taboos or unsaid issues in an organization

The Energy Model refers to the positive engagement that individuals or groups can bring to conversations and efforts around change. This can look like a willingness to listen and learn, genuine curiosity and open-mindedness, active participation in discussions (even if there is disagreement), and a focus on solutions and collaboration rather than conflict. The model underscores the importance of empathy and a focus on common goals in the face of resistance. Rather than seeing those who resist as obstacles or enemies, it encourages seeing them as part of the energy that can eventually be channeled toward positive change.

We have seen this reframing help leaders who are shifting evaluation policies toward greater equity. By anticipating the resistance to be expected whenever we try to change the status quo, leaders are ready to address concerns and keep the process moving. They can listen to colleagues who may be struggling with new expectations and meet them where they are to make a plan for growth. And for those like Angelica in Chapter 8 who are facing resistant leaders, the Energy Model helps to minimize burnout and frustration by positioning reluctance as the beginning of real engagement. When Elizabeth served as an equity director, she was often drained by the unwillingness of some to adopt more equitable practices. By realizing that colleagues generally only resist what they care about, she could leverage that care as a point of collaboration. And she didn't blame herself if people were reluctant. She asked for lots of feedback, made any necessary adjustments, and continued the work to make accountability systems more fair and effective.

Build Your Terrarium

With all this advice in mind, go back to Chapter 1 and revisit your Landscape Assessment. Now that you have read through the book, identify what your priorities are. What is your entry point? Where is the area of greatest need, and where might you have the greatest influence? Map out a plan of action and find an accountability buddy to go on this journey with you. Figure out what you'll plant and what tools you need. Don't forget to wear your gardening gloves to prevent blisters and splinters. Grab your favorite hat to provide shade from the sun. Allow the process to be challenging and joyful. We look forward to seeing what you've planted to transform the educational landscape—for the students and educators who deserve better conditions for learning, growth, and dignity.

Appendix A: Example Portrait of an Effective Educator

All educators exhibit strengths and growth areas that may fall into any of the categories listed below; in the classroom, more specifically, some teachers may find themselves emerging and developing in their skills even after having taught a long time, while others may find themselves exhibiting the strengths and qualities of a mentor or master teacher prior to achieving those years of experience. The following are broad descriptions that encapsulate the types of strengths one exhibits in each category. The following categories account for our work on Teacher Effectiveness as well as pull from current research related to state and national teacher performance standards.

Community Practices	
Characteristics	*Looks and Sounds Like*
Equity and Inclusion	• Through classroom and schoolwide practices, promotes the site's vision for equity in order to ensure that students and colleagues have what they need to be successful
	• Engages in one's own ongoing personal and professional development to develop skills and practices in service of the school's values of diversity, equity, inclusion, and belonging
Collaboration and Community Engagement	• Provides support (e.g., input, feedback, communication, time) to the community when needed and participates in community endeavors that serve students
	• Serves as a leader on collaborative teams and/or frequently provides useful and probing insights in content-area and course team meetings
	• Actively seeks to collaborate within and outside the content area or grade level and models thoughtful leadership on teams and in the school
	• Serves in an advising capacity in support of whole-student development and works closely with families and school community members to ensure student success

Professional and/or Curriculum Development	• Continues to develop a deep understanding of content-area-related skills and content • Individually, in teams, can develop a curricular scope and sequence using the principles of backwards design • Seeks professional development opportunities that deepen or highlight individual's growth areas and/or strives to present professional development within and/or outside the school
Innovation and Technology	• Tries and refines new methodologies/pedagogies to improve student learning and development • Demonstrates familiarity and facility with school-based and third-party party programs that impact student learning • Possesses a growth orientation related to technology and its benefit for student learning, including discernment around which technologies best support student learning
Mindfulness	• Whether through the development of one's own practice or through supporting the school's values, practices mindfulness skills to support student learning and growth • Approaches work with a learning mindset, staying open to new experiences, and skillfully managing the complex demands of working in a school

Classroom Practices

Characteristics	Looks and Sounds Like
Establishes a Safe Learning Environment	• Projects an authentic, welcoming, appropriately boundaried teacher persona • Invites all types of students to participate and makes space for different voices • Validates students while still redirecting and/or challenging them to meet high expectations • Shows awareness of group dynamic and individual needs in a range of ways that best meet the needs of students • Provides clear structure, communications, and expectations so that the class is directed toward learning

Designs Thoughtful Lessons	• Lesson has a clear and realistic structure that is developmentally appropriate for students • Lessons contain clear objectives in clear and transparent ways • Lesson demonstrates attention to skill development and content acquisition in a way students can clearly articulate • Lesson demonstrates attention to diverse learning needs and modes of expressing learning • Lesson contains effective pacing and transitions while also remaining flexible and adaptive • Activities are intentional, and the teacher clearly communicates intentions to the students
Utilizes Diverse, Effective Pedagogies	• Taps students' funds of knowledge and experience in a range of ways • Uses a variety of multimodal, student-centered, culturally responsive, and sustaining teaching practices that best meet learners where they are—and challenges learners to meet high expectations • Checks for understanding through a broad range of formative assessment strategies • Is responsive to what is happening in the room and makes adjustments to classroom practice
Respectfully Interacts, Challenges, and Engages with Students	• Demonstrates passion for subject matter as well as for learning and teaching; that passion is contagious in the classroom setting • Pitches content at a level that engages and challenges students • Consistently asks thoughtful and thought-provoking questions that encourage critical thinking and collaboration among students • Demonstrates genuine curiosity for students' point of view and is able to draw out a range of students • Demonstrates understanding of individual students' developmental needs • Offers feedback that validates and/or redirects the student response in a way that is encouraging

Evidences Sophisticated Content Understanding	• Through the questions posed and answered, shows multi-level understanding of subject matter • Able to answer most questions about the material—or knows how to find answers—particularly from non-traditional sources • Uses pedagogical content knowledge to help students access and master the material • Able to connect material to students' lives in ways that are complex and meaningful
Provides Intentional and Fair Assessments/ Feedback	• Develops assessments which effectively address skills and content taught/reinforced during the unit • Provides (or co-creates) and discusses the evaluation criteria (i.e., rubrics) for assessments with students; monitors student understanding of this criteria before, during, and after the assignment • Provides timely, actionable feedback that students can apply to improve skills and understanding • Analyzes student performance on assessments and makes informed adjustments to lesson plans/pedagogy • Models growth by asking for regular feedback from colleagues, supervisors, and students, and making changes to the course/ pedagogy informed by feedback (includes explaining how feedback was incorporated)

Appendix B: Professional Learning Choice Cohort Sample

Timeframe: one semester, meeting every third Wednesday from 3:35 to 4:50 (four meetings total)
This year's cohorts will be:

- *grounded in classroom practice and topics that center equity*
- *informed by relevant research*
- *structured around peer and collaborative learning*
- *differentiated based on teachers' needs*

Teachers will select their cohorts based on how they wish to engage and learn. Through a choice of approaches, each teacher will draw on their direct experiences of the classroom as a foundation for learning. Through a balance of classroom practice and current research practices, we will deepen our ability to reflect on and discuss how we might increase our efficacy for students, particularly those with significant barriers to learning.

Each cohort will establish agreements for their meetings, work to center trust and psychological safety, and discuss the ways they like to receive feedback (where applicable).

There will be four PLCCs, each of which offers a different vehicle through which we will learn together:

1. **Observation Partnerships**: Teachers will be grouped in observation partnerships and will develop their skills as observers, listeners, and givers and receivers of feedback. Using a variety of tools and approaches to observation, partners will observe each other's classrooms and review lessons together. They will examine data, offer growth-oriented feedback, and provide strategies for growth.
2. **Video Observation and Analysis**: Video can be a powerful tool for learning about classroom practice. In this group, teachers will use structured protocols to observe, share, and analyze both their own teaching video clips and those of others in the group. We will offer options for different ways in which video can be used and shared according to a range of comfort levels.
3. **Student Work Analysis**: Teachers will use structured protocols to collect, analyze, and learn from student work and data. Teachers will gain new insights into the thinking of their students, identify strengths and weaknesses in their assignments, and gather data to inform future instruction.
4. **Action research**: Action research is a form of investigation aimed at improving an aspect of classroom practice through systematic observations and data collection that are used in reflection, decision-making, and the development of more effective classroom strategies. Using the five phases of action research, teachers will (1) select an area of focus, (2) collect data, (3) organize data, (4) analyze and interpret data, and (5) create and implement action plans. Teachers in this group will also be asked to study professional research around their area of focus and will be invited to share their findings with their PLCC.

Once teachers have selected their PLCC and established community agreements, each teacher will then determine their area of focus (aligned with our portrait of an educator). Examples include but are not limited to:

- *using the science of learning to create differentiated lessons*
- *classroom culture strategies that inspire student learning*
- *exploring strategies that foster productive struggle and high expectations*
- *increasing student literacy and vocabulary acquisition*
- *explore modes of feedback that best meet student needs*
- *more equitable forms of assessment for the school's math competencies*

Each cohort will follow a similar structure:

- *Teachers will be asked to identify an area of focus (e.g., how can I increase students' opportunity for productive struggle without intervening too soon) for each semester.*
- *Teachers will work within the methodology of their cohort to explore their focal question.*
- *Facilitators will be provided with protocols, suggested agenda structures, and pacing guides. Each cohort will have one or two facilitators.*

Appendix C: Book Questions, Concepts, and Tools

Ecosystem Component	Essential Questions	Key Concepts	Tools and Activities
Equity: Lay the Foundation	• How do we define equity? • What does it look and sound like in practice? • What conditions need to be in place to support educators in an equity-centered environment? • What do leaders need to know and practice to foster equity?	• Culturally Responsive School Leadership (CRSL) • Critical Self-Awareness • Disrupting Deficit Thinking • Teacher Efficacy • Belonging as a Foundation	• Vision for Equity • Pre-Assessment: Are You Ready to Lead Your Vision for Equity? • Social Identities Portrait
Well-Being: Nurture the Soil	• How do we define well-being? • What is the portrait of an educator at our site? • What does an educator need to be fully affirmed in their dignity, experience, and professional practice? • How does this portrait align with the vision for equity? • What conditions need to be in place to support educators' well-being? • What do leaders need to know and practice to foster well-being?	• Well-Being as Foundational • Dimensions of Collective Well-Being • Dimensions of Individual Well-Being	• Dimensions of Well-Being Self-Assessment • Assess Your Well-Being • Portrait of an Educator • Build, Sustain, and Repair Relationships

Growth: **Cultivate** **Continuous** **Learning**	• How do we define growth? • How will educators grow? • How might leaders support educator growth in ways that are equitable, differentiated, and personalized in support of well-being? • What structures will promote growth? • How do leaders model their own growth and promote a culture of learning?	• Growth Cultures in a Healthy Ecosystem • Leadership to Cultivate Growth • Cultivating a Growth Cycle	• Developing a Growth Philosophy • Gardening Tools for Growth: Self-Directed, Small Group, 1:1 • Structures to Implement Growth
Evaluation: **Tend the** **Ecosystem**	• How do we define evaluation? • What is the model of evaluation that is aligned with equity, well-being, and growth? • How will educators be evaluated? • What will be the measures of effectiveness? • How will evaluators be prepared for the process? • How will leaders tend to the ecosystem of their sites, including their own evaluation?	• Reimagining Evaluation • Finding an Effective Observation Structure and Process • Adopting a Warm Demander Stance	• Transformative Equity Practices Assessment Framework • Teacher Student Relationship Quality Matrix • Integrated Classroom Practices for Equity Rubric • Process for Reimagining Evaluation

For Product Safety Concerns and Information please contact our EU representative GPSR@taylorandfrancis.com
Taylor & Francis Verlag GmbH, Kaufingerstraße 24, 80331 München, Germany

www.ingramcontent.com/pod-product-compliance
Lightning Source LLC
Chambersburg PA
CBHW070757230426
43665CB00017B/2400